The Seductions of Community

**School of American Research
Advanced Seminar Series**

James F. Brooks
General Editor

The Seductions of Community

Contributors

Peter Brosius
Department of Anthropology, University of Georgia

Gerald W. Creed
Department of Anthropology, Hunter College and the Graduate Center, CUNY

Kate Crehan
*Department of Sociology, Anthropology and Social Work,
College of Staten Island, CUNY*

Miranda Joseph
Women's Studies, University of Arizona

Aisha Khan
Department of Anthropology, New York University

Susan H. Lees
Department of Anthropology, Hunter College, CUNY

Gyanendra Pandey
Department of History, Emory University

Michael Watts
*Department of Geography and African Studies,
University of California, Berkeley*

Mary Weismantel
Department of Anthropology, Northwestern University

The Seductions of Community
Emancipations, Oppressions, Quandaries

Edited by Gerald W. Creed

School of American Research Press
Santa Fe

James Currey
Oxford

School of American Research Press

Post Office Box 2188
Santa Fe, New Mexico 87504-2188
www.press.sarweb.org

James Currey Ltd

73 Botley Road
Oxford OX2 0BS

Co-Director and Editor: Catherine Cocks
Manuscript Editor: Margaret J. Goldstein
Design and Production: Cynthia Dyer
Proofreader: Sarah Soliz
Indexer: Catherine Fox
Printer: Cushing-Malloy, Inc.

Library of Congress Cataloging-in-Publication Data:

The seductions of community : emancipations, oppressions, quandaries / edited by
Gerald W. Creed.
    p. cm. – (School of American Research advanced seminar series)
  Includes bibliographical references and index.
  ISBN 1-930618-68-9 (cl : alk. paper) – ISBN 1-930618-69-7 (pa : alk. paper)
  1. Community. I. Creed, Gerald W., 1958- II. Series.

HM756.H43 2006
307.01–dc22

                                    2005035647

British Library Cataloguing-in-Publication Data is available
ISBN 10: 0-85255-440-0 (James Currey paper)
ISBN 13: 978-085255-440-1 (James Currey paper)

Cover illustration: Pedestrians crossing street, Shibuya, Tokyo, Japan. © Getty Images.

Contents

Figures

Acknowledgments

This volume began as a deconstructive project to interrogate the term *community*, but our efforts ended up constituting a community of participants, confounding the very objective that inspired us! Such is the community conundrum. A large part of the blame for this complication must go to the School of American Research (SAR), which financed the effort, provided a lovely environment for its actualization, and even coordinated community-building social activities. In this idyllic setting, it was hard not to feel like a community. We all express our gratitude to the SAR staff—including those at the press, who kept us on track after we left the community incubator of the SAR seminar house—for funding and facilitating our project.

Of course, forced interaction does not necessarily lead to collectivity, so the communal result must also be blamed on the participants: an amiable group that was able to pursue very different approaches, insights, and contributions without giving up on mutual understanding. This group actually made the notion of a scholarly community seem plausible. We thank each other for providing inspiration and feedback in a truly cooperative atmosphere. The group includes Elizabeth Chin, who participated fully in the seminar but was unable to contribute to this volume. It also includes two people who joined our group anonymously by reviewing the manuscript. Their careful and critical reading helped us improve the final product, and we are extremely grateful.

In addition, the editor wishes to thank another intellectual community where the idea for a seminar first took root—the Agrarian Studies Program at Yale University. Most of the research for chapter 2 was completed during a fellowship year there in 2000–2001. It was in conversations with other fellows, as well as with the stimulating students, faculty, and staff who attended the weekly seminars, that the extent of the community conundrum became apparent, provoking the proposal to SAR for an advanced seminar.

These experiences confounded the community cynicism that inspired them, and while they have seriously diverted the original project, they have done so for the better. Such is the potential of community and why it is so seductive, even for a skeptic.

The Seductions of Community

1

Reconsidering Community

Gerald W. Creed

This book is about an obsession—one with global reach that occupies politicians, activists, scholars, and laymen alike—the obsession with community. Whether we see it as the nostalgic desire for a lost past or the creative reformulation of a postmodern society, the focus on community has become ubiquitous in the way we talk and think about life in the twenty-first century. Political and economic projects, from rain forest conservation to urban empowerment zones, focus on "the community" as the appropriate vehicle and target of change. Social movements to resist these very efforts often constitute themselves around the same concept, as do others trying to assert a claim on the resources that community recognition promises. For many, social identities define communities (and vice versa), suggesting a proliferation of potentially overlapping entities, while others see a decline of community and predict dire social consequence (for example, R. Putnam 2000). The public currency of the concept has expanded its use in social analysis, provoking one political scientist to conclude that "interest in community is *a* major turn in current thinking, if not somehow *the* turn" (Fowler 1991:ix).

In all this talk and text, what actually defines a group of people as a community is rarely, if ever, specified, and even when it is (for example, Calhoun 1980), the proffered definitions are rarely adopted by others. This is because the term has become part of the commonsensical way we understand and navigate the world. Community does not *need* defining, and this is precisely why scholars need to pay attention to it. Such common notions reveal the taken-for-granted understandings of the world that are so internalized or routinized as to escape comment and specification. It is essential, then, to look inside this seemingly transparent term and discover the associations that are, as it were, hidden in plain view. Moreover, when notions acquire such an aura of facticity, their uncritical use can actually reproduce the "reality" they supposedly just describe or, in the case of community, aspire to supersede. No matter how casually it is used, then, the notion of community may be doing sociological and ideological work—work that ranges from simply reinforcing the status quo to challenging systems of oppression to provoking communitarian violence and genocide. As these options imply, collectivity and exclusion are two sides of the same coin, and to understand either, we need to look at them together— community is the coinage.

While this concern is now critical, it is not novel. One of the most fascinating elements of the community notion is the repeated cross-examination it has sustained. For anthropologists, the most memorable instance is the scathing attack on the community study method popular in the 1950s. This critique challenged community assumptions and helped propel a paradigm shift to world systems models in the 1970s. Despite this and subsequent challenges, the term continued to expand in usage, and discredited assumptions reinsinuated themselves. A major barrier to fully and permanently reforming the community concept is its complex constitution, which includes at least three component meanings: a group of people, a quality of relationship (usually with a positive normative value), and a place/location. While each meaning represents a possible autonomous usage in contemporary English, a history of usage in which these multiple meanings were often combined diminishes the autonomy that usually pertains for multiple definitions of a word. As Raymond Williams explains, "the complexity of community thus relates to the difficult interaction between the tendencies originally distinguished in the historical development: on the one hand the sense of direct common concern; on the other hand the materialization of various forms of common organization, which may or may not adequately express this" (1976:76). Given the lack of referential discretion, people who deploy the term in one sense may unavoidably, if not intentionally, invoke the other qualities popularly associated with it. All references, then, may conjure to some degree qualities of harmony, homogeneity, autonomy, immediacy, locality, morality, solidarity, and identity, as well as the idea of shared knowledge, interests, and meanings. This situation accounts for why the term is loaded with affective power, or as Williams puts it, why it is always a "warmly persuasive word" and "unlike all other terms of social organisations (state, nation, society, and so on)...seems never to be used unfavourably, and never to be given any positive opposing or distinguishing term" (1976:76). This is also why it is so powerful and important.

By the end of the 1990s, the growing popular and scholarly appeal to community had once again provoked reaction from a number of scholars. Nikolas Rose (1999) correlated the community obsession with the collapse of the socialist project and the global victory of capitalism. Drawing inspiration from Foucault, he saw community as a new means of governance in the changed geopolitics of the 1990s (think, for example, about "community policing" or "community liaison officers"). Miranda Joseph (2002) turned instead to Marx to explain the popularity of community by its imbrications with the economy—a two-way process in which community facilitates the flow of capital, while capital provides the very medium in which community is enacted. Interestingly, Joseph's conclusion would also articulate with Rose's attribution of community popularity to the post-1989 triumph of capitalism. Zygmunt Bauman (2001) draws upon other social dislocations and transformations to explain the appeal of community as a source of hope and security. For him, the concept encapsulates lost qualities of society that live on as goals for the future. While this spin is more positive, he also acknowledges that the embrace of community demands a sacrifice of freedom that merits caution.

The idea for this book began as a seminar proposal with objectives similar to these efforts. By the time of the actual seminar in April 2003, the aforementioned publications and a few others (Amit 2002; Kelly and Kaplan 2001) had confirmed the importance of our motivating concerns and significantly informed our discussions in Santa Fe. These works allowed us to push further than we originally aspired. We were able to spend more time assessing the consequences of community in empirically grounded and culturally nuanced contexts. In addition to cases where community is used generally and generically, we purposefully included comparative contexts where the notion of community was less pervasive (even nonexistent), as well as cases where it was an official legal category of administration. This approach allowed us to correlate the deployment of community with other qualities and characteristics. We were also able to integrate the foci of earlier critiques and extract new insight from the articulation of previously distinctive explanations. Thus we examine not just how community facilitates governance or capital accumulation but also how community articulates these two forces in local and translocal contexts. Finally, prior efforts allowed us to take the reflexive enterprise to another level and to consider not just the unintended consequences of deploying community but also the potential consequences of criticizing that very fascination, as some of the dangers of challenging community were already apparent (Brosius, this volume). In sum, we are not interested in refining the community notion or in reaching an evaluative assessment as to its value, either analytically or sociopolitically. Rather, we aspire to understand the various ways community is deployed and what work it does in different contexts. In so doing, the essays demonstrate the critical value of using community as the focus of analysis rather than simply an empty category of heuristic or descriptive convenience.

LOOKING BACK TO MOVE AHEAD

On one level, the sighting of a community obsession is somewhat illusionary, as it is based on simple lexical usage rather than meaning, which remains so diverse and contested that David Kirp (2000:6) characterizes the word as a "Rorschach blot upon which myriad hopes and fears are projected." In fact, a range of meanings has characterized the word community from its early usage in the fourteenth century. But as Williams (1976:75) points out, from the seventeenth century, and especially during the nineteenth century in the context of larger and more industrial societies, the term acquired a sense of immediacy and locality. "Society," a term that had been used to distinguish the body of direct relationships from that of the state, came increasingly to signify larger encompassing categories, and community more narrow direct relations. This distinction informed the prospect of "community studies" in the twentieth century but still failed to generate a precise consensus. By 1955 a survey identified more than ninety definitions of community (Hillery 1955) with very little in common. In the decades that followed, observers recognized that the term had acquired so many meanings as to be meaningless (Plant 1978:79–80). Extensive use without shared meaning turned the word into an empty, although inherently positive, signifier available to any petitioner, which in turn assured that it would be used even more extensively, adding more divergent meanings. Community became the default term whenever "group" seemed inadequate.

This situation developed almost imperceptibly as a rather generic notion was used in more and more contexts, but the critique of culture as a uniform, homogenous, and discrete (that is, essentialized) category, beginning in the 1980s, catapulted community to the forefront as a stand-in for the popular but troubled notion of culture. This process helps account for the expansion of community in scholarly discourse around the same time others (Bauman 2001; Joseph 2002; N. Rose 1999) see political and economic explanations for its popular expansion—that is, in addition to being an analytic response to the expanding popularity of the term, its scholarly expansion has its own dynamic. The dangerous potential of the culture concept was exposed in the emergence of culturally defined racisms (Balibar and Wallerstein 1992; Stolcke 1995) and ideas about the clash of civilizations (Huntington 1998). Community seemed a safe generic alternative. This volume confirms that it is an alternative, but not always or altogether a safe one; many uses reproduce the problematic qualities and dangers of culture.

One response to the plethora of meanings of community might be to insist on distinguishing different uses of the term, such as "geographical communities" and "political communities," but since these dimensions often overlap, such distinctions could hardly be sustained. Instead, we endeavor to retain the concept's inherent obscurity and to make the user more aware of its uncertainty so that it does not automatically evoke any preconceived ideas but rather requires specification. Whether preconceived qualities haunt all invocations of community; if so, to what effect; and whether they can or should be exorcized are at the core of the community dilemma and this volume. Clearly, many people use community as a heuristic designation of convenience with no particular qualitative intentions. But can such uses completely escape the associations listed above? My framing essay, which follows, sees a romantic doppelgänger wherever community is invoked. The subsequent essays complicate this claim by showing how different historical contexts condition these elements in very distinctive ways with different consequences, often animating them but sometimes overwhelming them. Together they confirm a broader lesson: the terms used to delineate, describe, and motivate associations, relations, and identifications are neither coincidental nor inconsequential.

In sum, it is clear that Rose has targeted an important element of community—its engagement with modern governance. The success of modern rule owes much to its articulation of an expansive authority (in both degree and distance) in a language of community; states traffic in the emotional elements of community to establish consent. This emotionalism clearly informed Benedict Anderson's choice of the term community to understand the attachment of nationalism, but his association of community with nation obscures a quality that makes communities so useful for governance—that they usually remain subordinate to the state. Certainly, the definition of community allows for its use at the state/societal level, but that is usually not the implication, which is why Anderson must qualify the nation as an "imagined" community. Reversing Anderson, one may posit that the hegemony of the nation-state (which traffics in the notion of community) as the only imaginable form of political organization has contributed to the emotive resonance of the community notion, which then paradoxically makes his formulation so resonant.[1] Regardless, the fact that communities carry such emotion while remaining subordinate to the state makes them particularly useful as a mechanism of governance.

But modern rule is not possible without access to economic resources. Following Joseph's analysis of community's imbrication with capital accumulation, we might suspect that community attains some of its emotional resonance and significance for rule through its role in a system of resource extraction and mobilization. The contemporary study of consumption supports this conclusion, showing how many of the vectors defining communities (race, class, ethnicity, gender, urbanity) are articulated in consumption practices, which in turn provide a motor for capitalist growth (Davila 2001; Halter 2000; Miller and Carter 2001). The degree to which consumption practices correlate with the boundaries of communities cannot be coincidental. The implication of communities in the economic operations of capitalism then materializes the notion of community for members in a visceral way. Embodied through consumption, this emotional experience translates into the utility of the term for political mobilization by the state.

The association of community with contemporary statecraft and capitalism might seem at odds with the earliest theorists who blamed these same forces of modernity for eradicating community (for example, Durkheim, Tönnies, and Weber). In this model, traditional community ties were undermined by the commercialization and bureaucratization of social relations. Actually, however, these two views reinforce each other. Community becomes more central to state governance as its political and economic power is displaced. Put more directly, communities become useful and central for the state after they have been politically eviscerated and transformed into mere units of consumption and representation. The role of communities in this modern political economy then reinforces unidimensional understandings of community. James Scott (1998) points out that states can administer effectively only by simplifying and homogenizing the local context so as to make it legible to the state. To the degree that community is promoted by modern statecraft, then, it is likely to be a problematic idea of community as uniform and homogenous. Hence, some categories of political significance, notably religious and ethnic/racial ones, are hard to imagine as not communities. Communities that do not fit such images are abandoned by the state (Brosius, this volume), discredited as antimodern (R. Rose 1999), or defined by terms other than community (Khan, this volume). For example, even though the attraction of youth gangs in the United States is often explained by teenage desire for belonging, gangs are more commonly cast as family surrogates and blamed on family failures. Likewise, certain manifestations of capitalism (Watts, this volume) operate in ways that seem anathema to the positive image of like-minded consumers, and the community notion is noticeable by its absence.

Of course, community also allows for contrary mobilizations

against state and corporate interests (Weismantel, this volume). Still, the very notion of community may be self-limiting as a revolutionary force because it is defined by (and acquires emotional valence from) its subordination to the state. Can global and virtual mobilization of community challenge this quality? On the one hand, internationalization of community as a focus of NGO and IO activity clearly articulates with and reinforces the notion of community as subordinate to the state, as communities are often the focus of aid projects expressly to circumvent state/political barriers.[2] On the other hand, some global mobilizations and movements appear to be creating effective communities of interest that supersede states and influence state and international policies (Edelman 1999). These changes may authorize new images of community no longer subordinate to states. However, their ultimate success may connect to other components of the community notion. Unrealistic expectations of community may preordain disappointment, in which case supra-state communities will also fail to sustain a challenge to state power.

In relation to the state and international arenas, the notion of community clearly connects to issues of rights, which provides further explanation for community obsessions. Because of their role in governance, communities may also make claims on rights at state and international levels, which renders the definition of community a highly contentious issue. This situation is most explicit in cases where communities constitute an official unit of administration (usually found in terms of "indigenous communities"). These special cases, however, should sensitize us to the way more informal notions of community may also be implicated with struggles over rights. How communities are defined and who gets designated or recognized as a community is determinant of political rights of representation precisely because community is central to governance. When this factor is taken into consideration, arguments about inclusion and exclusion can be appreciated as more than just issues of prejudice and culture clash. They are contests over power and the resources such power affords. The emotive nature of community, however, cannot be ignored here as it contributes to the reaction and affront that people feel when political designations fail to mesh with emotive ones. Some community crises, then, may be redefined as a clash between different definitions of community (Lees, this volume), in which case simply promoting the idea of community may exacerbate the conflict. Here we can see that notions of community are at the crux of the tension between individual and collective rights. The resonance of community blurs the distinction between these arenas precisely because community attains a more emotive connotation simpatico with the individual, even though it references a collective.

Clearly part of the problem with the community concept is the complex relationship between academic and popular uses of the term, which has heretofore not been closely examined. There is a disjuncture between scholarly uses of community, which are assumed to be free of erroneous assumptions, and popular uses, which traffic explicitly in the emotive conceptions purportedly purged from academic discourse. However, those popular images can often be traced to scholarly (even anthropological) sources (Weismantel, this volume), and many scholarly analyses of community are actually interested in the term's popularity. The latter reintroduces unreformed images of community into scholarly discourse by default. In addition, some scholars traffic knowingly in stereotypical images of community in the hopes of having more political or social influence with the politicians and bureaucrats who operate with similar ideas. This situation maintains an image of community consistent with that implicated in governance and corporate accumulation despite quite contrary objectives. Activists are especially important as interlocutors between scholarly and popular fora, and their extensive use of the community notion facilitates a continual cross-fertilization of scholarly and popular images. This complex relationship helps explain why repeated critiques of community in the scholarly arena, including the most recent, have not had popular impact, and why they have even failed to completely reform notions of community among scholars. The scholarly engagement with community provides numerous openings for popular influence. For these reasons we cannot assume that current deployments of community have been inoculated by previous criticisms.

PROVOCATIONS

Our project, then, recognizes that community is not a thing, or simply a concept, but rather a moment in modern rule, a moment saturated with affective power. While articulating discipline and accumulation, it nevertheless holds the promise of escape from the conditions of its own constitution. The question of whether this promise can ever be achieved, or whether inherent expectations of community inevitably hamstring such efforts, fueled seminar discussion, and we did not reach consensus. We did, however, agree that the greater actualization of such potential depends upon a thorough interrogation of the term and a detailed specification of what the notion conveys, explicitly and implicitly, empirically and conceptually. We also agreed on three reactive strategies to achieve this goal.

Against the fetishization of community, we insist on examining the making (and unmaking) of communities. Marx used the term "fetishism" to convey how the products of human labor were seemingly removed from the social relations of their production. Just as Marx traced the perpetuity of exploitative productive relations to an ignorance about the nature of these social relations, we suspect that the disciplining and accumulative work of community hinges on the unreflective assumption of community as natural, organic, and perhaps sui generis. Such assumptions, for example, seem to authorize the conceptual possibility of a "crisis of community," which might seem nonsensical if the term were simply heuristic. Thus a powerful step is to look at the history of particular collectivities, to examine when they began to acquire an identity (internally and externally) that merits the community appellation. What are the qualities and relations that justify this specification, and what forces generated them? Of course, just as important, are examinations of parallel contexts or forces that fail to generate such labels. We then have to follow through to see the degree to which the constitution of community perpetuates itself quite apart from the forces that brought it into being, or how changes in those forces challenge and redefine communities. Violence, for example, seems particularly effective at constituting opposing communities. If violence defines communities vis-à-vis each other, does internal violence inevitably mark/invoke community decline and redefinition? Put more broadly, do the historical forces that constitute communities continue to shape their destiny, or does the notion of community itself establish expectations that shift subsequent developments?

Against the normative presumption of community as positive, we acknow-

ledge diverse and often unintended consequences generated by invocations of community. As already mentioned, Williams (1976:76) recognized that the term community seems never to be used unfavorably. While this idea might be challenged by bringing his historical method forward to include subsequent developments, such as communitarianism (Pandey, this volume), we accept that a positive valence is common-sensical and part of the popularity and utility of the community concept. Any effort to understand the dynamic of community must challenge this evaluation. This means examining diverse invocations and subjecting progressive projects to the same deconstructive efforts directed at essentializing ones. The invocation of community for any objective may be affected by the term's baggage. In fact, the same positive valence that makes community attractive may provoke discontent and dissatisfaction when such ideals are not realized. The same sentiments that generate community attachments clearly authorize exclusivity on the part of communities. This process may not be inherently negative, but it certainly has negative potential and clearly limits the flexibility of such units under changing circumstances such as increasing globalization. This quality helps explain why we can have both a profusion of community discourse and laments of community crisis. The fascination with, and desire for, community may be inadvertently generating disappointment, alienation, fragmentation, and segregation.

Against the objectification of communities, we maintain that communities are constituted by and constitutive of different regimes of knowledge. Communities are not things. Community is a loaded term for designating groups of people, and the designation is realized by different constituencies. It is not exclusively a term of self-ascription, and even if it were, the popularity of the choice clearly relates to the lack of satisfactory alternatives (at least in English). This situation demands that we be sensitive to how community fits within the authorized forms of knowledge that shape how we understand and experience the world. Following Foucault, we recognize that these regimes of knowledge are tied to vested interests and configurations of power so that the deployment of community, or an alternative designation, has ideological significance. The question remains as to whether we have reached the point of a "community discourse" tied to a current hegemonic project, or whether we are dealing with distinctive invocations of community from very different and contrary discourses. Perhaps more significant, can community provide a counter-hegemonic discourse without serving the interests of a hegemonic one that draws heavily on the same lexical tool? Drawing on different historical and geographical contexts, the essays in this volume carry through these interrogations of community with different assessments and conclusions.

FROM ROMANCE TO REALPOLITIK

Realizing the intentions set out above requires strategies of inquiry that can circumvent the snares of community. We developed a collection of important questions (not all useful in every case, obviously) to help get at the content and impact of community without reifying it. First, it is crucial to discern who is deploying the term and with what objective (if any). What do people who identify themselves as a community think the concept implies? Are there disjunctures of meaning and intent between actors using the term in the same place and time (for example, the anthropologist, local activists, state representatives, NGO/IO workers, and local residents)? How do such conceptualizations differ over time? Is community the translation of an indigenous term? If so, why exactly is community used as the English equivalent? Are communities constituted by the research techniques used to study them? What are the relationships between concepts of community and identity vectors such as race, class, gender, family, and nation? Do communities fulfill particular roles in political organization or the mobilization and distribution of resources? Do violence and conflict help constitute, destroy, or redefine notions of community? Is community implicated with other complex notions such as culture, minority, diaspora, authenticity, or development? If so, how?

Miranda Joseph builds upon her earlier interrogation of community and capitalism (Joseph 2002) by examining connections between ideas of community, debt, and incarceration. In this model, the discourse of community crisis, with its associated disappearance of trust, operates as performance aimed at encouraging people to establish creditworthiness (which requires debt). The connection of debt to the expansion/infiltration of capitalism is obvious. Historically, as credit/debt became a way to constitute the individual liberal subject, default on debt stopped being redressed by incarceration, but the notion of prison as payment for debt continued in the popular belief that criminals owe a debt to society, paid in time, because after all, time is money. Efforts to reform and redress the excesses of the criminal justice system in the United States now explicitly employ ideas of community. But romantic assumptions in the program of these "restorative justice" efforts can conceal the structural relations and causes of high incarceration rates, with the dangerous prospect of actually reinforcing the structures of power they protest. The point is that romantic aspects of community are dangerous, but their ultimate impact depends upon other factors surrounding their deployment.

These "other factors" are central to the chapter on Nigeria in which Michael Watts offers a direct attack on idealized notions of community by considering the possibility of violent communities. There is nothing romantic or "warmly persuasive" here (except perhaps the dream of oil riches), yet the results are more fractious than those driven by the search for harmony or unity. He shows how the political economy of oil prevents the constitution of communities that could facilitate governance and capitalism. If communities are central to these modern processes, then the impossibility of such communities may explain why Nigeria has been unable to constitute an effective modern state. Watts demonstrates clearly, however, that the failure is not due to the lack of potential community entities, which have in fact proliferated, but the inability of these fractious violent units to be integrated into a single national community due to the role of indigenous ethnic groups in the political structure and the nature of oil-claims-making. While romantic expectations of community may be a force of fragmentation and political disappointment in some contexts, in Nigeria the overwhelming forces of political economy explain similar, but more severe, outcomes. At the same time, the oxymoronic feel to the notion of "communities of violence" confirms the presence of quite different expectations for the term.

Kate Crehan, who has also written about fractured communities in Africa (1997) as well as the problematic notions of community held by aid workers there (2002a), turns to the inner city of London and finds uncanny parallels in the community rhetoric of urban regeneration. Focusing on a community arts project—the construction of a large mural in a public housing estate—she highlights the role of material expressions and representations for people in identifying community. Initiated by despair over the decline of community, the project mobilized people (and a moment of community) to produce a mural that is now, ironically, permanent evidence of subsequent community decline. As Crehan notes, the home of community is often the past, but the same romantic nostalgia we might easily refute with historical facts provides the basis of efforts that actually produce moments of community experientially. This idea should give us pause about dismissing nostalgia as historical fiction, as it has its own generative power, and not only with conservative or nationalist results.

Aisha Khan shows how particular assumptions about community led researchers to conclude that Afro-Caribbean populations lacked communities, while Indo-Caribbean peoples had them by default (and perhaps to a fault, albeit a faulty version). In short, preconceptions about community interacted with assumptions about different cultures of origin and the differential impact of slavery and indenture to shape the scholarly profile and social policy of the area. Through synecdochical reasoning, the dominance of Afro-Caribbeans determined the characterization of the region as lacking community, while the exception of Indo-Caribbean communities operated to fit Indians into a governable slot within the hegemonic social structure of a purported mixed ("callaloo") nation. The latter could then easily accept other communities once new analytical models of transnationalism and diaspora began to redefine the notion of community around political resistance and justice, which opened up the Caribbean to being full of communities. But Khan finds continuities even in such radical rethinking. Assumptions people have about community lead them to emphasize particular aspects and elements of their new or innovative community experience. Diaspora seems to break with territorialized notions of community, but instead those expectations operate to redefine diasporic communities in terms of a territory—the homeland. Here we find not a wholesale shift in the notion of community but a shift in some qualities of community, while other ideas persist and actually influence the outcome of innovation.

Khan's formula for the importance of homeland may also shed light on the role of Zionism in the Jewish diaspora, where different attitudes toward Israel differentiate Jewish communities. Susan Lees, however, takes a different tack and shows how Jews living in the town of Tenafly, New Jersey, come to loggerheads precisely over their different ideas of community. A conflict over the public posting of religious symbols pitted Orthodox Jews against an alliance of assimilated Jews and gentiles in the town. The latter interpreted the public symbols of the Orthodox (and the public presence they facilitated) as a ghetto-like disruption to their image of the town as a single, integrated community. Assumptions of what a community should be led the multiculturalists to view the Orthodox not as a diverse component in the Tenafly mosaic but as a separate, autonomous community, which actually reflected Orthodox desires for their own community. The presence of assimilated Jews (and their somewhat deracialized status as "white") prevented many residents and leaders from interpreting their opposition to Orthodox symbols as cultural or ethnic intolerance. Here, notions of community are clearly more than just derivative outcomes of political struggles—they provoke the conflict, illustrating exactly why the simple appeal to community is not the solution to contemporary troubles.

Mary Weismantel provides an example where the idea of community has a more explicit structural history—the indigenous Andean *ayllu*. Even here, though, the term's flexibility operates against the clarity and precision such formalities might seem to promise. Moreover, the history of the term in Andean studies mirrors the reification of "community" as recounted by Creed (this volume). Weismantel uses the ayllu to track the theoretical shifts in Andean anthropology and political activism over the last fifty years, a history she divides into three moments: the modern, the postmodern, and the antimodern. These moments, however, are not linear, autonomous, or exclusive. In short, it is the romantic image of the ayllu reified by modernist anthropologists in the twentieth century that provides the inspiration for twenty-first-century antimodern struggles by Andean activists (as well as a collection of new age enterprises!). The activists find the essentialized ayllu of modern anthropology, which was rightly criticized by postmodern critics, to be a useful symbol of the future they seek to (re)establish. Like Crehan's community nostalgia, the value of the ayllu is its ability to will itself into being as a political project.

The utility of a romantic community for Andean activists, and the possibility of achieving it for even a fleeting moment in a London housing project, should certainly give us pause regarding the critique of the community concept. Peter Brosius provides us with another warning from the world of conservation. He examines the recent shift from a community-based model of resource management to a regional one. The former emerged in recognition of the need to engage local populations in the protection of their own environments. However laudable, the assumptions conservationists held about "communities" produced programs that could never work. Many scholars (including Brosius himself) rightly castigated this model for mythic, unrealistic assumptions about community. Unfortunately, practitioners responded by moving to a higher level of abstraction—the region—and redefining their focus as "natural" communities. Not only are people rather irrelevant here, but the qualifier "natural" also implies a subjective evaluation. Natural communities are basically those that do not refute or contradict the assumptions about community held by the conservationists who identify them and, not coincidentally, work with the new technologies for monitoring conservation. The communities defined and delineated by community-based conservation programs did not facilitate governance or capital productivity (via the accounting demands of conservation funders), so they were redefined into units both more compatible with statecraft and more amenable to financial regulation.

Gyanendra Pandey notes the recurrent evaluation of community according to natural and unnatural criteria. In India, as elsewhere, the "natural" came to be defined as the "national" through the naturalization of the nation-state political form. The idea of the nation as the paradigmatic natural community sets the framework for how other communities are evaluated (see also Kelly and Kaplan 2001). Thus the contemporary notion of community has become essentially political in aspiration or potential. But to be effective in this political action, communities need to be recognized as "natural units." It is this tension between natural and political that marks the discourse of community for Pandey. His contribution then looks at this tension in relation to the politics of gender, caste, and communalism.

The essential political dimension to community that Pandey underlines is evident in each of the chapters. The question remains as to whether these efforts facilitate modern governance or not, and if not, with what consequence? Clearly Nigeria's proliferating "violent communities" do not constitute avenues of modern governance, but they hardly present a desirable alternative to it. The Andean ayllu may offer such promise, but we should not lose sight of the difference between actual relations on the ground and the ideal images of community. The utility of the latter must ultimately be evaluated by their products, and the weight of history does not suggest optimism. Still, it is important to remember, as the examples described by Watts and Lees illustrate, that behind the failure of one community is often the success of another.

From most of these discussions, it is clear that the political role of community cannot be understood apart from considerations of scale—that is, how units conceived of as communities articulate with smaller and larger units of identification and analysis. To be simple, the cases confirm that the positive and unproblematic image of community seems to be essentially bound to hierarchical organization. Communities must nest into each other and then into larger units such as society and nation.[3] It is this nested hierarchy that allows a "debt to society" to be paid with "community service." A nested hierarchy allows for differently identified communities to constitute part of a single tolerant Tenafly community, itself a microcosm of the American national community. This also explains why the notion of ghetto is anathema. Similarly, when residents of a public housing estate are forced to represent what it is that makes them a community in their mural, they settle on their pride as Londoners! The focus on family disruption among Afro-Caribbeans made it hard to imagine them as communities precisely because communities were assumed to be constructed of families. The lack of communities, in turn, made it impossible to see Caribbean countries as "societies." The possibility of Indo-Caribbean communities, however, could nest within a "callaloo" or composite nation, although their possible affiliation and allegiance to another nation/homeland, into which they also nest as nationals abroad, causes hesitations and political problems. The possibility of hierarchical nesting verifies the contribution of the community to the nation-state, itself then imagined as a community writ large. The bigger picture of the nested and segmentary nature of communities explains why it is easy to have multiple and overlapping community memberships, because they are ultimately components of a single larger community. The communities that are problematic, then, are the ones that defy such nesting or segmentary integration and thereby interfere with fidelity to larger communities. This is where the notion of communalism is invoked and where, as Pandey and Watts point out, community finally loses its "warmly persuasive" connotation.

While each of the papers reveals something about community that is rarely recognized or specified in contemporary community discourses, they also show us how treating community critically opens up new *empirical* insights. By focusing on community, we gain insight into the limitation of Gandhi's politics. We learn why petro-capitalism produces particular social dysfunctions. We gain new appreciation for why notions of homeland figure so centrally for diasporic communities. We begin to appreciate the different political prospects of related social movements such as "restorative justice" and "transformative justice," or more generally why projects with very similar complaints and objectives can produce different impacts. In other words, while we may begin with the community as subject, by cross-examining it we gain unexpected insights into the contexts where it is (or is not) deployed. This may be the most compelling case for redeeming the term.

NO SOLUTIONS

Any effort to reexamine the notion of community must justify itself not only in relation to current community enthrallments but vis-à-vis previous efforts. To some extent, this project is motivated by the juxtaposition of these two considerations. We recognize and appreciate the numerous prior challenges and corrections to the community notion (many of which are reviewed in the next chapter). However, it is equally clear that this attention has ironically contributed to the uncritical embrace and use of the term in contemporary research and politics. Repeated critiques have created a perception that everyone is fully aware of the problems of the community concept, and this perception authorizes its continued uncritical use, even when this use retains assumptions supposedly left behind. In a way then, the perception that this critique is "old hat" is part of the very dynamic we attempt to understand—it has become part of the problem. Another problem is the way prior critique has removed noncompliant work from serious consideration among those who might challenge it. For example, when

I cite the work of Robert Putnam (2000) or Amitai Etzioni (1998) as evidence of unreformed idealized notions of community, cognoscenti respond by dismissing these works as naive and beneath serious consideration, even though they are extremely popular and influential among political leaders designing social policy (*including those in the White House*). Those of us who have internalized prior community critiques cannot afford to simply dismiss those who have not, especially given the sociopolitical resonance of the community notion in the contemporary world.

Obviously, this project follows from a belief that current circumstances render the community issue more significant than ever. We see a critical conjuncture in which liberal, progressive projects are proliferating the notion of community as a means of staking claims and expanding rights, at the same time a more traditional movement of civic republicanism, which fails to recognize these as community efforts, diagnoses a crisis of community and advocates community resuscitation in different terms. There is a confluence of community adulation from diverse agendas and objectives, and one could end up inadvertently supporting the other. At the same time there is a shift created by the current neoliberal context that designs to devolve responsibilities to communities but also explains the status quo as the successful product of social Darwinism. In this context, the proliferation of communities creates its own competitive antagonism rather than a common project. In other words, the changed social context of the twenty-first century may reshape the impact or consequences of community proliferations, even those driven by very progressive objectives. Clearly, the current forces of globalization and "deterritorialization," driven by capitalisms and imperialisms, have contributed greatly to people's desire for the moorings and attachments offered by community. If these same communities are mechanisms of governance and capital growth, then we are in a terrible dilemma. Our own efforts at redress underwrite the very system and forces that generate our discontent. This is why the current fascination with community is more significant than earlier ones and why more attention must be paid to ensure that efforts in the name of community are moving toward the objectives to which they aspire. We cannot simply rely on earlier exhortations—they need updating and rehearsing.

Given the pervasive and ever-increasing investment in community (both politically and socially), this collection makes no pretension toward resolving the problems it depicts. The term is far too popular and powerful to be completely redeemed or displaced, as multiple efforts have shown. Indeed, we could not even agree among ourselves about the ultimate political (f)utility of the community project. The objective is rather to expose the diverse work that the notion does, often imperceptibly and unintentionally, and thereby instill a sense of caution and reflection. The difficulty of our project is captured by two divergent metaphors used in the following two chapters. My review of community critics equates the notion to a tar baby that can absorb all assaults, while Crehan pictures it instead as an illusive unicorn. The dilemma lies is this potentially dangerous combination: a self-sustaining and binding term employed to convey illusive and uncertain objectives. *Community is an aspiration envisioned as an entity.* If we're not careful, the entity can tie us down even when the desires that conjure it are soaring and ethereal. The essays here aim to loosen the strictures of community so that we can get closer to its lofty ideals.

Notes

1. It is no coincidence, then, that Anderson's use of community has provoked several recent efforts to reconsider the term (see Amit 2002; Creed 2004; Kelly and Kaplan 2001).

2. Although the fact that such efforts rarely succeed underlines just how implicated communities are in state governance despite images of depoliticization (Ferguson 1994).

3. C. J. Calhoun (1980:124) appeals to the breach of this quality—"the breakdown of the structure of hierarchical incorporation"—to explain why English communities shifted toward class-based connections in the nineteenth century.

2

Community as Modern Pastoral

Gerald W. Creed

In the preceding introduction, I argued that invocations of community conjure a collection of romantic associations. Following Raymond Williams's (1976) approach to "keywords," I accept that such semantic profiles can be traced to the conditions of historical usage, and one such condition is the opposition central to another of Williams's classic works, *The Country and the City* (1973). The collection of romantic sentiments in the idea of community can be traced to the urban bias and evolutionary assumptions of many of its formulators—urban intellectuals reflecting on an imagined and essentialized rural past they alternately desired and disdained. The concept of community crystallized the positive elements of rural life free of its attendant "idiocies," to use Marx and Engels's famous summary. Most uses of the term, then, envision a cosmopolitan replacement for a lost rural idyll.

Thus I suggest an additional supplement to the trio of capital, governance, and security (Bauman 2001; Joseph 2002; N. Rose 1999) to explain the attraction and proliferation of community: urban hegemony. The dominance of the urban gaze and subject position—the degree to which the urban condition has come to define and filter interpretations of the contemporary global situation—has expanded the foundation upon which earlier and formative notions of community were built. In other words, the conditions that provoked prior community romantics are now much more pervasive and popular. Until we recognize both the urbo-centric foundations of community ideas and the hegemony of the urban gaze in contemporary critical analysis (see Creed and Ching 1997), we will not be able to break through the robust romanticism of the community concept.

To help do so, in this essay I pursue a critical and deconstructive agenda that is untempered and unrelenting. I first demonstrate the historical urban basis of community romance and then show how these assumptions were sustained in subsequent deployments of the term despite concerted efforts to avoid them. This is not to deny the redeeming potential of community projects and research—the "lofty ideals" mentioned in the preceding introduction. Nor is it an arrogant denial of the important advances made by the pieces I examine. Rather, this is an admittedly desperate effort, in the face of such compelling narratives, to highlight the term's potentially dangerous discursive complexity. Deconstruction alone, however, is insufficient; it must be combined with investigations of how actual people in actual places interpret the notions and issues being examined (in this case "community"), and how they respond. This essay, then, is intended as a provocation to which the subsequent essays should be read as elaborations and correctives. Their greater success at capturing the nuances is testimony to one of our central conclusions: that the notion of community can be adequately and usefully apprehended only in particular historical and geographical contexts. That is why an edited collection is a useful way to present this argument and why the ultimate lesson must be drawn from the volume as a whole, rather than from this essay or any one that follows.

THE PRIMORDIAL COMMUNITY

According to Williams (1976:75–76), the notion of community began to acquire romantic qualifications, or as he puts it, "a sense of immediacy and locality...based on narrow direct relations," from the seventeenth century. This tendency intensified with industrialization and associated social dislocations of migration and population growth (that is, urbanization). Thus *community* took on an intense interactive connotation as that very characteristic became less common or taken for granted, and therefore more deserving of identification. *Community* came to represent what was apparently lost. It was then associated retroactively with the living embodiments of that past—the rural countryside and the village—despite the fact that these "communities" had experienced their own diminishing cohesion as a result of earlier enclosure movements.

This basic distinction is evident in the binary penchant of social scientists in the nineteenth and early twentieth centuries (A. Cohen 1985:22). Most posited a dichotomy between two types of society: Maine opposed "status" to "contract," Durkheim contrasted "mechanical" to "organic" solidarity, and in what is the most influential dyad, Tönnies distinguished the direct, dense, and significant contacts of gemeinschaft from the instrumental, formal, or abstract social relations of gesellschaft. One could also align Engels's opposition of primitive communism to state capitalism and Weber's distinction between enchanted and rational/bureaucratic societies along the same binary. In keeping with the evolutionary gestalt of the period, the opposed types were historically sequenced, and since most of these thinkers were concerned about contemporary social ills, the shift they delineated provided a potential explanation for the problems of society (although they saw positive as well as negative changes, and some emphasized the former). The family resemblance of these models reinforced the foundational binary even as the debates over details and causation formed distinctive theoretical schools of thought. In all the models, the notions of consensus, conformity, and solidarity constitute part of a disappearing past, whether applauded as the triumph of liberalism, accepted as a step toward working-class consciousness, or bemoaned as the source of anomie. Even models that emphasized stratification in the past assumed a sort of harmony because people knew their place. These are the images that were attached to the community concept.

The rural-urban opposition fit easily with these distinctions, and rural society provided a living replica of the past. This situation was not the result of rural people celebrating the idea of community or even the empirical observation of rural societies by urban intellectuals, but rather the latter's projection onto the countryside of the antithesis of their own urban conditions. Community as gemeinschaft was attributed to rural society or the village. As Plant (1978:81) has pointed out, over the last two hundred years, "the notion of community has been used almost universally by social and political philosophers to point up some of the drawbacks and baneful characteristics of urban industrial society and to point the way toward new and more humane forms of social relations." Despite these negative qualities, however, the city retains its evolutionary superiority as the hallmark of civilization—few advocate going *back* to the countryside. Instead, the suburbs emerge as an alternative that fuses qualities of rural and urban life. The interstitial location of suburbs as neither urban nor rural is then reflected in the ambiguity of their community character: they are alternately imagined as locations of collective hyperactivity and extreme family isolation (Hummon 1990; Scherer 1972; Thorns 1976). Moreover, an unambiguous characterization of suburbs as communities becomes more likely when they take on the bounded and corporate (romantic?) qualities found in "gated" or "planned" communities (Low 2003). In many respects, then, the trajectory of the community concept follows that outlined by Peter Stallybrass and Allon White for other categories, such as "the forest" or "the savage":

> The bourgeois subject continuously defined and re-defined itself through the exclusion of what it marked out as *low*—as dirty, repulsive, noisy, contaminating....But disgust always bears the imprint of desire. These low domains, apparently expelled as *Other*, return as the object of nostalgia, longing and fascination....These contents, or domains, are subject to misrecognition and distortion precisely because idealization and phobic avoidance have *systematically* informed their discursive history. (1986:191)

The validation of a community associated with the countryside does not translate into a defense of rural society or culture precisely because there is little empirical rural reality behind it, but rather an imagined ideal conjured to shape and improve urban life. James Ferguson (1992) has demonstrated how this same dynamic developed in postcolonial Zambia, where the village is used by urbanites as a moral image first to help purge the city of its colonial character and then to discipline urban behavior. The concept of community takes on this role in a context where rural/village associations carry negative baggage. The term community extracts elements of rural life for emulation without upsetting the cultural hierarchy of urban superiority that authorizes intellectual social analysis. The community phenomenon was produced by the dovetailing of an antirural evolutionary logic with sociological recognition of urban problems. It allowed analysts to prescribe certain qualities *thought* to inhere in rural milieus without the associated negative values of traditionalism and forced conformity antithetical to liberal society. Unfortunately, the positive elements of community associated with the rural past were no more empirically valid than the negative ones, yet they remain elements of the community concept and project.

This dynamic is evident in the work of the Chicago School of urban sociology, to which major installations of the community concept in social scientific theory can be traced. The rural/urban distinction is central to this work, but its role is hardly unequivocal. Sydel Silverman notes that the diverse communities studied by the Chicago School and its contemporaries were treated as a common type, even though they included factory towns and rural villages: "Surprisingly little contrast was drawn among the communities, as diverse as they were" (1979:50). Anthony Cohen (1985:25), however, claims that the early founders of the Chicago School equated rural society with the idea of community in an effort to underline urban distinctiveness and superiority. Both assessments are in fact true, reflecting the combination of rural attraction and distain conveyed by Stallybrass and White, easily accommodated by a notion of community that was already multivalent.

Gerald Suttles (1972) maps the dynamic in more detail. According to his interpretation, Robert Park and Ernest Burgess developed the concept of "natural community" to characterize urban neighborhoods that were not planned or artificially constructed, but rather were developed as the accumulated outcome of independent personal residential decisions. However, the "natural" qualifier all too easily acquired a sense of primordial solidarity unaffected by culture or administration, to which no urban neighborhood could lay claim but which could be imagined to exist in the backward countryside, especially by urban intellectuals. This process had the effect of linking the concept more immutably with the village as distinct from the city. Subsequent urban sociology then became obsessed with the absence of community relations (Stein 1960; Nisbet 1953), the reprise of which continues to haunt us today (Putnam 2000; Etzioni 1998).

In the interim, urban sociologists and anthropologists responded by identifying a plethora of urban communities, but this response simply reinforced the romantic ingredients associated with the concept's bucolic exemplar. They focused on ethnic enclaves, close-knit neighborhoods, and cliques where elements of uniformity, solidarity, and consensus could still be found. This approach is most explicit in the title of Herbert Gans's (1962) classic study of Italian Americans in Boston: *The Urban Villagers*. Grounded in ideas of consensus and uniformity, the subsequent and seemingly laudable drive to re-create community actually became a vehicle of segregation. Morris Janowitz's (1967) study of the community press offered an alternative concept defined by "limited liability." It avoided the problems of diversity and conflict by revealing the limited role that communities actually play in a city and recognizing that a sense of community is maintained by a limited number of custodians, such as the local press. This approach still reproduced the romantic image of community by limiting the concept to a vanguard that met these specifications. All the diverse studies that defined urban communities as components or building blocks of the larger city left rural community assumptions intact by simply applying the term to urban units where its (rural) romantic standards could be met.

In what must be a worse violation, however, Robert Redfield, also at Chicago in the 1950s (and Park's son-in-law), used these imagined ideas about the countryside to characterize peasant society—in short, he embraced the retrospective projections of urban researchers as the theoretical foundation of his investigation of the peasant (Redfield 1941, 1955). Peasant society became the "little community," and the distance from the city calibrated with the degree of community (a formula conveyed in the folk-urban continuum). The challenges to this view posed by the material reality of peasant life no doubt led Redfield and his disciples to focus more on worldview and less on the troublesome economic dimensions of peasant societies (Silverman 1979). The model was reinforced nonetheless, and it reached its apogee in anthropology with the development of the so-called community study method, in which the community (usually a village) became both object and sample for the researcher (Arensberg 1961).

For anthropologists looking for the equivalents of tribes and lineages in peasant societies, the community seemed the logical choice (for example, Arensberg and Kimball 1940), and it came with many of the associated assumptions of corporateness, insularity, and solidarity that anthropologists had attributed (often incorrectly) to kinship groups. This focus, evident in Redfield's work, clearly reinforced the association of community with rural villages and also enhanced the geographical dimension of the community concept, which had not been as central or essential to studies of more mobile nonagricultural societies. It is noteworthy that the community study approach in anthropology is closely associated with the discipline's expansion into European and Asian studies, where geographical units appeared more clearly and permanently defined. The community study method reinforced them further by focusing on internal activities to the near exclusion of external relations. Community became further equated with peasant villages, and the emphasis of community studies on the coherence and integration of peasant society fueled the consensus model. Terence Byres and Henry Bernstein see this process creating a "peasant essentialism" constructed around "the solidarities, reciprocities and egalitarianism of (village) community, and commitment to the values of a way of life based on household and community, kin and locale" (2001:6). Of course, such equations can be read from both directions: "peasant" and "community" were mutually constructed as interdependent essentialist categories. This association of community with romantic/Redfieldian notions provoked Anthony Leeds (1973) to make one of the first appeals to replace the term, offering instead the more neutral term "locality" (compare Appadurai 1996). His alternative was hardly a panacea, but the effort shows early recognition of the problem, while its apparent lack of impact suggests significant scholarly resistance.

FALSE STARTS, NOBLE EFFORTS, AND NEAR MISSES

Predictably, thesis led to antithesis, and researchers challenged the romantic image of peasant community with reports of conflict-ridden and competitive villages with little or no solidarity. Oscar Lewis (1960) returned to one of the sites of Redfield's own research to drive home the difference, while Edward Banfield (1958) spawned a whole cottage industry of criticism with his image of a southern Italian village as a collection of backstabbing nuclear families. These models, however, painted pictures of conflict and opposition so extreme that the very concept of community, already infused with discursive power, seemed inappropriate, leaving it largely unreformed and still in the hands of the romantics. Thus, rather than challenging our understanding of community, Banfield's "*amoral* familism," to use the most notorious example, seemed to suggest that the village was not a community at all. He begins his book with the fantastic claim that "most of the people of the world live and die without ever achieving membership in a community larger than the family or tribe" (1958:7). Here community is cooperative, and any unit that's not is not a community.

More recent work maintains this formula. Frank Cancian's (1992) book on the history of community in Zinacantan re-creates the urban community collapse model nearly whole cloth in a rural context, suggesting that urban problems have now affected the cradle of the community itself. Modernizing forces have destroyed community even in the countryside. What is especially interesting in such accounts is how previously linked elements in the concept have become unlinked. But rather than destabilizing the assumptions inherent in these links, decoupling has allowed more thoroughly romantic connotations to survive. Notions of location have been rendered less important. For Cancian and Banfield, living together in a village is no longer a factor defining community, but the expected, cooperative nature of relationships, once erroneously associated with that type of place, remains determinant. The romantic ideas once thought to result from particular types of place (communities) become the determinant elements in defining community. Cancian's analysis provoked a rebuttal from Jeffrey Cohen (2000) based on research in Oaxaca, where he found community alive and well. This community, however, is still defined in the same explicit romantic terms of "cooperation." Both sides of the argument reinforce an explicitly romantic notion of community, and their debate deflects attention from the underlying assumption of community as cooperation, which they share.

A few anthropologists have attempted to establish some middle ground, looking at how degrees of corporateness related to particular historical and external conditions (Wolf 1957; Nash 1967), but these insights failed to destabilize romantic concepts of community, showing the power of the community model. In fact, Eric Wolf's effort to show how different political and economic histories create different types of community was reinterpreted as a general typology of community and applied in places lacking the historical specifics Wolf saw as causal (Popkin 1979; Skinner 1971), forcing Wolf to write a corrective (1986), which also failed to break through. James Greenberg (1995:68) suggests that the failure of ethnographers to fully explore the implication of Wolf's model probably stems from a "certain romantic fascination with native cultures," which I would suggest is linked to their notions of community as well.

A more promising intervention is offered by William Roseberry (1991), who clearly appreciated Wolf's approach and attempted to apply it to community relations in rural England from the premodern to modern periods. He argues that England saw a movement from a more community-based form of production characteristic of late feudalism to a more household-based form of production in the early modern period. He nonetheless acknowledges that communities of a different character probably preceded the strong communities of late feudalism, and he warns against romanticizing the latter. Yet in the end, he is also seduced. Once the more corporate and collective community associated with the three-field rotation was established, he sees its decline under an expanding commercial economy as a decline in community rather than another shift in community relations: "*[D]ifferentiation* within village communities, always a characteristic of the feudal village, could become *class formation* within villages. The community was increasingly a shell that was finally cast off with enclosure" (1991:44). Class conflict apparently cannot exist within a community (a notion that resembles politicized understandings of community common in the twenty-first century). This conclusion contradicts his earlier comments about community, which insist it is a relationship rather than an essence and describe it as a problematic category, the meaning of which differs "according to—and even within—modes of production" (21). The point here is to show how an effort that explicitly recognizes the problems of the community concept can still be victimized by them.

Social historians have done their part to disabuse us of romantic images of community. In detailed accounts of local communities, practitioners of the Annales School often drew upon conflicts for their primary source material (for example, Le Roy Ladurie 1974). Latin American historian Florencia Mallon has taken the project further by documenting a sophisticated relationship between conflict and hegemony in the production of peasant communities (Mallon 1983, 1995). However, as with the historical debate about English communities, the correct association of such conflict with the development of capitalism and/or state expansion unintentionally allows (if not requires) an ideal, less conflictive community to exist theoretically in the past or under different political-economic conditions. This result is not the intent of these historians, but rather it is an unintentional product of the discursive field surrounding the notion of community. It is reinforced, however, by scholars who continue to document communities in predominantly cooperative, collective terms. For example, Nikolai Mikhailov (2002) suggests that Russian village commune traditions were reconstituted in new forms when peasants moved to town as workers and that these traditions, not agitation by intellectuals, account for revolutionary mobilization. This is a laudable effort to recognize worker/peasant agency, but in that very effort it reconfirms a notion of community as collective and communal, which can be traced *intellectually* to the Russian countryside/past. A similar conclusion is deducible from Karen Hansen's (1994) discussion of community in antebellum New England. Alan Macfarlane (1977) apparently anticipated such traps when he warned social historians against adopting community studies.

Other historians challenge the romantic interpretation of community by describing the dreadful constraints that rural communities imposed on their members in the past (Wall 1990; Worobec 1991). They point out that life in places with strong community traditions was often hard to bear. However, the evolutionary association of this community with a rural past, and its historical disappearance or erosion, is still the central thesis. Helena Wall (1990) suggests that community relations on the wane in Europe were reproduced in the American colonies: "Highly conscious of their strange environment, fearful of departing too far from European society, the colonists clung to their received ideas about the community....Indeed, these ideas may have drawn added urgency from the disorder of a new society and the colonists' apprehension of failure" (1). She shares a romantic notion of community based on "stability, order and cooperation." It is qualified by a developed understanding of the conflict and consequences involved, but ultimately conflict and community are incompatible: "The persistence of tensions in community life, and the failure of means such as arbitration to lessen them, fueled questions about the nature of community and the sacrifices it demanded" (29). These strains emerged "in religious controversies and malicious lawsuits and witchcraft accusations—and in a concern for reputation that bordered on the obsessive. This remained true until the late eighteenth century when traditional community life lost much of its coherence and community ridicule lost much of its sting" (48). In this model, communities struggle to reestablish consensus when faced with conflict, and when that is no longer possible, community is lost. I am not suggesting that these characterizations are historically or ethnographically "wrong," just that the way they utilize the notion of community in making their case reproduces and sustains a romantic image.

By the 1800s, the image of America is not "forced communion" but Tocqueville's voluntary associations. What is in some ways a very different animal from the community of colonial America gets redefined *as community* by late-nineteenth-century thinkers. The emphasis on volunteerism becomes the urban community surrogate, and in the process community begins to lose one of its rural qualities—territoriality—while romantic notions of consensus and solidarity get reinforced and enhanced. As previously noted, this "moral" notion of community was reterritorialized in the work of urban sociology during the 1930s, where community as neighborhood was a localized space of habitation (see also N. Rose 1999:172) but never completely (Banfield 1958). Furthermore, the fact that these locations were often ethnically defined exposed community to various political and intellectual currents in the 1960s. As ethnicity itself came under increased attention and scrutiny and primordial notions were challenged by instrumental and constructionist views, the concept of community also acquired more fluid manipulability. The social movements of the time also embraced the concept in their effort to represent and mobilize like-minded constituencies. Ironically, these political communities were constructed on the primordial assumptions of their rural exemplars and conformed to Tocquevillian reconceptualization of American community and liberal notions of individuality.

Other political and religious projects, such as utopian communities, also played a role by providing living examples of idealized communities. Here, mythic, romantic ideals inspired efforts to build such communities, from hippie communes to the Israeli kibbutz. Their fame, in turn, served to reinforce the idealized conceptions upon which these communities were built (Kanter 1972; see also S. Brown 2002). When these efforts collapsed, failure was often attributed to selfishness, which reinforced the notion that community and self-interest are incompatible (Schwartz, Lees, and Kressel 1995). Interestingly, the utopian element of such communities was not their romantic conceptualization of what community means, which was shared by most other deployments of the concept and thus not utopian, but rather their effort to actualize it in a territorially defined location, which was an improbable effort to reestablish community's historical rural origins. This effort ran the risk of generating all the horrible negative elements of rural communities shucked off the political concept. The will to community was omnipresent, progressive, and politically practical; the effort to ground it was potentially retrograde and utopian.

The new community expansions (conceptual and concrete) spurred a flurry of academic interest in the concept during the 1970s (for example, Clark 1973; Plant 1978; Scherer 1972). These notions of community were based on a complete consensus of political objective and uniformity along the particular lines that defined the community or association. Community then becomes nearly synonymous with identity, but an identity that was political and elective, so that the concept lost any residue of the inevitability that characterized village or lineage communities. Thus Fran Markowitz (1993) feels compelled to qualify the rather disorganized and underpoliticized group of Soviet Jewish émigrés she studied as "a community in spite of itself." Even the inevitabilities of race, class, gender, and sexual orientation failed to automatically define a community but required some political involvement and self-ascription. Moreover, these identities crosscut one another, which prohibited the kind of consensus and uniformity increasingly expected of community, provoking ever more narrowly defined units. Thus Kath Weston (1991) suggests that the embrace of the concept of kinship by gays and lesbians beginning in the 1980s was partly a response to the failure to build a gay community (see also Joseph 2002). In the absence of clear territorial boundaries defining communities, members of political and elective communities became increasingly consumed with boundary definition and maintenance (Li 2001), often based on consensus and uniformity. My concern is that this view of community actually creates a crisis of community as people aspire to an improbable ideal that never figured in the rural villages and small locales that inspired community imaginings. The nostalgic desire for such community generates social fragmentation.

Perhaps the strongest challenges to the sanctity of the community concept have come from a diverse collection of environmental/ecological research. Frustrated by the substantive failures and ethical ambiguity of governmental and global conservation efforts, states and international organizations embraced the concept of community resource management, which supposedly allowed communities to manage (read "preserve") their own local resources. While this process potentially empowered local populations, the romantic assumptions about communities that validated this approach ran afoul of local practice, provoking a collection of critiques and qualifications (Agrawal and Gibson 2001; Brosius, Tsing, and Zerner 1998; Li 1996; Oates 1999; Zerner 1994). These critiques rightly point out that communities are beset by differences of ethnicity, gender, and class and are not automatically good environmental stewards. As Arun Agrawal and Clark Gibson put it, "the existing literature on community-based conservation reveals a widespread preoccupation with what might be called 'the mythic community': small, integrated groups using locally evolved norms to manage resources sustainably and equitably. Such characteristics capture the realities of few, if any, existing communities" (1999:640).

These environmental critiques provide a launchpad for rethinking the community concept, but they also allow for its reinforcement. The realization that community is a problematic concept for conservation efforts because of its romantic assumptions has led conservationists to either abandon the approach or to look for communities that do conform to their preconceptions, rather than rethink their notion of community (see Brosius, this volume). This is hardly surprising when other environmental theories engaged with communities emphasize and reinforce the challenged elements of the concept (for example, Di Chiro 1996). Moreover, romantic assumptions may actually apply if communities are redefined or constituted in relation to the demands of such conservation programs, as Donald Moore (1998) intimates, or if local groups use the concept to constitute "communities" defined by shared political interests (Li 1996). This strategy may produce communities that conform to the expectations of state or international organizations (uniform and cooperative), a result that fits frightfully well with Miranda Joseph's (2002) and Nikolas Rose's (1999) focus on the notion's imbrication with capitalist accumulation and state governance.

IDENTITY POLITICS: NATIONAL AND OTHERWISE

Many of the examples already discussed reveal the link between the concept of community and what is often glossed as identity politics.[1] In many cases, these interests are nearly synonymous, but the conscious use of the community notion for political goals does not necessarily escape the term's discursive constraints and consequences. An interesting case is presented by the notion of "indigenous communities" in which the community may be defined legally by the state, which grants particular political rights and obligations. In such cases we should not be surprised to find that assumptions about the nature of community play a significant role (see, for example, Fondahl 1998; Gray n.d.; Weismantel, this volume). Jeffrey Gould (1998) shows that after promising to avenge misdeeds to Nicaragua's indigenous communities, the Somoza government in power decided that the communities had indeed been destroyed and thus did not qualify for land restitutions. Here, a decline in the cooperative and collective relations assumed to characterize community became evidence of community extinction, which delegitimized the economic demands of indigenous groups and contributed to the political project of building a homogenous nation. In such cases, assumptions of what a community is may determine the outcome of community-based claims. In any case, the arguments on both sides may simply reinforce erroneous assumptions about what constitutes community. These issues are also evident in Kate Crehan's (2002a) discussion of South African NGOs and their difficulties with the community discourse (see also Crehan, this volume).

Tanya Li (1996) maintains that the community concept, while obviously problematic, is still politically useful for oppressed people, who can knowingly use it to acquire resources or rights from powerful people with naive romantic images of community (see also Weismantel, this volume). Yet because of the concept's popular and discursive power, the expectations it carries come back to haunt the people who attempt to manipulate it for a utilitarian political project. Much as Peter Berger and Thomas Luckmann (1966) characterize the social construction of reality, the projection or externalization of the community idea runs the risk of objectification, which can then come back to make demands on the people who deploy it strategically. In fact, this situation is almost inevitable, since the term is already so thoroughly objectified and reified in the circles where it can be usefully politically invoked. By embracing the notion, the group itself, or its spokespeople, can end up answering to the implications carried by the term. It is like a monster that will not be controlled: energized by progressive political goals, its dangerous side emerges to strangle the unit(y) it was animated to support/foster. The Janus face of romance is gothic horror. Calling yourself a community and trafficking in the assumptions that are implied risks a subsequent exposure to those very assumptions, which is especially problematic when they are romantic ideals that can never be met.

This process renders community less useful in Gayatri Spivak's important tactic of "strategic essentialism" (see Spivak 1996). She suggests that images of subalterns that operate in an essentialized way may be developed to interrupt the discourses of exclusion yet also to reveal internal contradictions so as to prevent this essentialization from being reproduced by the powerful groups whose discourses were the target of intervention. Not only has little attention been directed to creating such complex images of community (the agenda of this volume), but in contrast to other categories, such as ethnic group or race, assumptions about community seem to deny the very contradictions that Spivak insists have to be included.

Perhaps no one has made these points as strongly as Iris Young (1986). Responding to an earlier and explicitly romantic use of community (such as Roberto Unger's [1975] claim that it represented a political alternative to personal love!), Young suggests that the notion denies difference and is thus more in league with racism and ethnic chauvinism than progressive politics. She advocates the abandonment of the term altogether. Although the article was reprinted twice, its impact was surely weakened by the author's association of community with "face-to-face relations." She finds evidence for community's "denial of difference" in the parallel "denial of time and space distancing," which privileges face-to-face relations. Obviously, this idea has been disproved by the subsequent proliferation of community projects that do not demand or even desire such contact. She did not foresee the potential of "imagined" or virtual communities, and thus like Maurice Stein's (1960) prediction of the eclipse of community, the gems were thrown out with the baubles. It is not the face-to-face relations that are important but rather the quality of relationships assumed to inhere in these types of relations, and this assumption is related to the urban imaginary that viewed the rural primordial community of face-to-face relations as harmonious and collective, when in fact they are often conflictive and antagonistic. Young notes that face-to-face relations can involve separation and violence as much as communication and consensus but simply says that theorists of the community emphasize the latter, without examining why. An effort to explain this preference would have led her "back" to projections of an imagined rural exemplar by the likes of Redfield. She unwittingly verifies this rural foundation when she suggests that the actualization of community as face-to-face relations "would require dismantling the urban character of modern society" (1986:18).

The final blow, however, is her suggestion of "city life" as the alternative to community: "I suggest that instead of the ideal of community we begin from our positive experience of city life to form a vision of the good society" (1986:20). This alternative completely re-creates the urban gaze (and the rural/urban opposition) that imagined the community as the problematic entity she sees it. The urban interpretation of the countryside is part of why community is conceived in the way she suggests it is (denial of difference). To turn to city life to escape the community conundrum is to miss how an urban perspective of the rural created the problem. She, of course, does not see this effect, because the rural has ceased to figure in her view of the modern condition (and she does not look at the history of the term).

To recognize "difference" within a community is certainly a step in the right direction, but it does not automatically challenge romantic ideas if it does not instantiate conflict and opposition as potentially constitutive of the community. To say that a community is divided by ethnicity, race, class, gender, generation, religion, or sexuality (to name only a few) is more likely to lead to proposals for redress, mediation, and reconciliation than recognition that such conflict is part of community. For the same reason, community has become more resonant with increasing spatial separation—it is the separation that allows the romantic elements that can't persist in face-to-face groups to flourish. The uniformity is actually increased by separation and difference, which allows for more selectivity and more denial of the anticommunity sentiments of conflict, tension, and even contempt. So the fact that community has expanded its popular, political, and scholarly resonance with movement, diaspora, and separation is verification of the assumptions that underlie the term. These assumptions are more sustainable with separation! The current fortunes of the community concept reveal its underlying assumptions. Thus, contra Young, denying difference has been facilitated/enhanced by acceptance of "time and space distancing."

Even the promising idea of "communities of difference" (Whitt and Slack 1994; Di Chiro 1996), which is defined explicitly against the assumptions of community unity, can easily end up replicating Durkheim's view of organic solidarity if the differences are cast as complementary elements within a diverse multicultural whole, which takes on a unity not so distinct from the homogenous community it was intended to debunk. Thus the community of difference can revert to what Homi Babha distinguishes as "diversity" rather than "difference" because of the assumptions inherent in the community concept (Rutherford 1990).

The comparison with the concept of culture is instructive (see also Khan, this volume). The idea of culture as a shared set of uniform beliefs or attributes has been thoroughly discredited by some of the same interventions listed above, yet the community concept has survived with much less effect. In some sense, community has become the new locus of sharing and cohesion within diverse and fragmented cultures. The relationship between community and family is also illustrative. Banfield's statement quoted earlier verifies that the qualities of community are often the same ones expected of "family" (see also Scherer 1972:ch. 7). For Hegel the family constituted the basic community (see Pandey, this volume). For Orthodox Jews the ability to move freely within their community on the Sabbath requires redefining neighborhoods as family or household spaces (Lees, this volume). In efforts at restorative justice, the family is tapped as the essential link to reconnect the offender to the community (Joseph, this volume). Given pervasive domestic conflict, the family-as-community template could provide an opening or avenue for quite unromantic characteristics, but this transfer does not seem to occur. The family model for community must involve a family that is integrated, cooperative, and harmonious. Thus dangerous collectivities in Africa are described as "a *crummy* family," which is antithetical to community (Watts, this volume), and unstable Afro-Caribbean families are presumed to prevent the formation of communities (Khan, this volume). Family seems to provide a model or base of community only when the family conforms to romantic preconceptions about community.

Perhaps the best evidence of community's enduring romantic foundation is its negation. If community is not defined by any of the qualities I posit here, then what does it mean? Current uses rarely depend upon the territorial designations that once dominated its meaning. There is certainly no common use of the term in which contrary qualities of conflict and contention are foundational.[2] So if we remove romantic elements from the notion of community, we are left with little more than a synonym for "group." Yet most people would feel uncomfortable with that equation. C. J. Calhoun (1980) offers an alternative based on the social relations and organization that produce collective action. A community leads people to alter their actions on the basis of their social relations to each other. Or put differently, people constitute a community when they behave this way. But what are we to call groups to which people express a sense of belonging without an evident impact on their actual choices of action? Are these not communities? When it comes to specifying the differences between communities, Calhoun returns to such issues as familiarity, obligations, and the density, multiplexity, and systematicity of networks (1980:117–118). These are qualities that have been elemental to romantic images of community. Making them variables that distinguish degrees of communalism between communities certainly diminishes the expectation of extreme closeness, interaction, and cooperation in *every* community, but it hardly dislodges these qualities from the notion. In fact, it seems to facilitate a hierarchy of communities that works easily with the decline/disappearance narrative. A different response might be to insist that the essence of community varies by context—that it is a locally contingent category. I completely concur, but if this is the case, why do scholars (not to mention popular commentators) rarely feel the need to specify what community references in different places?

Benedict Anderson's (1991) popular conceptualization of nations as imagined communities is a perfect illustration of many of these qualities (see Creed 2004). What is being imagined is a romantic "deep, horizontal comradeship" (B. Anderson 1991:7), which must be imaginary because it reaches beyond the rural village where it is possibly real (6). The popularity of his thesis, then, certainly suggests that these assumptions about community resonate with most scholars. Partha Chatterjee is an exception (1993). He offers an alternative take on community that is neither imagined nor synonymous with the nation but rather a national quality that survived colonial domination to distinguish the nationalism of the colony from that of the colonizers. In his effort to refute the colonization of consciousness model advanced by other postcolonial theorists (Comaroff and Comaroff 1989) and to temper his earlier critique of nationalism as a derivative discourse (Chatterjee 1986), Chatterjee focuses on community as a reflection of the spiritual dimension of Indian society and culture that was not completely erased or reformulated by colonialism. This is a compelling move toward more contextualized notions of community, but it also supports, and in fact depends upon, the problematic evolutionary image of community decline in Europe.[3]

Aisha Khan (this volume) suggests a similar reading of Paul Gilroy's idea of a black Atlantic community, and Mary Weismantel (this volume) shows how Andean activists have employed the indigenous notion of *ayllu* in the same ways. The qualities of this community are the same as those of the romantic model, and they correspond again to the binary distinction between rural (colony) and urban (metropole). These postcolonial arguments embrace a romantic concept of community to contrast it with the colonizers, who ironically have made the same contrast between their own past and present (as recounted in the discussion of Roseberry, above). The use of community for decolonizing consciousness actually reinforces evolutionary views, since the places of such community are the very places one would expect from the ethnocentric evolutionary image of primordial community: "less developed" and predominantly rural. That rural India was one of the important foci of earlier community studies projects and paradigms is probably not insignificant to this essentialization, which may in turn have encouraged observers of the Caribbean to find community survival among Indo-Caribbeans, in stark contrast to their interpretation of Afro-Caribbean life (Khan, this volume).

If our concept of community carries *any* of these ideas, then they are likely to influence our analytic interpretations of anything we call a community. Moreover, as John Kelly and Martha Kaplan (2001) illustrate, the potential negative consequences of the romantic view go beyond the limited arenas of social science. They show how the nation in Fiji was not so much imagined as it was constructed by colonization and decolonization. The legacies of colonial "divide and rule" policies interacted with the international commitment to the nation-state system after World War II to produce a particular version of the Fijian nation. In this historical reconstruction, we see how assumptions about communities likely played an important role. The notion that "essential" differences were a natural basis of community distinctions underlay the "divide and rule" strategy. The same assumptions would then mandate that one such group be the basis for defining a national community, dismissing Asian populations. The representations of community thus influenced the construction of the Fijian nation.

This example, like Gould's (1998) analysis of Nicaragua, shows how dominant ideas of community can marginalize groups within a nation-state. It can also lead to national fragmentation and even genocide as people strive for communities that are harmonious, uniform, and cohesive. These expectations inspire division and repression in response to conflict, just as we have suggested for communities defined by identity vectors such as ethnicity, race, or sexual orientation. This suggestion opens the door for conspiracy theories in which the political encouragement to community becomes a means for limiting the political influence of groups who appeal to it for progressive political goals.

Nikolas Rose's (1999) provocative discussion of community as a form of governance suggests a similar outcome without conspiracy. He locates contemporary uses of community in what he calls the "third space" between the state/market and individuals (perhaps most recognizable as civil society, which constitutes only one of his examples). He then tracks the popularity of this community to the decline of the "social state." As the state shirks social responsibilities, individuals, firms, and organizations (which are themselves being relieved of state regulation and control) are made responsible for taking up the slack via notions of individual morality, organizational responsibility, and ethical community. He then suggests that this concept of community has been made technical through expert discourses and professional vocations evident in "community development programs" run by "community development officers," protected by "community policing," and analyzed by sociologists pursuing "community studies." Rendered technical, community can become a means of governance (N. Rose 1999:176–177).

While the ethical dimension ensures self-governance, the political technologies constitute new forms of authority over this new space of natural associations with newly instrumentalized forces to govern conduct. As community becomes a valorized political zone, a new political status has been given to the indigenous authorities of community. "To govern communities it seems one must first of all link oneself up with those who have, or claim, moral authority in 'the black community' or 'the local community'" (N. Rose 1999:189). Such natural authority is often more difficult to contest than more explicit laws or professional experts.

I will conclude with a recent attempt within anthropology to offer a solution to such dilemmas of community. Vered Amit's (2002) collection *Realizing Community* in many ways replicates the project of this volume. She takes issue with Anderson's imagined community notion, but her main complaint, reminiscent of Calhoun (1980), which she also directs toward Arjun Appadurai's (1996) notion of "locality," is the lack of attention to material social relations. Communities are imagined, but they are also embodied in social relations. Imagined communities are lived and experienced in very real ways, if only with a segment/ sample of those included in the imagined collective. These personal relations give the concept meaning and resonance and account for

43

people's emotional attachments to the larger category. Without further deconstruction, however, the idea of "sample" relations standing for the whole runs the risk of re-creating and validating prior notions of community as a microcosm or sample of a larger society. The parallel logic here is discomforting—Amit suggests that a selective set of relationships can stand for social relations with the community as a whole and account for its meaning among community members. Studying these relationships, then, tells us about community. But again, it is prior, internalized notions of community that lead people to see this projection—that is, to interpret their relations with a few as the basis for a larger collectivity. This leads people to select out some relations and not others as the basis for imagined or extended communities: those that conform to preexisting community ideals! It thus becomes self-fulfilling and self-validating. The notion of what a community is makes possible the linkage. Thus, in her discussion, as well as in some of the volume's chapters, the lived social relations foundational to community evince many of the same romantic elements discussed previously. Without further deconstruction of the term, efforts to look at real social relations focus primarily on the collective, harmonious, homogenous types that conform to romantic community notions.

I agree with Amit's conclusion that the outcome of past community analyses has been a detachment of the concept from social relations. Appadurai's (1996) distinction between locality as phenomenological (in contrast to actual neighborhoods) follows Cohen's (1985) effort to define community as a symbolic construct, which ironically dovetailed with Anderson's (1991) formulation of a Marxist imaginary, to produce a major conceptualization of community as a structure of feeling and quality of sociality/identity, detached from social relations. Clearly, the move away from real social relations is what made it possible to sustain the romantic elements I'm complaining about. But here again, we need to go further. When something is labeled or conceived of as a community, members' expectations of what community relationships *should* be like are potentially consequential, leading them to sever, break, or seek alternate social relations. The point is that the meaning of community can affect social relations, not just vice versa. Thus we ultimately disagree on the problem with Anderson's project. Amit focuses on his "decoupling" of the idea of community from an actual base of interaction. But I say he invoked a romantic image of real community relations and suggested they could be projected onto others. The projections are still those associated with intensive social relations of a romantic community. Amit's insistence on reinserting social relations into imagined community notions also runs the risk of re-creating some of the problems that Young points out with the notion of community as face-to-face relations—to wit, "[i]t presumes an illusory ideal of unmediated social relations, and wrongly identifies mediation with alienation" (1986:15). It may also create yet a new dichotomy of face-to-face versus imagined communities, which bears an uncanny similarity to the rural/urban one.

FINAL THOUGHTS, OR THE NEED FOR NEUROSIS

The way insightful critiques can also reinforce community preconceptions verifies that we have created a conceptual web around the community concept that is so dense and intricate that it is hard to escape. Every attempt to challenge elements of community ideology reinforces other elements; every effort to dislodge assumptions gets absorbed by it—it has become the tar baby of social analysis and cultural theory. I do not expect this, or any other, intervention to break through or escape the traps that have checked previous efforts. Indeed, the tar baby analogy is intended to underline just that impossibility, and the history recounted here would support such skepticism. However, I cannot second Young's or Leeds's suggestion to abandon the word altogether—an easy decision given the obvious lack of success with this strategy and the even greater entrenchment of the concept in politics and society. Moreover, the chapters that follow provide compelling examples of community's political utility (especially those by Crehan and Weismantel), as well as powerful warnings about what a post-community world might be like (notably those by Brosius and Watts). As Gyan Pandey (this volume) notes, the alternatives to community are equally worrisome or equally elusive. Instead I advocate a thorough deconstruction of the term (begun here) to be followed by a reconstitution with particular specifications (the project of subsequent chapters). I am encouraged by what appears to be a gathering momentum of scholarly involvement with this project, much of which has been discussed here. Unlike earlier efforts, these criticisms cut deeper into the concept. The fact that all fall short of a difficult goal does not diminish their contribution to a cumulative critical mass. Again, the concept of culture offers a parallel. The concept is as popular as ever, and essentialized qualities still figure prominently among its uses, but the various critiques of the concept have fostered greater consciousness of potential negative consequences and pitfalls. The same outcome for the concept of community would be a great success.

The reason the romantic foundation of community needs to be exposed now is, ironically, because it is now more likely to be achieved. People can now "imagine" communities based not only on their shared experience of the popular press, radio, and television but also on their visits to the world wide web (Castells 1997). The latter has facilitated the formation of "virtual" communities connecting people globally along the smallest or most narrowly defined interest (see Wilson and Peterson [2002] for a useful review of "online community" research). These new possibilities render the qualities of uniformity and consensus as virtual realities, which may serve to justify those images retroactively and more broadly. The ability to selectively create communities that conform to the notions of uniformity and harmony, and to select only interactions that confirm this formula through specialized chat rooms, makes it possible to conform to the ideal model—a model not of face-to-face relations but of the romantic qualities incorrectly assumed by urban intellectuals to inhere in face-to-face relations. This historical confluence—culturally ascendant romantic views of community meeting new possibilities for creating communities that approach such an ideal—has contributed to the dangerous trend toward fragmentation. The romanticized *ideal* has become *real*, or at least realizable.

According to Zygmunt Bauman (2001), it has also become more appealing due to the other insecurities of postmodernity. This suggestion puts the search for community in the United States in league with gun and SUV ownership as a popular response to fear and anxiety. So people are in desperate search of a community still defined in romantic terms, just as technological changes make it possible to virtually create such categories. As James Fernandez (1965) suggested long ago, the search for such communities may actually threaten existing communities based on the "gut feeling" of coordinated interactions (the ones people live in). Of course, fragmented, narrowly defined, virtual communities are not the inevitable outcome. Some of these "new" communities are more interactive than predecessors based on nation or locality, and some people suggest that new information technology even increases interaction in grounded neighborhoods (Doheny-Farina 1996; Hoffert 2000). Other studies examine the potential, as well as the problems, of the World Wide Web as a space of democratic community (Jones 1999; Nakamura 2002). Regardless, the lesson of this essay is that an appreciation of "online communities" will require attention to the underlying notion of community.

This objective is hampered by the very pervasiveness of the term. In what may prove the term's ultimate, and most perverse, protection, its popularity becomes a justification for inattention. With so many different uses, the temptation is to assume that there is no common meaning deserving analytical attention, which allows implicit meanings to go on doing ideological work. In a similar case, Sylvia Yanagisako (1979) once suggested that we should see "family" as simply an "odd-job word." The consequences of that attitude in an era of "family values" hardly require specification. A recent commentary by Anthony Cohen (2002) suggests a similar danger for community. Exhausted by attention to the notion and strangely disgruntled that his classic book on the topic has eclipsed his more substantive contributions to anthropology, Cohen concludes that "[t]he most we should allow here is that communities may now differ from their prior forms—nothing very startling about that—and that the nature of people's belonging to various communities with which they identify may also have changed....But let's not waste time and energy on semantic neuroses and anxiety about the word" (2002:169–170). This argument is all the more surprising following his recognition that the concept "seems to have become a normative rather than a descriptive term" (169). It is as a normative concept that the danger of the notion lies and why it should indeed provoke anxiety (if not neurosis)!

Notes

1. Consequently, it is no surprise that "community" and "identity" share many conceptual limitations (see Brubaker and Cooper 2000).

2. One might suggest the notion of the "scholarly community" as such, but while argument and conflict pervade such relations, the scholarly community is primarily about what is shared among combatants rather than their disagreements. This idea may help account for the continuity of well-known arguments even after they have been shown suspect (Hamilton 1996). Popular theorists and thinkers provide the shared knowledge that makes community possible. This may also explain why particular theories become pervasive and hegemonic out of proportion to their originality or analytic utility.

3. Kelly and Kaplan (2001:98) also find Chatterjee's use of community problematic, although for somewhat different reasons.

3

Hunting the Unicorn

Art and Community in East London

Kate Crehan

"How do I know what I like until I see what it is possible to have?"

—*Richard Hoggart (2002), quoting—and modifying—E. M. Forster*

I am currently working on an ethnography of a community arts organization, Free Form Arts Trust (subsequently Free Form), based in Hackney, one of London's poorest boroughs. In this chapter I examine a Free Form project on an aging and run-down council estate[1] that was carried out some twenty years ago. The Free Form ethnography represents something of a shift for me, since most of my previous fieldwork has been in rural Africa. And yet, as I read more urban regeneration (sometimes urban renewal) literature, I am struck by how similar the language often is to that of the development literature with which I am so familiar. Nonetheless, despite the many commonalities, the two discourses are normally understood as referring to two quite distinct spheres. Both may take as their object problems of poverty and social deprivation, but "development" is normally understood as the answer to a purely southern predicament; "urban regeneration" to a purely northern one. One interesting commonality in the context of this volume is the shared belief in the importance of "community" as an agent of progressive change.

For instance, to take urban regeneration first, in 2001 we find Britain's Labour prime minister, Tony Blair, giving "the community" a starring role in a speech delivered at the launch of the government's National Strategy for Neighbourhood Renewal. The launch was held at a dilapidated, interwar council estate, Ocean Estate, in Tower Hamlets, a London borough bordering Hackney and equally associated with social deprivation. "Over the last four years [since Labour was elected to government in 1997]," Blair announced, "we have laid the foundations for what I believe will be a new era of prosperity for this country. An era of prosperity in which I am determined communities like Ocean Estate will share." He went on to explain that "so much of the policy of the 1950s era failed because it was top-down, paternalistic, well-meaning, but failed to challenge. It is now very clear that doesn't work. But it is also clear what does work. *What works is when communities are empowered to control their own destiny and shape it*; where the opportunity is matched by responsibility" (Blair 2001, italics added). A 1989 World Bank document demonstrates a similar belief in the potential power of "the community" among development planners and policy makers:

> Many basic services...are best managed at the local level—even the village level—with the central agencies providing only technical advice and specialised inputs. *The aims should be to empower ordinary people to take charge of their lives, to make communities more responsible for their development*, and to make governments listen to their people. (World Bank 1989:54–55, quoted in Thomas, 1992:133, italics added)

The shared assumption here that there *is* an entity, "the community," with the power to "take charge" of its life, if only it is given the opportunity, reminds me irresistibly of Rilke's unicorn, "a creature there has never been," willed into being through people's determination that it *must* exist.[2] Mapping the effects of this determination, and the specific forms it takes in particular times and places, can perhaps allow us to understand a little better the phenomenon of "community," an entity that seems to be simultaneously so fiercely believed in and so illusory. My primary story here is a London story, but I want to begin with a brief look back at some of my earlier South African research, in the course of which I interviewed a number of land and housing nongovernmental organization (NGO) fieldworkers (see Crehan 2002a). The history of community as a political concept in South Africa is interesting in this context partly because it throws into relief the rather different, and less clear-cut, role that the notion of community has played in Britain.

"COMMUNITY" IN SOUTH AFRICA

Community is a particularly powerful term in the South African context, and I was curious as to how the NGO fieldworkers I interviewed both understood and used it. I interviewed them in 1997, three years after South Africa held its first multiracial elections. The expectations of black South Africans, newly enfranchised but still impoverished, were high, and the new state, dominated by apartheid's old foe, the African National Congress (ANC), had called on a number of NGOs to help it deliver on these expectations. As a result, many NGOs that had spent years locked in struggle with a racist state now found themselves an integral part of the new state. For land and housing NGOs, a particularly important possibility in the new South Africa was land restitution: returning to black South Africans land from which they had been forcibly removed under apartheid. Crucially, the entity that can claim land back in post-apartheid South Africa is a community—a "community" is a legal, rights-bearing entity in the new constitution. The centrality of community was also reflected in the fact that the NGOs with which I worked defined their aims in their mission statements and other literature as serving the needs of poor "communities." The problem for the fieldworkers was that while opposition to a brutal, racist regime had indeed created powerful communities of struggle, once land was actually going to be returned, the "community" tended to dissolve into competing groups and individuals. Running through my interviews is a tension between the rhetoric of community and the experiences of the fieldworkers, for whom the "communities" of their mission statements often seemed as hard to find in the real world as Rilke's unicorn. And given the reality of the community as a legal entity in South Africa, its tendency to vanish when looked at too closely presented NGOs with a difficult dilemma. The problem of identifying the needs and desires of such fragmented entities was particularly challenging.

In the old South Africa, things had in a sense been simpler; there was one overriding need, the destruction of apartheid, and communities could unite around this need. Determining a "community's" needs or wants in the new South Africa is far more complex. One female interviewee talks interestingly about this situation in the context of gender. She is reflecting here on the problem of identifying the needs of women in impoverished rural communities:

> These things need, I believe now, a lot of disaggregation. Obviously, in many places it's a place to live....And then the next, the next things [are]...a crèche, a clinic...and then there are a list of things. They're social services in a way that are particularly relevant to women. Now...I've begun to think that...those things—if one were to work with women around those things—need so much disaggregation, because that [a crèche] was one of the things identified in this community. In fact there were about five people who were child-minders. Now...were they saying that that isn't good enough, that they want a building? Were they saying they want to be free so they can go out to work? *Is* there work? Were they saying, ja, you know: "We see in the white suburbs crèches, so we want one of those as well."...So every need that they identified to me, needs *massive* disaggregation. Is it like a fashion or is it that we want to be in competition with the child-minders? Is it, "I don't think the child-minders do it well enough—can we improve this?" Is it, "*I* want," you know, "to make an income in a crèche?" So you're talking about six women and oh, they want, "we've identified a crèche." Is that because they think they'll get an income every month if they have it?...I don't trust those needs that are being identified like that. I don't trust them. I'm sure they have a kernel but we've never...disaggregated enough to find out what is the kernel. Maybe the kernel is as simple as they want something *better* for their children—right from the word go?

This problem, of course, is not specific to women—although teasing out "what people want" may be particularly difficult when the group concerned is a subordinated one. Men, too, articulate their desires in light of what they think legitimate, appropriate, possible, and so on. All of us come to know what we want within a dense network of real and imagined constraints, and an equally dense network of positive pressures pushing us toward what our particular time and place defines as appropriate desires. Even when those desires are ones we are told we should resist, the very fact that in any given time and place it is assumed that we will have certain forbidden or antisocial fantasies helps shape the particular landscape of desire we inhabit. However much we may feel we know what we want, our desires are always grounded in a specific economic, political, and social context and in our understanding of that context; unless we know what is possible, how *can* we know what we want? And given the often fractured nature of "communities," in what sense does *the community*, as opposed to the different individuals and groups of which it is composed, have desires and needs?

At this point, however, it is time to shift from South Africa to London, from the sphere of development to that of urban regeneration, and from attempts to serve the needs of rural "communities" to a community arts project in an impoverished, inner-city borough.

THE MAKING OF A COMMUNITY ARTS ORGANIZATION

Free Form, the community arts organization that carried out the project, was born in the counterculture years of the late sixties and early seventies, developing out of a small group of London-based visual artists' rejection of the elite gallery world of high art. The founders, Martin Goodrich, Jim Ives, and Barbara Wheeler-Early, were all trained at leading British art schools but had come to feel alienated from an art world they saw as incapable of reaching out to populations living beyond its self-referential gallery circles. Convinced of the liberatory value of art, these artists wanted to find a way of making art that would be relevant and accessible to those living in the kind of public housing in which Goodrich himself had grown up: "The great housing estates in England where art meant nothing. The great, vast areas of the population that had no exposure to art," as he put it, stressing that he himself had not been introduced to the arts while growing up.

Free Form was not alone in its aspirations to take art out of the gallery; it was part of a larger community arts movement that was itself one element of the wider political and social struggles erupting across the world in the 1960s. What constituted community arts was much debated. On the one hand, there were those who believed it should be an explicitly revolutionary enterprise, defined in unambiguous terms. On the other hand, there were those—and these included the Free Form founders—who felt it was more important to keep the nascent movement as broad and inclusive as possible and to refrain from over-precise definitions. In the context of this chapter, it is significant that Free Form never felt it necessary to define community in any precise way, accepting rather that there are many kinds of community, some defined by geographical proximity and some by shared interest, and that all of us inhabit numerous different communities and inhabit them in different ways. This pragmatism is possible in part because in Britain a community is not a legal entity, as it is in South Africa, nor has the term been central to political mobilization.

Community certainly does have considerable power in the British context as an imagined reality, conjuring up often rather romanticized notions of tightly knit, working-class communities woven together by powerful threads of kinship and shared hardship, but these assumptions tend to be unstated and implicit. As a result, while this sense of community, with its aura of authenticity, is undoubtedly present in the political and social landscape that community artists inhabit, in general they do not have to confront the contradictions between the rhetoric of community and an often fractious social reality quite as directly as do South African NGOs. In practice, what constitutes "the community" in any given community arts project for Free Form tends to be defined in the particular context of that project. At the same time, the popularity of the concept of community with urban regeneration professionals makes it an important term to use in funding applications. Over the course of its thirty-year life, Free Form has become very adept at framing its projects in terms of the urban regeneration language of the day. This is not to say that the organization's use of the term community is purely cynical. Inevitably, given the power of community as a concept, some kind of loose bundle of positive associations is likely to be part of the mental furniture of the various Free Form artists and in various ways to shape the work they do.

In Free Form's early years, much of their work had a strong performance element—this was the era of festivals and happenings—and the performance work was used to draw those outside the art world into the projects. Over time, however, the focus shifted increasingly to projects that sought to improve the built environment of those living on often grim and desolate housing estates, and the artists employed began to include architects. The group's current company profile defines it as "a multi-disciplinary practice established in 1969 to undertake Community Art and Architecture projects as a way of involving people with artists in improving the physical and social urban environment." However, it still draws on participation techniques developed during the initial performance years, and the current mission statement is close to the original vision of the founders, two of whom, Goodrich and Wheeler-Early, still lead the organization. Free Form has grown considerably over the years: by 2002 it was a registered charity with a board of directors and a grant income of just over a million pounds, plus three-quarters of a million in earned income. By this point it was providing employment for approximately seventy arts professionals (including permanent employees, commissioned artists, and trainees), as well as running a regular training program for community and public artists.

A number of community art practitioners, including Free Form, claim they can provide mechanisms whereby nonexperts can play a genuine, if modest, role in shaping their environment. This claim has important implications that reach beyond the realm of "art." It may well be that those who live in a particular environment, such as a dilapidated council estate, know very well what the social and environmental problems are; the problem is that devising *effective* solutions requires the skills of a design professional. A standard design professional, however, is not trained to tap into the visual and social imagination of those who inhabit public housing. The community artist is. Following Antonio Gramsci's theorization of the nature and role of intellectuals,[3] we could think of the artist in a community arts organization as an intellectual who attempts to transform vague aspirations for something "better" into design solutions that genuinely reflect the cultural life in which those aspirations are rooted and that improve the environment in ways that those who live in it recognize as "what they wanted."

PROVOST

To examine this claim, and in what sense this claim, even if success-ful, could be said to reflect the aspirations of the *community*, I have selected a single Free Form project, the Provost project. My account of it is based primarily on interviews with some of the Free Form artists involved and a small group of Provost tenants. Unless otherwise indi-cated, all the following quotations are from interviews conducted in 2002 and 2003. It should be noted that the Provost project was carried out almost twenty years ago, so the accounts represent people's memo-ries of it, not necessarily how they experienced it at the time. What my interviews do reflect, in the case of the tenants who have been living with the results of the project, is what that work has come to mean to them. For the artists, who have moved on to other projects and other places, my questions gave them a chance to revisit some early work that they had neither seen nor thought about much for many years.

The Provost Estate, on which the project was carried out, was built just before the Second World War and is still social housing owned by the local council (originally Shoreditch, now Hackney), although its management, in line with the general move to privatization in local government, is now contracted out. Hackney has long been one of the poorest boroughs of London. For most Londoners, and indeed Britons, it represents the archetypal East End, conjuring up images of cockney barrow boys, London underworld figures such as the Kray twins, and the extended working-class families long celebrated in British films and by sociologists such as Young and Wilmott (1962). East Enders and many others tend to regard those from the East End— one of the oldest parts of London, located just east of the city—as the most "authentic" Londoners. This attitude is reflected in the definition of a true London cockney as someone born within the sound of Bow bells (the bells of the city church of St. Mary-Le-Bow). The familiar image of lovable, characterful cockneys living in a tight-knit, working-class "community" is perpetuated in the popular television soap opera *EastEnders*.

For many years, Provost was indeed characterized by the presence of extended, intergenerational, and intermarrying families. Until the 1970s, it was the policy of many local councils to favor the relatives of existing tenants when reallocating vacated flats to those on the often long waiting lists for council properties. This policy undoubtedly favored the development and perpetuation of close-knit "communities," but it also ensured that estates such as Provost would remain enclaves of white working-class families, often distrustful of outsiders and downright hostile to "foreigners," particularly dark-skinned ones. Hackney and the East End in general have a history that reflects an ugly side of "community": Shoreditch and neighboring Dalston (also part of Hackney) were the primary strongholds of Oswald Mosley's black shirts, Britain's homegrown fascist movement in the 1930s. It is probably not coincidental that the East End has a long history of immigration—in the nineteenth century, mainly Jewish and Irish; since the mid-twentieth century, Caribbean and South Asian. By 1991, 29 percent of Hackney residents had been born outside the United Kingdom (Rix 1996:27).

As the East End became ever more ethnically and culturally diverse, a housing policy that virtually ensured that estates would remain white enclaves was seen as increasingly problematic. In the 1970s the policy was reversed, and a deliberate attempt was made to diversify the population of estates. By the time Free Form began working on Provost in the early eighties, a small number of primarily Afro-Caribbean and South Asian families had moved in, to the dismay of some white residents.

The layout of the Provost Estate is typical for interwar British social housing: five-story blocks of flats, with approximately forty flats in each block, grouped together on a common plot sandwiched between a series of main roads (see figure 3.1). The blocks were by and large well built, and with the fall from favor of the high-rise, the virtues of their more human scale, with individual flats leading off walkways, are once more being recognized. Nonetheless, by the 1980s, the more-than-fifty-year-old Provost Estate was in serious need of renovation. The external spaces were particularly bleak; what had been intended as communal open space with grass had deteriorated into an ill-lit, muddy no-man's-land. To make things worse, the most direct route to the local shops was blocked by a tumbledown wall, its sorry state presumably the result of the tenants' habit of climbing over it to avoid the long detour around it.

FIGURE 3.1

Provost Estate showing mural. Photograph by Kate Goodrich.

THE PROVOST PROJECT

The Provost tenants first encountered Free Form through the Shoreditch Festival. For several years beginning in the late 1970s, Free Form had organized a series of festivals, each culminating in an elaborate bonfire. This was against a background of increasing racism throughout much of Britain and growing support, especially at the local level, for neo-Nazi, anti-immigrant parties such as the National Front. One aim of the festivals was to bring together the different Shoreditch estates, on many of which racism was rife, in the context of a more positive and friendly rivalry. Each festival had a theme and culminated in a grand parade around all the estates. At the end of the parade, each estate would make its own contribution to the bonfire. Free Form worked with a number of tenants associations, including Provost. The tenants I spoke to more than twenty years later still remember how Free Form had helped the children make Halloween lanterns: "You got the little night lights in them and they paraded as proud as they could be. They paraded around the streets with their little lamps."

In 1982 Free Form was approached by a group of Provost tenants who were looking for help in improving their estate. In an attempt to "make the professions available to people," as Wheeler-Early put it, Free Form had recently established a Design and Technical Aid Service to provide tenants associations and others with free advice and practical suggestions on how estates could be improved. Funding, primarily from the Hackney Council Urban Programme, allowed three core artists, including an architect and a landscape architect, to be employed. The service lasted for ten years and led to Free Form's working on more than 100 estates. The projects varied greatly in size, from small to substantial, sometimes involving successive projects over a number of years. Groups such as tenants associations were able to use Free Form's expertise to decide how they wanted to improve their estates, and then applied for funding for Free Form to carry out the work. The organization's core funding allowed it to provide its services at a highly subsidized rate.

The Design and Technical Aid Service fulfilled a crucial function: the Greater London Council (GLC, abolished by the Thatcher government in 1986) had made money available for environmental improvement through a special program to which tenants could apply. Tenants had to come up with an acceptable proposal, however. They had to know not only exactly what they wanted but also how to write it up as a funding proposal with a budget, all of which required skills not necessarily possessed by tenants associations on impoverished working-class estates.

Once approached by a group of tenants, members of the Design and Technical Aid team would visit the estate and hold meetings to explore ideas and possibilities: What were the estate's major issues and problems? How could they be solved? Which problems could, or should, be tackled, and in what order? As on Provost, this work might represent the first stage of a process that would continue for several years, as trust was established, a program of work was decided on, money was raised, and the work itself was carried out. The consultation with tenants, however, did not simply involve meetings between the Free Form artists and the tenants association. Building on their long years of experience of drawing people into projects, Free Form ran workshops that introduced people to different techniques and helped them think in new ways about how their estate might be improved visually and socially. At their most successful, such "participation techniques" enable those without any formal design skills to tap into their vague and often incoherent ideas about their built environment in ways that allow them to contribute to design solutions for problems they have identified.

When Free Form began working on Provost, the total number of tenants involved was very small, a core of about ten in the tenants association, with thirty or so attending estate-wide meetings. A complicating factor with Provost—one common to many such "communities" —was that the estate held two main factions, each centered on a powerful family and each wary of the other. The Free Form artists remember a lot of time spent walking between flats and talking separately with different individuals, attempting to mediate, stressing all the while the importance of getting more people involved. With any such project there are always limits to the extent of participation; certain groups will tend to be overrepresented and others underrepresented. For instance, it is easier to get children to participate in "art" workshops than to get adults, in part because making art tends to be seen as something, except in the case of professional artists, that children, not adults, do. Another interesting bias is that of gender. Often, it seems, the work that goes into making "the community" a more pleasant place to live, which frequently involves a lot of unpaid voluntary labor, is seen as somehow the responsibility of women, part of their maternal role as "homemakers." It is noteworthy that on many of the estates on which Free Form has worked, the key activists among the tenants have been women. Participation can take many forms, however, and people can have a sense of ownership of a project without necessarily physically working on it.

The first problem the tenants identified was that of the badly lit and muddy open spaces between several of the blocks. The key to solving this problem, Free Form suggested, was a fundamental reorganization of the communal spaces between the individual blocks of flats. How this kind of space is organized shapes how people move about on an estate, how they enter and leave it. All too often, the planners who lay out estates are more concerned with the formal geometry of the space than with how those who live there will in fact use this space. At the heart of Free Form's suggested improvements was the rethinking of the layout of the estate's open spaces through the creation of "desire line paths": well-designed paved paths with benches and good lighting that would follow the routes actually used by people and create natural meeting places. For example, an opening would be made in the wall the tenants were currently clambering over, with a paved path leading up to it. Free Form's plan was agreed to, and a successful application for funding was made to the Hackney Urban Programme Fund.

This work, however, was concentrated on one area of the estate, and the problem remained that only a small number of tenants were actively involved. Free Form's solution was to offer everyone on the estate a window box to be placed on the balcony walkway outside his or her flat. Free Form would install the boxes (a fairly complicated procedure given the safety concerns of attaching the boxes securely), and individuals would be offered a choice of planting plans for their boxes. Since the tenants were by and large lifelong flat dwellers with little or no knowledge of gardening, Free Form organized a trip to a nearby stately home with a famous garden, Syon Park, and arranged for a gardener to run workshops on how to take care of window boxes. The window box initiative was very successful in getting people from across the estate to participate. About 150 window boxes were distributed; perhaps one-third are still in place twenty years later. In my interviews with tenants, the window box initiative, which had in fact happened two years into the project, was the first thing mentioned: "The first thing we thought of was the window boxes....It was to get neighbors there, to be neighborly, they'd talk about their plants...and then they started getting interested."

Quite early on, the Free Form team felt that although the creation of the paths, the new lighting, and so on was central to improving the estate, the project needed something more; it needed a focal point. The new layout of the paths created a natural corner, the main feature of which was a blank brick wall with crudely drawn goalposts, against which the children of the estate played football, a source of considerable irritation to those living in the flat behind the wall. To the eyes of the Free Form artists, this corner cried out for some kind of visual statement, possibly a mural. Initially, however, the tenants were not convinced, and one of the two rival camps on the estate was quite hostile—in part because murals were sprouting up on many council estates in the early eighties, particularly on so-called sink estates, those desolate and despised estates on which "problem" tenants were ghettoized. In addition, many tenants were convinced that anything put up would rapidly be graffitied or destroyed. Faced with this hostility, the Free Form team did not press the idea but concentrated on other aspects of the project while trying to build support for a mural.

It should be stressed that while Free Form artists see work on estates like Provost as genuinely dialogic, with tenants contributing to the final shape of the project in substantive ways, they do not see their role as being simply the realization of tenants' existing understanding of what they want or need. The aim is rather to provide mechanisms and a process through which those living in a particular place, at a particular time, can *discover* what it is that they want. Let me stress here that it is not that those living in social housing are assumed not to know what they want because they are poor or working class. In the highly complex contemporary world of proliferating experts and ever more differentiated areas of knowledge, knowing what is possible in any given context grows harder for all of us.

Free Form did manage to get support for an idea it had used on another estate to stop children playing football against a wall: decorative railings enclosing a small area of planting in front of the problem wall. But as Free Form artist Hazel Goldman remembered, "The idea that you could put a decorative feature there that would work, took a long time. And I remember we said, well you know, it's no problem, we won't do it yet. Because it was like, yes, they'll say no if we push it too fast." Building support for a mural involved above all convincing people that what Free Form had in mind was not the kind of mural people were familiar with from other estates. The tenants agreed to explore the possibilities through a mural workshop organized by the artists. People were asked to bring favorite images of themselves and other images they liked. Using these as a starting point, the artists posed the question of how the people of Provost thought of themselves, what they valued about who they were. One common thread was their pride in being Londoners. I have already mentioned how East Enders tend to think of themselves as the most authentic Londoners. The artists focused on this perception, exploring the different meanings that London had for people. The proposal that emerged from the workshop was a mural celebrating London. The specific theme, since everyone agreed on the centrality of the Thames, was to be how London relates to its waterways.

One problem the artists faced was how to create a mural that would be aesthetically satisfying to the artists while accommodating the rather different aesthetic of the tenants. For Goodrich, who ultimately came up with the basic design, the challenge was in

> making images that they could respond to and understand, and wouldn't just see as children's drawings. Most of them, even if they saw a Picasso, they'd say "that's children's drawing."... It was also moving them away from their images about what they think is beautiful, because they were stereotypical basically. So it's how to actually create the vehicle by which there was a realistic way that you could put the elements in they wanted; the water, the plants, the flying swans, and the other little bits and pieces they liked, but you could put them as a very small element or within the context of how London relates to its waterways.

There was also the challenge of finding a technique that would enable the tenants to participate in making the mural.

The solution the artists came up with was a mural telling the story of the tenants' lives as Londoners. The mural would be comprised of a mosaic and a series of low-relief tableaux cast in concrete and then painted, a technique one of the Free Form artists had been using in her own work, although on a much smaller scale. By this time, after more than two years of working on the estate, Free Form had established a good rapport with the tenants, and people had begun to come around

FIGURE 3.2

Provost mural detail: London landmarks. Photograph by Kate Goodrich.

to the idea of a mural. What was needed was a practical demonstration that the casting technique could produce something "good." The artists organized another workshop and asked everybody, including children, to bring small objects—small enough to be held in one hand—that to them represented aspects of London, a Dinky Toy car, for instance. The idea was that these small, everyday objects—which had to be able to make an impression in clay—could be used to create a narrative. A china ornament someone had brought, a Bo Peep shepherdess in a crinoline, was used to demonstrate the casting process. Once cast, the shepherdess lost her "kitschyness" while continuing to be recognizable as the original ornament. The cast of the shepherdess was agreed to be a success—the daughter of one of the tenants I interviewed had it hanging on her wall until just a few years ago. The idea of a mural that told stories using children's toys and other found objects began to take hold.

Goodrich then produced a preliminary drawing for the mural, inspired in part by old maps of medieval London. The mural was to be made up of two halves: the lower a mosaic representing the River Thames, bordered at the bottom by riverside plants; and the upper a double row of 300-square-centimeter cast concrete panels, thirty in all, featuring major London landmarks such as Tower Bridge and scenes of London life (figure 3.2). The drawings for some of the panels, particularly those showing major London buildings, were very detailed, but many were more like suggestions for possible stories. Using objects people had brought in—toy cars, plastic animals, a Barbie doll's bed—Goodrich and the other Free Form artists demonstrated how you could put together different scenes: a waterside pub (the Barbie bed helping form the facade) with a cricket match going on outside; a man fishing in the river; someone else going for a walk (figure 3.3). Goodrich, who can be quite charismatic, used his drawing and the demonstrations of the technique to make the idea come alive, convincing the final doubters that it could indeed work.

In the mural workshops, and in the development of the stories on the panels, the artists continually talked about what worked as images, what did not, and why. They discussed more generally what makes a picture and what makes a painting "good." From the earliest days of the organization, the founders of Free Form were determined not only to make art available to "the great housing estates in England where art meant nothing" but also to *explain* what art is and what it can do to those to whom it had never been explained. For the artists, the Provost mural was not merely about the creation of a mural; it was also a process through which those who had not been exposed to art were able to discover its power and learn how it can be used to tell stories, much as the artists themselves did at art school. Let me emphasize that the goal here is not to foster an appreciation of art that will allow people to enjoy the high art found in galleries, but rather to show people how the language of art can be used to tell their stories, to provide representations of their world rooted in their own day-to-day experiences.

It was agreed that the picture of London should not be a romanticized one; a major roadway with all the cars was included, as was a housing estate and a scrap merchant complete with a demolition ball. The artists were determined that the mural should represent the diversity of London, especially given the background of local racial tension; one panel, for instance, shows the Notting Hill Carnival, London's annual celebration of Caribbean music and culture, next to a local

FIGURE 3.3

Provost mural detail: waterside pub and cricket match. Photograph by Kate Goodrich.

street market (figure 3.4). Clearly, the artists had their own notion of London as a "community." Also included, at a time when the Tory government was moving to abolish the Greater London Council, was a small plane flying over Tower Bridge and trailing a banner declaring, "Keep the GLC Working for London."

The technique of telling stories through making impressions in a

FIGURE 3.4
Provost mural detail: street market and Notting Hill Carnival. Photograph by Kate Goodrich.

clay block was one that was particularly successful in enabling children and those without any artistic training genuinely to participate, under the guidance of the artists, in creating the images. As Goodrich put it, "It was actually quite a marvellous device because all of a sudden they could all participate, they could all find something—even if they didn't find something they could still participate: 'Oh yes, I can make that impression. Does that really work that way round?'"

I asked Goodrich how he would characterize the role of the tenants in shaping the imagery of the mural. As he saw it, they were essentially "the guardians of taste. It was like, well we're not having that. Well I'm not sure about that. But there was a lot of persuasion that went on.... And we also acquiesced, you know, the swans went up. I might have said, over my dead body, but they went up." In one interview, Goodrich talked more generally about the relationship between the community artist and the "community." For him, artists are fluent in a sophisticated visual language that allows them

> to interpret the raw ideas that come through a participation mechanism. And a lot of our successful projects, the most successful ones, which have actually achieved a high degree of sophistication, are very much to do with participation by local people, which has then been further interpreted by artists who have created the means, the skills, whereby people's contributions can actually achieve a high standard. You simplify [what the local people have produced] so that artists can take that and transform it into something else, but the original contribution is still recognisable within it and local people can proudly claim ownership.

He also stressed the need to work within a structure, such as the series of cast concrete panels making up the Provost mural, and the educative role of the artist:

> I think that Free Form has tried in all its work to provide the structure whereby people can succeed and not expose people to failure because they can't cope with that. The point is that they can make a contribution and see that they've achieved something highly satisfactory on their own terms and that the [artists] who are then going to take that and do something else with it, value it. It is valued rather than just lost. Unless you provide that structure you don't get good work. You end up with inarticulate drawings and messages. So it's this whole thing about providing people with the use of the language, you have to do that; you have to play the "teacher" role. I don't think of this as an enabling role, I'd rather see it as a master/apprentice role. You know something they don't but you're willing to share what you know with them so they can participate. It's a giving relationship....Sometimes pieces of work become much more to do with the artist than the original participants. I think that's fine as long as the integrity of that work is still recognised by

the people who have participated in it. So even if it's radically changed, as long as they genuinely feel that they participated I think it's perfectly okay.

Goodrich's concern to share his artistic knowledge can be seen in part
as a way of replicating his own discovery of art at art school.

Clearly, there are going to be times when the artist and "the community" do not see eye to eye, and Goodrich talked about that as well,
explaining how he would distinguish between Free Form's approach
and that of some other community artists. For him, the community
artist is not some simple conduit through which the community
expresses itself in an unmediated way. For instance, if "a community"
wanted to do a piece of work that was racist, "you're not going to stand
there and say, 'Oh, yes, we'll go and do a piece of work that's racist.' No,
you're going to put your foot down and say, 'No, we're not going to do
that.' And why. And then have the argument with them and then say,
'Okay, well, what we need to do here is talk about racism…let's understand our culture and the culture of other people, of how we integrate
and who we are'…you have to be able to have that conversation with
people."

The Provost mural was cast and fixed to the wall over the course of
two summers. It was then left to dry out fully before being painted the
following summer. The painting process and the making of the mosaic
of the river illustrate the kind of structured participation that Goodrich
talks about. The mosaic was made of vitreous glass tesserae and tiles,
and the children of the estate were set to work cutting up sheets of mirror and glass into small fragments out of which the image of the river
was created. Applying them, however, was very structured, as Goodrich
explained: "Each [artist] would have three or four kids and say, 'We're
going to do this bit today and then we're going to do it like this and
then you can repeat that over there.' So they would get a little thing
going, so you'd get this sort of patterning here that would happen."
The painting of the cast panels, which was really more of a subtle tint-
ing, was quite a challenge. Key to the artists' control, Goldman
explained, was a very detailed, color rendition of the whole mural that
Goodrich had produced. Everyone loved this drawing, so in Goldman's
words, "It wasn't 'Oh, you can't do this because I don't like you and you

can't do it.' It was 'Come on, let's look at the drawing again and see what we're trying to achieve overall.' So you're getting people to see it's not just about the little bit you're doing, it's about the whole thing. And people could buy into that because it had such a good design overall." As the artists remembered it, those who worked on the mural developed a strong sense of ownership both of the mural as a whole and their particular corner of it. Both Goodrich and Goldman stressed how much the making of the mural depended on a basic relationship of trust between the tenants and Free Form, whereby the tenants had faith that the artists would come up with something the tenants could be proud of and that would be "theirs."

THE MURAL AND THE TENANTS

So far my account of the mural has been based primarily on the recollections of the artists involved. They began the project knowing in general terms, if not in detail, what they wanted to achieve; as the mural took shape, it made sense to them, as an image and as an event, in a way that it cannot be assumed to have done for the tenants. Both the artists and I were interested in how the Provost tenants they had worked with, and those who had moved to the estate in the intervening years, now felt about the Free Form project, particularly the mural. I tried to explore this question in my interviews with tenants. In addition, Goldman and I spent a Saturday afternoon sitting in front of the mural with two of the women I interviewed, chatting with passersby. While it is not possible to draw definitive conclusions from such limited data, they do begin to tell us something about what the mural "meant" to the tenants.

One indication that tenants value the mural is that it has not been vandalized or graffitied in the twenty years of its existence. It has also become a popular backdrop for photographs. One woman who moved to the estate some ten years ago told us how much she appreciates the mural, photographing visiting family and friends in front of the Tower Bridge section, telling them, "Now you've seen Tower Bridge, we don't need to go to there." In general, the response to the mural was very positive: "It's beautiful" was the general sentiment. Two women and two men who had worked on the mural as children walked by while we were sitting in front of it; all four stressed what a memorable event of their childhood the creation of the mural had been. One older woman was negative about everything connected with the estate with the sole exception of the mural, which she felt Provost did not deserve, remarking, "It's a shame it can't be moved to somewhere nicer." But this comment from an earlier interview with tenants was more characteristic: "Even though you live there and it's been up that long, you walk along that grass, and you still look around and look at it. All those years, you still look at it."

Goldman had brought some photos of the project in progress. I asked the tenants what the mural "meant" to them now. One woman, initially opposed to a mural, told us how she had not expected a mural to survive long: "I didn't think a mural would stay there this long. I thought once you'd all gone that would be gone too, but it hasn't." She went on to explain, as she leafed through the photos, what the mural had come to mean to her and to the others who worked on it:

> I think of all the little kids that—a lot of them have got kids of their own now—that were doing that, all the little toys, my grandsons and that was Danny and Paul, all my grandsons with their little motors and other kids coming out, some bits of broken toys, "Can I put that in, miss? Can I do that, miss? Look can I do that there, miss?" And all that, they were so involved in it and it was a community brought together for that. They were really brought together with the mural and with the planting, but with that mural everybody had a little bit of it. "No you can't do it on this, it's my one, I've got to do it there." You know how kids talk, and it meant so much. We see them come past, look that's my house on there. That's the one I did up there, or that's what I did there. I put that bit of glass there....But then again you look at the picture of Peter, how healthy and young and fit he was then, now he's on dialysis all the time. You know, and you think of all those sorts of things and people that were there and died since. But they were there, there's a part of them still going on because everybody was involved in the mural.

The mural, therefore, has a special meaning for both those involved in its making, for whom it embodies a part of their history, and those who encounter it as an existing part of their environment, for whom it seems, as it was intended, to be a focal point for the estate. But what does the Free Form Provost project tell us about Provost and its "community"?

THE PROVOST "COMMUNITY"

One thing the tenants I interviewed agreed on was that Provost had once been a community but no longer was. The very fact of the mural's survival was evidence "that people weren't that bad then as they are now." Then, Provost really had been a community. Now, however, all those people had moved away, and there had been an influx of "new" people—"new" here being a euphemism for immigrants. One elderly man, less concerned with political correctness, put it more bluntly. For him the problem was "Africans, they destroy anything they want. They aren't used to anything." Another tenant described the effect of the changes as follows:

> It broke up a community really badly because [there were] people that have lived there for years, and it's like losing someone in your family because you were so close with them. They weren't just neighbours, they were friends....You got to know one another, more than you are now, people are pretty antisocial now.

I pressed her on what exactly had broken up the community. She replied: "New people coming in and people weren't ready to accept such a drastic change, and that's all I can say it is, a drastic change."

Interestingly, as Goldman and the other Free Form artists remember it, twenty years ago when they were working on the estate, tenants had made exactly the same complaint—that Provost used to be a real community but no longer was. Goodrich and Goldman remember Provost as being a very difficult place to work, with the same problems of young men on drugs—at that time there was a lot of glue sniffing—and generally out of control. As evidence of the problems they faced, Goldman remembered how they always made sure there were several Free Form artists working on the mural, since if there were only one or two, some of the rougher young lads were likely to harass them. As for the tenants' insistence that the community had been broken up by everyone moving away, although I do not have any precise figures, this situation was far from apparent during the time Goldman and I spent on the estate. For example, of the twenty-three people shown in one of the photographs of the installation of the window boxes, something like a third were identified by the interviewees as either still living on the estate or having died there. And in the few hours Goldman and I spent sitting by the mural on a Saturday afternoon, four people who had worked on the mural as children and still lived on the estate happened to pass by—evidence of a certain continuity.

The tenants' insistence on the lost community of Provost points to the way that the home of "community" is so often seen as the past, a roseate image of how people should live, and once did, but no longer do. In this instance, it probably also reflects a genuine shift from a more stable East End world in which, as one tenant put it, "This is how people were. They settled in their place and that's where they wanted to stay. They were quite happy to stay there, but now they're not." The past may not have been as stable as this statement suggests, nor the present as fluid, but it is true that the old tightly knit, ethnically and culturally homogeneous East End housing estates have become far more diverse and that this process has accelerated in the last twenty years. The Afro-Caribbean families who had just begun to live on Provost at the time of the project have been joined by many other "new" people, among them Africans, South Asians, Eastern Europeans, Portuguese, and Turks.

The key point, I would suggest, is that there was not some preexisting Provost "community" with which it was Free Form's task to connect. Rather there was a multitude of both social networks and narratives of identity and belonging that different people might or might not claim. How people saw themselves in relation to Provost, London, a particular family, and so on was not something fixed; at different times, in different contexts, they might think of themselves as connected in many different ways to different "communities." The Free Form project can be seen as providing a space in which it was possible—but by no means inevitable—for a particular sense of community to emerge. It provided this by improving the physical infrastructure of the estate in a very tangible way with new paths, lighting, and seats, and by providing mechanisms, such as the window box scheme, that brought people together to work on common projects that nonetheless offered individuals something of their own—their own window boxes with a planting plan that they themselves had chosen. The mural, too, was a common project but was made up of a series of elements on which an individual, or a small group of individuals, worked. Providing opportunities for people who might otherwise have little to do with one another to create something together was particularly important given the incipient racial tension on the estate. As the photographs taken at the time show, the Afro-Caribbean tenants were very much part of the project, but Goodrich and Goldman remember a number of Afro-Caribbean teenagers who at the beginning had to be reassured that this project was something for them and that they would be welcome. In addition, particularly with the mural, Goodrich and the Free Form artists set up a process by which the "community" could arrive at a collective representation of itself, even if only for that moment. Drawing on the array of images and narrative threads presented to them, Goodrich and the artists created an integrated London tapestry that the tenants could recognize as "their" London. Something Gramsci wrote in a rather different context seems to me to capture something of what was going on. Writing in a 1919 issue of *L'Ordine Nuovo*, the revolutionary newspaper of which he was a founding member, on the relationship between the newspaper's readers and its editors, he observes:

> The workers loved *L'Ordine Nuovo* (this we can state with inner satisfaction) and why did they love it? Because in its articles they rediscovered a part, the best part, of them-selves....Because its articles were not cold, intellectual struc-tures, but sprang from our discussions with the best workers; they elaborated the actual sentiments, goals and passions of the Turin working class, that we ourselves had provoked and tested. (Gramsci 1977:293–294)

It is important, however, not to exaggerate what was achieved. We are a long way from communities "controlling their own destinies." Nonetheless, finding mechanisms through which people can signifi-cantly shape even a tiny corner of the public space they inhabit, and have a sense of ownership, represents, it seems to me, a genuine achievement. In hunting the elusive quarry of the community, it is important, I would argue, to relinquish the illusion that there is in fact some continuing entity, "the community," that exists independently of a specific historical context. That "community" is as mythical as the unicorn. Communities are probably better thought of as collectivities of many different types that come into being in the context of particular circumstances in response to particular issues and concerns, or some shared history. They may have only a momentary life, or they may persist in one form or another for long periods. Whether or to what extent it makes sense to talk of a particular community is always an empirical question. Equally, how individuals inhabit communities and in what sense they define themselves as belonging to a given community are also empirical questions. And there are no definitive answers. The "communities" of the apartheid era in South Africa, for instance, which came into being in the context of that regime, cannot be assumed to persist unchanged in post-apartheid South Africa. Similarly, individuals' relationships to any given community are not fixed or permanent but shift over time, assuming different forms in different contexts.

In what sense, then, was Free Form working with the Provost *community*? The comparison with South Africa is interesting here. The notion of community may not have been central to political mobilization in Britain in the way it has been in South Africa, but there is an implicit assumption that those who live together in the same neighborhood necessarily constitute a community. The rhetorical power of community in the language of urban regeneration depends on this assumption. The fact that the community is not a legal entity as it is in South Africa makes it easier to maintain this fiction. It is interesting, for example, that the question of just how it is possible for a community that numbers several thousand to "participate" in any substantive way is rarely raised. In general, it seems clear that participation through the established channels of elected officials is not what is meant; it is difficult to imagine that those, such as Blair, who advocate communities "seizing control of their destiny and shaping it" are simply referring to gaining control of existing representative bodies through the electoral process.

The community with which Free Form worked on Provost, to the extent it existed, was undoubtedly more of a moment of community, with which different tenants identified in varying ways and to different degrees, than any kind of homogeneous entity persisting through time. A project such as the Provost mural should not be seen as articulating a sense of "what it means to be a Londoner" or the meaning of living on Provost that already existed in some unexpressed, submerged form, but rather as a *process* that allowed certain Provost tenants to contribute their threads of memory, meaning, and desire. The artists wove these memories and desires into a coherent image that the tenants recognized as "theirs." They recognized it both because they had worked on it and because it reflected their aspirations. In this sense the project did perhaps capture at least some of the needs and desires of the Provost community. It is said that the way to catch a unicorn is to show it a reflection of itself in a mirror. To conjure the mythical beast of community into some kind of precarious, temporary life, it needs perhaps to be presented with an image of itself that it can recognize.

Notes

I would like to record my gratitude to the artists of the Free Form Arts Trust and to the residents of Provost Estate for their generous cooperation with my research. I am also grateful to the Arts Council, UK and PSC-CUNY for their support.

1. Housing built and managed by local councils. Until the Thatcher revolution, this was the standard form of social housing in Britain. Being an anthropologist, I have tended to use the local British terms, such as council estate and flat, rather than their American equivalents in presenting my case study material.

2. See Rilke's (1946) *Sonnets to Orpheus*, Second Part, IV.

3. See Crehan 2002b for a fuller account of Gramsci's theorization of intellectuals and the production of knowledge.

4

Ayllu

Real and Imagined Communities in the Andes

Mary Weismantel

For anthropologists who work in the Andes, the word *ayllu*, which has often been glossed as "community," calls to mind a long history of rather arcane debates about the definition and function of a remarkably elusive social formation. These discussions, once rather heated, have faded out of earshot recently: ethnographers have lost their enthusiasm for the ayllu, as they have for other Quechua terms, such as *ayni* or *tinkuy*, used as shorthand for sociological concepts. After accepting the invitation to the seminar behind this volume, I ran into an Inca specialist who had written about the ayllu in the past, and I told him about my proposed paper topic. His response was less than encouraging. "The ayllu?" he asked, surprised. "But that's so...so *seventies*."[1]

And indeed, in the 1980s, such modernist anthropological pursuits as elucidating kinship systems, debating the "closed corporate community," or defining the ayllu faltered before the challenge of postmodernism. Not only does it smell of fusty antiquarianism, the ayllu carries the taint of colonialist exoticism. If asked to specify the reasons for their distaste, those who see an indefensible claim to empiricism would provide the harshest critique: where scholars thought they were *observing* an institution, they were in fact *creating* one. A workhorse word, used in everyday life to describe various sorts of ad hoc social arrangements, had been reified into the signifier of an ineffable fundamental principle, much as happened with its English approximate in "community studies" (see Creed, this volume). An even more tenuous claim had then been erected on the first one: that this deep structure of purely indigenous thinking provided evidence for unbroken cultural continuities with the pre-Columbian past.

A more moderate critique would allow the ayllu some basis in fact, at least in remote rural areas until perhaps the mid-twentieth century. Still, critics would hold, by century's end, that what little might remain of such institutions had become largely irrelevant. Orin Starn (1992, 1994) attacked ethnographers for "missing the revolution" through their obsessive concern with documenting vanishing continuities with an imagined past instead of focusing on the emerging social and political realities of the present. He mocked Andean anthropologists for their devotion to an ideology of *lo andino,* or "Andeanism," which he characterized as an ahistorical and essentializing vision of Native South Americans similar to Said's notion of Orientalism.

Although Starn's article aroused a firestorm of angry response at the time, recent scholarship has largely followed the research agenda he proposed, looking for, and finding, Andean people fully engaged with modernity. Disdainful of talk about ayllus and tinkuys, academic researchers have turned their attention instead to such phenomena as education and immigration, NGOs and state bureaucracies, even beauty pageants and television personalities—presumably following the Natives' lead.

Ah, but there's the rub. For just as the ayllu was abandoned on the pages of ethnographies, a chorus of indigenous voices from across the Andes began to proclaim its significance: the ayllu has staged a comeback, championed by political activists who have brought it onto a much bigger stage and reintroduced it into scholarly venues as well. In 2001 the *Journal of Latin American Anthropology* published the following statement:

> The ayllu is a model...whose reach stretches to almost all the

indigenous peoples of the Andean region: Colombia, Ecuador, Peru, Bolivia, and Chile. It is...*jatha*, the "seed" from which civilization and political structures such as Tawantinsuyu [the Inca Empire] were germinated. The ayllu...is until today the unit that forms the fabric of our social and political organization. (Choque and Mamani 2001:207)

The essay in which this statement appears stands out not only for these bold, sweeping assertions but also because of the pronoun *nuestro/a* (our), which modifies—and electrifies—dry noun phrases such as "social and political organization" and "state-level organization."[2] Choque and Mamani are indigenous Andean names; the authors are members of a Bolivian Aymara organization dedicated to scholarship and activism, the Taller de Historia Oral Andina (THOA; the Andean Oral History Workshop).[3] Publications such as this mark the collapse of a long-standing racial divide between social scientists who study Native Andean communities, and the Native Andeans they study.

From Ecuador, a short essay on the ayllu by nationally known indigenous political leader Luis Macas reveals similar emphases:[4]

The llacta-ayllu is the organizational nucleus of indigenous society...the fundamental basis on which culture, society, politics, history, and ideology are concentrated and processed....The llacta-ayllu is also the historical institution that became the basis of indigenous resistance and a vital component of our identity, as many outside social and political commentators have noted. (Macas 2000)[5]

Macas is one of a new generation of indigenous leaders who have achieved national and even international prominence, as Native peoples and parties across the Andes, long excluded from electoral politics, have suddenly gained visibility and legitimacy. In Ecuador, the country with perhaps the most vicious and recalcitrant history of overt racism, the indigenous presence on the national scene began with massive uprisings, protests, and even a brief presidential coup, and then turned into resounding electoral victories. In Peru whiteness has become a political liability, as demonstrated by the successful campaigns of the last two presidents, both of whom campaigned on racialist appeals to nonwhite majorities; Toledo, the incumbent, used the help of his Quechua-speaking anthropologist wife to orchestrate public events filled with Incaic imagery. Academy-trained indigenous intellectuals, the THOA scholars among them, have attained the most recognition in Bolivia. In every venue in which these new leaders promulgate their message—political platforms, slogans, and speeches; scholarly conferences, classrooms, and journals—references to the ayllu abound.

Anthropologists have been quick to welcome these changes, to publicize them, and—to the limited extent it is in our power to do so—to augment the spaces in which they can happen. But while we are very glad to see the messengers, we are less able to respond with equanimity to every aspect of the message. Some anthropologists working in the Americas—Kay Warren, Joanne Rappaport, Stefano Varese, Les Field, to name a very few—have fully embraced the challenge, taking indigenous activism as the topic of their work and successfully navigating the contradictory roles of advocate and researcher. Many more, however, unhappy with what they read but reluctant to criticize, stay carefully away from direct response. For much to our horror, anthropologists discover in the rhetoric of indigenous politics a romantic vision of an unchanging Indian culture that exceeds our own worst excesses—and one that partly or perhaps mostly originates from our own texts. The ayllu is described in terms that make us uneasy: as a survival from the ancient past, a symbol of steadfast Native resistance to change through five long centuries. While other anthropologists and historians insist on viewing the Andes through the lens of modernity, indigenous scholars celebrate an institution they see as premodern in origins and explicitly antimodern in conception.

One response to this new rhetoric is cynicism: like the language of "community" elsewhere, twenty-first-century talk about the ayllu can be dismissed as impotent fantasy. The forces of late capitalism in the Andes have surely finished what conquest, colonialism, and the depredations of the nineteenth-century republics began, fracturing and devouring what little remained of traditional cultures and social formations, which today exist only as ghostly memories. Even the emergence of new indigenous political movements that assert the significance of the ayllu is but a local response to global developments that originated far outside rural South America. Furthermore, the preconquest Andes was a place of enormous cultural diversity and political turmoil, in which social and political formations were constantly undergoing rapid and often forcible alteration; there was no singular, stable, shared social form in the first place for postconquest Native peoples to inherit from their ancestors.

But such a reaction seems ill advised, and not only because it puts the foreign researcher on a collision course with indigenous scholars. The rebirth of this almost moribund idea is now a social fact, one that emerged from precisely the kind of hybrid cultural spaces that have been the focus of postmodern theorizing: between North and South, the academy and the street, political cultures and cultural politics. The intellectual and political history of the word *ayllu* and its recent deployments, then, should reveal some of the tangled interconnections at play within these spaces. This history might enable us to see anthropological thought and practice from a critical distance not always available to us—and thus might give us some perspective on our own intellectual priorities in regard to such overworked concepts as community or modernity.

THE MODERNIST AYLLU

As described in most anthropological writing of the latter half of the twentieth century, the ayllu certainly sounds like a community: a group of people who share an identity based in descent, residence, and ethos and who have erected upon those shared characteristics a social institution with both economic and political functions. By century's end, however, doubts had crept in. In 2001 American anthropologist Andrew Orta summarized the state of the ayllu as follows: "Though often glossed as 'community,'" in reality the formation to which the term refers "does not always map easily onto" the concept as used by anthropologists or historians (2001:198). His hesitation is a response to recent critics who distrust the social scientist's "community" as something that "can exist only in an ideal model, not in the real world." (See, for example, Isbell 2000:249.) But it also stems from earlier debates about the ayllu, which even in the heyday of structural and functional analyses had proved obstinately recalcitrant to precise definition.

At first, the social organization of Andean rural communities seemed almost disappointingly straightforward, especially in contrast to the knotty problems found in Africa and Native North America. Here, there were no large polygynous households, no matrilineal descent systems, no rain queens or leopard skin chiefs. Instead, the rural Andes was a landscape filled with small, scattered households, each occupied by a monogamous married couple and their children; radiating out from each household was a dense network of real and fictive kinship ties, binding each unit to those around them (Mayer and Bolton 1977; Mayer 2002).[6] There were few formal suprahousehold institutions, making the ayllu, which existed in many regions, especially in the south, a focus of scholarly attention.

This consensus view of Andean social structure was hammered out in the middle decades of the twentieth century, and it produced a wealth of ethnographic and historical studies. As these proliferated into the 1980s, however, disagreements cropped up; Incaic kinship in particular proved as impenetrable as anything found in Africa. A further, tragic complication ensued in the 1980s as political violence erupted in the southern highlands of Peru, killing some 20,000 rural residents and sending another 500,000 fleeing to the cities. Anthropologists, too, evacuated the Inca heartland, the locus classicus of Andean anthropology; when they returned in the mid-1990s, it was to a vastly different social and political landscape, and the research agenda changed accordingly. It no longer seemed possible or appropriate to search for stable social structures or write of a timeless "ethnographic present" in a place where the effects of history were so recent and so savage.

Earlier in the century, debates arose over how the communities actually functioned, but consensus formed around the role of the ayllu as a conceptual building block in Andean thought; it is largely in this latter guise, as principle rather than practice, that it would later prove so valuable, and so contentious, as a political tool. Interpretative studies of cosmology and research on social structure and political economy developed in synchrony, each shaping the other.

Much of the impetus for ethnographic and archaeological theorizing came from ethnohistory, especially from the work of three men, John Rowe, John Murra, and R. T. Zuidema, and their students. Working in a Marxian framework, Murra (1975, 1978) built a picture of

Andean political economy under the Incas that challenged conventional political thinking by breaking with the assumption that polities inevitably control contiguous, bounded territories. He argued that the great ayllus of the southern Andes—as large as independent states—were organized according to a principle of territorial dispersal into "vertical archipelagoes" to allow better exploitation of the sharply differentiated ecologies of the high Andes. Murra's work sparked a rash of studies that fused economic anthropology with the nascent field of ecological anthropology. By documenting twentieth-century systems of verticality, a young, international group of scholars worked to demonstrate the vitality of indigenous communities and the continued existence of a rich, flexible, and eminently practical cultural tradition (Brush 1977; Orlove 1977; Bastien 1978; Masuda, Shimda, and Morris 1985).[7]

Today, many American anthropologists see these findings as of only historic interest: changing demographic patterns, a depressed rural economy, and greater dependence on imported foods make agricultural systems seem less important now. But in arguing that Andean societies were organized according to unique principles poorly understood by outsiders, Murra had sounded a battle cry not only for those studying agricultural economics but for symbolic anthropologists as well. So too had his contemporary R. T. Zuidema, a Dutch scholar working within a European structuralist tradition; Zuidema's analyses of Incaic mathematical and spatial thinking were as important in symbolic anthropology as Murra's had been for political economy. And like Murra, Zuidema wrote about ethnohistory but trained a generation of ethnographers, who studied social structures such as the ayllu to find underlying conceptual principles that revealed a uniquely Andean way of thinking.

Verticality, for instance, was not only a pragmatic strategy for managing ecological zones but also a conceptual framework intimately related to the tradition of worshipping sacred places and ancestral tombs, in which ecological zones were represented metaphorically as parts of a larger whole, especially of a human body. Similarly, the peculiar scalar nature of the ayllu was studied both in terms of function and symbol. Pragmatically, ayllus may range in size from tiny hamlets to entire ethnic groups with hundreds or even thousands of members;

they are nested in structure, smaller ayllus within larger ones, from a group of households that share common descent from a local ancestor to entities with all the functions of a state polity. Catherine J. Allen sees in this system of nested units a form of "synechdochal thinking," pervasive in Andean culture, that "comprehends the world in terms of mutually enveloping homologous structures that act upon each other: ayllus are contained in ayllus; places are contained within places....The scale of one's purview can expand or contract endlessly. Every microcosm is a macrocosm, and vice versa" (1997:81).

For political anthropologists, however, the variable size of the ayllu and its long history made defining the term difficult. The functions of corporate landholding and management of inheritance that characterize a "microayllu" of a few related families are quite unlike the massive mobilization of resources for defense and military aggression undertaken by the enormous and powerful "macroayllus" that fought the Inca. Too, in enduring the vicissitudes of life under Incaic, colonial, republican, and modern states, the ayllu was repeatedly refashioned. Each successive political regime tried to destroy the ayllu's political power and wrest away its resources; even rare state attempts to preserve or reconstruct the ayllu transformed it, regularizing disparate local systems into conformity with an externally imposed order. For some, this variability renders the concept of the ayllu useless.

In the area of kinship, the dichotomy is even more marked: ferocious disagreements over social realities nevertheless produced surprising consensus about fundamental symbolic structures. Almost all researchers describe descent from shared ancestors as the primary defining characteristic of the ayllu. But while early authors assumed that descent was patrilineal, in the 1970s Enrique Mayer established that most twentieth-century kin systems were bilateral, and Zuidema (1977) argued that the Inca had a system of double or parallel descent —a structure that Billie Jean Isbell (1978:108–112) among others (for example, Collins 1986:658) believed to have persisted into historic times in rural communities. Historian Catherine Julien (2000:24–26) has recently revived the debate, attacking Zuidema and reintroducing the argument that the Inca were in fact patrilineal. And Denise Arnold (1988, 1997, 1998) has steadfastly reminded scholars about the existence of structures of descent and social organization based upon relationships between women.

Where researchers agree is on the moiety structure of the ayllu, traditionally divided into *hanan* and *hurin* ("upper" and "lower") and ruled by two leaders. Strongly influenced by Claude Lévi-Strauss (whose legacy is deeply inscribed upon South American ethnography), Andeanists elaborated this concept of duality or binary opposition, extending it from the domain of kinship to everything from textile design to tinkuys. The latter is a Quechua term for the joining together of opposing forces, variously applied to ritual battles between ayllus, the tumultuous meeting of water from two streams or irrigation canals, and the act of sex.[8] Together, dualism, synecdoche, and verticality were seen as giving rise to a vision of the universe in which each living thing is both internally multiple and externally expansive, since it contains divisions and is itself a division within a larger entity. These studies of Andean cosmological thought made major contributions to anthropological understanding of Native America, and of non-Western religion and science. At the same time, however, it is when writing about duality that anthropologists have been most likely to indulge in creating an imaginary Andes in which putative cultural continuities erase the specificities of history. Social scientists, then, have produced and consumed both rosy visions of the timeless ayllu and hard-edged assessments of actual beliefs and practices; and this dialectic between romanticism and realism prevails outside the academy as well.

THE POSTMODERN AYLLU

I began this paper in the belief that the biggest problem with the writings of indigenous intellectuals, from a scholarly point of view, was the assertion of an unbroken continuity between the precolonial past and the present, somehow passed on in undiluted form through an ineradicable racial memory. But when I reread the THOA article quoted above with care, I found few areas of substantive disagreement after the first, rather overblown assertions.[9] If anything, these authors (and others like them) are at pains to emphasize the fragmentation of the ayllu over time. They describe their own decision to join Bolivia's ayllu movement, in which local groups resolve to reorganize according to their understanding of traditional Aymara leadership structures, as "an abandonment, almost vertiginous" of the familiar forms of local political organization extant since the revolution of 1952.[10] Like academic historians, they recognize the ayllu as a historical memory,

not a lived actuality—but a powerful one, precisely because it demonstrates both the alterations and diminishments that Native communities have suffered, and their determined capacity for survival, flexibility,
and resistance.[11]

Indeed, indigenous intellectuals' assessment of the ayllu's current
state may be more accurate than some American anthropologists'
understanding of its past. Orin Starn, for instance, harshly criticizes
Andeanism as "a way of seeing in which the highlands of Bolivia,
Colombia, Chile, Ecuador, and Peru appear as an alien, fascinating
land untouched by the West and modernity...an island of Otherness
removed from the world" (1999:19–20). He locates the origins of this
fantasy in the tourism industry on the one hand, and the romantic
primitivism of American anthropologists in the period between 1960
and 1980 on the other. Many other scholars, myself included
(Weismantel 2001), have pointed to the relationship between anthropology and travel writing. But here Starn is holding the wrong end of
the telescope: the sources for Andeanism are not to be found in the
United States, or in the latter half of the twentieth century. Instead he
should look back in time, at least to the 1920s (although its origins are
much earlier), and to the Andes itself. In the pages of the Peruvian literary magazine *Amauta*, for example, he could have found far more
flamboyant flights of imaginative play. In 1927 the following meditation
upon the different meanings of the word "Andeanism" appeared there:

> ANDEANISM. Is a geographic expression...a sporting
> expression [referring to mountain climbing]...Andeanism,
> sport of the gods...Andeanism, purifying water, creator,
> blood of the ancestors, vertical breath of the earth. Life and
> culture germinated on the Andean plateau and in the
> Andean valley. (Valcárcel 1927:32)

These are the words of Peruvian intellectual Luis E. Valcárcel, a
founding father of twentieth-century *indigenismo*, one of the most significant political and artistic movements of Latin America—and the
single most important source of writings about the ayllu. Indigenist
writing by authors such as Valcárcel, José Carlos Mariátegui (editor of
Amauta), and José María Arguedas, as well as by lesser-known figures
from across the Andes, are filled with evocations and descriptions of
the ayllu as it was imagined to have existed during the preconquest era,

or in contemporary rural communities.[12] These writings, influential throughout Latin American between 1920 and the 1960s, are the source not only for the Andeanism that flourished in American anthropology beginning in the 1960s but also for indigenous intellectuals writing today—both directly, as part of their own national intellectual heritage, and indirectly through anthropology.

Like the ayllu of contemporary indigenous writers, Mariátegui's ayllu is twofold: in his polemical essays it is celebrated as a still-vital direct survival from ancient times, while in his analysis of Peruvian history it appears in a more realistic guise, subject to the vicissitudes of history.[13] Most *indígenista* writing about the ayllu was evocative rather than descriptive in intent; the desire was to inspire a change in deep-seated attitudes by creating powerful images of the Andean past and the Native American present. These authors celebrated the ayllu as it could be, not as it was; in so doing, they tried to will into being new nations that would no longer be dedicated to policies of violent extirpation and forced assimilation. Recent critical reevaluation of this movement questions the commitment and success of these writers' antiracism, but it was undeniably their avowed intent (see de la Cadena 2000; Zevallos Aguilar 2002). And in comparison with received opinion of the time about the racial degeneracy, moral depravity, intellectual inferiority, and utter degradation of the Indian, their celebrations of Andean culture appear radical indeed.

It is in this light that we should consider Murra and Zuidema, foreign scholars who were nonetheless deeply immersed in Peruvian intellectual life. Their students in Peru continued the attack: "Given the anti-Andean prejudices of...the intellectual tradition of Peru's elite... to search for, to demonstrate with ethnographic facts, and to portray a 'living' culture rather than dead 'survivals' seemed to those in my generation of fieldworkers to be a worthwhile task" (Mayer 1992:195). Starn's comparison of Andeanism to Orientalism, then, is singularly inapropos: while the two might share a romantic essentialism and a glorification of an imaginary and vanished primitive, the position of these two rhetorics within their respective colonial histories is quite different. Orientalism is quite simply colonialist, the creation of British authors who traveled to the Middle East as colonials and colonists; Andeanism, in contrast, is the product of national literatures produced by young postcolonial states as they struggled with the internal colonialism that still plagues them. In fact, Mariátegui explicitly posited indígenismo in contrast to "criollo" literatures that borrowed images of Indians to provide folkloric color and to revel in the image of a pleasantly colonial past in which the subaltern races did not pose a threat to white supremacy—what Renato Rosaldo (1989) would later refer to as "imperialist nostalgia." Andeanism, then, is better seen as conceived in opposition to colonialist Orientalism than as its South American counterpart.

Murra's Peruvian student, Enrique Mayer, criticizes Starn for his failure to recognize this history: in Mayer's account, it is Starn who appears unable to move from a foreigner's viewpoint to contemplate what it means to practice anthropology within a South American political context. Writing at the end of the 1980s, Mayer arrays on one side Peruvian novelist and political aspirant Mario Vargas Llosa, whose references to an Indian peasantry locked into pathetic ignorance identify him with a long tradition of conservative writing. On the other was Sendero Luminoso (Shining Path), the violent extremist group that claimed inspiration from Mao and Mariátegui. Each saw a Peru starkly and irreparably divided, and they differed only in which side they thought needed to disappear—whiteness and modernity, or the backward Indian.

Peruvian anthropology was called upon to support both these extremes. Vargas Llosa hired an anthropologist to lend authority to a condemnatory report that dismissed Indians as incapable of understanding the political world in which they lived—a report vehemently attacked by leading scholars. On the other side, Shining Path was full of anthropologists; one of the inner circle had been an anthropology professor in Ayacucho, and many early recruits were his students. When Abimael Guzman, the movement's leader, was captured in 1992, a book of essays by anthropologists and historians lay on his nightstand (Starn 1994:16). The uses made of Andeanism by ideologues on both sides operated at high stakes unfamiliar to American anthropologists. This dramatic politicization brings into view the circulation and reappropriation of anthropological texts—out of our sight, beyond our control, and in ways not of our choosing.

Starn cannot really be faulted for not perceiving the connection between American anthropological writing and its literary forebears in the Andes; modernist anthropologists were often loath to admit the unscientific sources of the ideas that filtered into their work. But in truth, the boundaries between discourses about the indigenous Andes have always been extremely porous, and continue to be so.

I was startled when I idly typed the word "ayllu" on Google to discover almost 3,500 hits. Some groups had just borrowed the name: Peruvian rock bands from the 1970s, an award-winning group of all-girl steppers in the United States, a few import-export businesses dealing in Bolivian textiles, and dozens of new age shamans and healers in half a dozen countries. Longer definitions, replete with detail, appeared as subheadings under more general statements about Andean culture, which tended to be earnest, didactic, and highly essentialized. These appeared on Web pages of not-for-profit organizations—some devoted to natural healing and neo-pagan religions, others to international development—as well as a site from a Peruvian legal society with a page about traditional concepts of law. And, of course, there were not a few syllabi for college courses.[14]

What was immediately obvious is that almost all of the former came from the latter. Whether a sorority member, an acupuncturist, a lawyer, or an expert on water treatment plants, the writers had all gotten their ideas about the ayllu from introductory anthropology courses—and then done with them whatever they wanted. Andean anthropology has apparently been more influential than we knew—and perhaps more so than we like. We scorn some interlocutors, such as the new age shamans, as beneath contempt; with indigenous intellectuals, in contrast, we listen hard but assume too much, and do not yet know how to speak. And as to the longer relationship between other Andean intellectuals and American anthropologists, we have been aware of it only in fits and starts through our own individual connections, oblivious to the larger social, political, and intellectual context in which we operate—and which has operated upon us.[15]

The history of the ayllu demonstrates that rather than standing on the outside, looking in and describing what we see—the modernist vision of anthropology—we work within intersecting collections of readers, writers, speakers, and actors that are at once the topic and the context of the work we do. The recent fissure between the anthropologists who described the ayllu, reified it, and then abandoned it, and the activists who have taken those descriptions and made them into stirring political rhetoric is only one moment in a long process of exchange. The anthropological vision of the ayllu has permeated popular culture, as demonstrated by my little excursion onto Google; but the very construction of that vision was itself shaped by literary and political works from outside the social sciences.

THE ANTIMODERN AYLLU

This history does not erase the profoundly divergent visions of the ayllu found in the writings of anthropologists and activists. However, by bringing to the fore the high political stakes involved in writing about Indians in Latin America, it does provide a vantage point from which to see the conflict more clearly. There is little disagreement about the current condition of the ayllu as lived practice; and broadly speaking, all parties writing about ayllus deplore the racism that afflicts Native communities. But while the antiracism of the foreign scholar may be abstract and theoretical, embedded within the project of description, for activists it is immediate, organizing everything around it—and fashioning the imagined ayllu as a weapon for struggle.

As social scientists, even the most humanistic anthropologists begin with a statement of what is: Indigenous communities as they exist today are the products of a modern history that in the Andes is five hundred years old. Without disputing that reality, indigenous political actors take a different starting point. They use the ayllu to call into being something that does not exist—but that could. For Macas, the ayllu matters because it can aid the "process of reconstructing our ancestral peoples and nations." The THOA authors, too, emphasize its immediate utility: "[T]he communities of the province of Ingavi...decided to return to organizing themselves into ayllus...thus re-taking the road of autonomy and indigenous liberty" (Choque and Mamani 2001:202).

Instrumentality is more significant than an author's race in shaping the kind of ayllu he or she imagines: some of the most radically essentialist statements about the ayllu appear in the writings of nonindigenous development workers, European and South American, whose visions of the ayllu are inspired by environmentalist and neo-anarchist as well as Andeanist thinking.[16] In Peru, Mayer recently noted that among some applied anthropologists, "the ideas of John Murra and his followers (myself included) [have] now become unquestionable ideology rather than research issues to prove or disprove" (2002:274). As an example, he offers a sympathetic but ultimately critical assessment of one such group. This small independent NGO devoted to resuscitating traditional Andean agricultural practices has as its stated goal "to let Andean culture's own vigorous flow purge it from the distortions that colonization has caused in it so as to reestablish its wholeness" (Apffel-Marglin 1988:xiv).

When the imagined ayllu is entirely instrumental in purpose, it has a different kind of relationship to time and to truth. Recovering the history of resistance in the past motivates the living and in so doing can change the present and the future. Thus the standard for judging a particular image of the ayllu is not whether it is an accurate description of what is or was, but whether it has the power to make itself become so— to will itself into being by capturing the imaginations of others (see Crehan, this volume).

This difference between description and action provides a context in which to examine the most intransigent difference between visions of the ayllu: the question of Western modernity, which most anthropologists view as all-enveloping and inescapable. The activists' vision of the ayllu, in contrast, is predicated upon the possibility of an Indian history, past and future, that is both non-Western and antimodern. Macas, for example, writes of deploying the ayllu as a weapon in an ideological struggle against those who insist upon "the superiority of 'modern civilization' over that of the indigenous world." The concept of the ayllu as an indigenous institution, he argues, is "indispensable" as part of a strategy of "build[ing] different terms of reference to those of western 'modernity' and all that that entails" (2000:1).

Such rhetorical oppositions between Indians and modernity trouble anthropologists; thus, when Andrew Orta, a Bolivia specialist, wrote an introduction to the THOA piece, he undertook a difficult job, for his readers would include both his anthropologist peers and the activists whose work he was discussing. His introduction emphasizes the positive aspects of THOA's work but expresses his unease, because the authors have positioned themselves within a

deep tradition in Andean studies of counterposing the

> ayllu/community to...modernity.... The claim here has
> classically been of a resistant tradition defensively main-
> tained.... This emphasis upon a sharp dichotomy between
> indigenous culture and Western modernity has fallen into
> disfavor among many Andeanists as among other sociocul-
> tural anthropologists. (2001:199–200)

In referring to this "deep tradition," he may be thinking of authors like
Allen (1988), whose lovely ethnography of the Quechua community of
Sonqo has the tragic quality of an elegy. Modern Peru intrudes only in
the epilogue, not as part of indigenous lived reality but as "an unpleas-
ant vision" of an inescapable future.[17]

Postcolonialist critiques of anthropology hold the romantic primitivism of an author like Allen to be politically pernicious and implicitly
racist. By fostering the image of Native communities as cultural isolates,
the argument goes, this sort of anthropology exacerbates the actual
exclusion of indigenous Peruvians, Ecuadorians, Colombians, and
Bolivians from their respective national societies and helps deny
them a role as historical actors. But these charges are rendered nonsensical when indigenous activists deploy the ayllu to be a bulwark in
the struggle for greater representation within the Andean states and
societies.

This dilemma is not new; Spivak's concept of "strategic essentialism" is one tool used to confront it. But we can do more than adopt
temporizing tactics that leave fundamental disagreements intact; scholars could instead more closely consider the ideological position being
taken here. Allen and other nonindigenous Andeanists, motivated by a
liberal multiculturalism, may have been attracted to the idea of the
ayllu as a refuge from modernity, but more radical authors such as
Macas look to it as a force that could actually deconstruct Western cultural hegemony. The difference in their positions can be perceived
only if we understand how modernity is being defined; here, too, the
difference is between description and action. Like "community," the
word "modernity," used and overused until it threatens to become
meaningless, regains its significance when we recall that, rather than a
statement of fact about the world, it, too, is actually an ideological
instrument: "'Modernity' is a murky term...inherited from what we

now call the West...that project[s] the North Atlantic experience on a universal scale that [it] helped to create....[Such terms] are not merely descriptive or referential. They do not describe the world; they offer visions of the world" (Trouillot 2002:220).

If most anthropologists have tended to accept "modernity" as simply a reality of twenty-first-century life, indigenous writers may be closer to Michel-Rolph Trouillot's perception of it as a political imaginary imposed upon lived experience. Hence the possibility of living outside modernity is not utopian wishful thinking but rather a matter of constructing a new template with which to view social life. The modernity in question is a specific one, held responsible for the ills wreaked upon indigenous communities by the West; and the antimodernity imagined as its antidote is tailored to address those wrongs. The antimodern ayllu is unlike other antimodernities: it is not a Luddite rejection of technology, the Wiccan's return to paganism, or the religious fundamentalist's desire for isolation from a morally bankrupt mass culture. Instead, it is structured around two basic tenets, antiracism and anticolonialism— the first principles of postcolonial scholarship.

Where Andeanist thought parts company with postcolonial studies is in its overt anticapitalism. As Donald Donham remarks, despite its nominally political intent, the scholarly literature on modernities and postmodernities is markedly less focused as a political discourse than its intellectual precursor, world systems theory. In place of the latter's "single-mindedly and perhaps simplifyingly economic and political enterprise...[scholars in the 1990s] talked instead of cultural flows, of cosmopolitanisms, and alter/native modernities." But, he says, the modern "and the anti-modern" can only be understood "when such ideas are placed within the context of global capitalism—with all its gaping differences in power, wealth, and life chances" (2002:254–255).

The rhetoric of the ayllu is precisely a discourse about global capitalism and its "gaping differences"—perhaps because, like world systems theory, its origins lie in Marx. Latin American intellectual life has been profoundly influenced by Marxian theory; in the Andes, indígenismo developed out of the ideas of communist writers such as Hildebrando Castro Pozo (1924), who asserted that the ayllu was a communistic institution. Mariátegui forcibly underlined the political origins for his work:

> Call me, simply, socialist....I confess to having arrived at my
> understanding of the value and the meaning of indigenous
> culture in our time...through the road—at once intellec-
> tual, sentimental and practical—of socialism. (1991:77)

The intellectual history of indigenous thought is less well documented,
but since communist organizers traveled to the rural Andes for
decades, indigenous intellectuals, like their white counterparts, have
been long conversant with the tenets of socialist thought. This history
shows that unlike the U.S. and European academic discourses to which
Donham refers, in indigenous intellectual discourse modernity is conceived explicitly as a specific political economy: the nation-state constituted in the service of an urban white bourgeoisie, and a capitalist
economy that creates poverty in the service of wealth.

The activists' ayllu, then, is an instrument in a particular political
project, as can be seen in the particular list of traits they have chosen
out of the descriptions found in ethnography and ethnohistory.
Although these authors make occasional reference to kinship and cosmology, they are far more interested in certain aspects of political and
economic organization. And unlike conventional structural-functionalist studies, political economy does not appear in activists' accounts simply as a natural part of a passively self-perpetuating social whole. Here,
social organization is overtly political, each of its parts critical to a
defensive strategy that protects community members against the cultural and economic incursions of a larger society perceived as unambiguously hostile.

Two aspects of the ayllu's economic organization are seen as critically important, and both are portrayed as aspects of a deeply felt cultural ethos antithetical to the profit motive. The first is a system of
exchange based upon the principles of *ayni* and *minka* (or *minga*), envisioned as a Maussian culture of the gift, in place of the capitalist culture
of the commodity. The second is collective ownership of the means of
production.

According to Murra and his students, the Inca state, unlike the
Aztecs, operated without markets; instead it was organized around
principles of ayni (reciprocal exchange) and minka (redistribution
and/or corvée labor). Colonial administrators and hacienda owners
adopted these principles to suit their own ends; within indigenous

social life, they survived in modified form well into the twentieth century, despite the steady incursions of the market. Mayer and other researchers compiled detailed documentation of workaday exchanges in which barter and cash purchases coexist; in contrast, symbolic anthropologists reified ayni and minka into fundamental Andean concepts intrinsically resistant to Western thought[18]—and it is in this latter guise that they appear in the activist literature.

While anthropologists, convinced that rural Andean life is now completely commodified, have largely abandoned ayni and minka as research topics, among activists the ideas are of growing importance. Macas (2000), without using the Quechua terms, invokes the sharing of goods and labor as one of the fundamental qualities of the "llacta-ayllu" that most differentiates it from the values of Western modernity. Evo Morales, head of Bolivia's largest opposition party, emphasizes "the traditions of indigenous people who have organized their communities collectively for generations"; a party member describes the party's economic policies as intended to "regain the philosophy of the Andean soul" (Forero 2003).

Even more significant is the ayllu's historic role as a landholding unit, with individual households having only usufruct rights. Such collective ownership was anathema to the liberal economic theorists of the nineteenth-century republics, who attacked the power of the ayllu with all the political force at their command. Most scholars describe this time as a period of great loss for indigenous communities, which were stripped of collective resources, and for indigenous individuals, many of whom were forced by economic circumstance to sell their land to white landowners and entrepreneurs. In the twentieth century, the pendulum swung back the other way, with governments enacting policies reinstating the indigenous community as an entity with distinct legal rights, including control over territory; this trend has accelerated rapidly in recent decades.

Thus the ayllu matters because of its political-economic functions as a unit that controls, manages, and defends productive resources. According to Choque and Mamani, this economic function has two faces. Internally, members recognize their lands to be inalienable collective property, although worked as individual parcels. Externally, this process then allows the ayllu to function as "the guarantee of the defense of indigenous territory" (Choque and Mamani 2001:211).

Defense of territory is deeply significant throughout the Andes—and Latin America—as the sign of the community's ability to protect its members against the predations of white society.[19] The ayllu has been, and could be again, a place from which to fight back on several fronts: economic, political, and military. Economically, collectivizing prevents the steady loss of indigenous lands to outsiders as individual community members fall into debt, and so functions as a defense against the pressures that bleed indigenous families of their land, wealth, and resources. Politically, the landholding ayllu makes a territorial claim that renders the Indian "nation" a tangible reality with which Andean states must contend. In Ecuador recently, indigenous communities have been flexing their muscles as polities by exercising juridical rights normally reserved for the nation-state, especially the right to try and punish thieves. Territorial boundaries are realized through military-style blockades at entrances to the community, with entry refused to representatives of the state, such as the rural militia, but not to journalists and television news trucks, until the trial is over. These actions suggest that under provocation, the indigenous community's role as a refuge from state and white/mestizo violence could be intensified, realizing its potential as a site from which to organize collective resistance to such violence (Weismantel 2001:13–14).

In sum, then, the rhetorical opposition between ayllus and Indians on the one hand, and modernity and the West on the other, becomes comprehensible in the context of its intellectual history and the political aims of those who invoke it. Unlike the structural-functional descriptions of modernist anthropology, this is an overtly antimodern project; but it is quite unlike the neoconservative antimodernism vilified by Rosaldo (1989) and others. There is no desire here to return to a fantasy world in which cultural difference flourished because everyone knew his or her place, as in the antimodern rhetoric of, for instance, older elites in the Ecuadorian city of Cuenca (Weismantel 2001). And while there are frequent invocations of rather mystical conceptions of culture and tradition, a strong materialist emphasis underlies this particular antimodernism. Although cultural survival is the goal, it will be achieved through alterations in economic structures, which in turn allow political and finally cultural autonomy to be achieved. Finally, this rhetorical use of the ayllu seeks and claims the possibility of changing history, now and in the past. The characteristics of the ayllu and its members in the past not only are different from those of Western modernity, as liberal anthropologists such as Allen might have it, they also embody an active opposition to that modernity that has constrained the ability of modernization projects to force unwanted changes on indigenous communities.

Understanding the emergence of a body of indigenous intellectuals who read modernist anthropology avidly but quite selectively, choosing some themes that we are eager to reject, requires more than the simple reflexive trope of writing ourselves as individual actors into our ethnographies, or a well-worn postcolonial critique that trots out tired denouncements of anthropology as the handmaiden of (neo)imperialism. What is needed is a form of reflexive practice that is both broader—looking at ourselves collectively rather than individually—and narrower, looking at the specific social history of our discipline within particular regions and nations, where the politics of scholarship often play out quite differently. Anthropology is a collective endeavor with multiple and often conflicting political engagements, one that involves national and foreign, indigenous and nonindigenous practitioners, all of whose products—books, videos, lectures, collections—go on to have a social history of their own, independent of their makers. Only from such a standpoint might we have even a hope of thinking through—and living out—the real and potential relationships that exist between the scholarly disciplines of ethnography, ethnohistory, and archaeology, and the social justice movements being forged by the very people we study.

Notes

1. Similarly, ethnohistorian Rachel O'Toole recently sent me a query about the ayllu's moiety structure; she opened her e-mail by apologizing for asking "such an antiquated question" and ended by asking, "Do anthropologists care about this anymore?"

2. I was editor at the time and solicited this article; I also solicited the introduction to it, written by Andrew Orta and discussed in this chapter.

3. As Choque and Mamani recount the history of their organization, what began as a scholarly endeavor with political ends—collecting oral testimonies and

documentary evidence about Aymara history so as to "decolonize Indian historical memory"—ended with a decision in 1993 to join Bolivia's ayllu movement, which had been growing since the 1980s (Andolina 2001). Abandoning the archives for the moment, they reinvented themselves as "activists in a decolonizing process" (Choque and Mamani 2001:204–207).

4. These similarities are not incidental; NGOs have arranged for increasing collaboration between Ecuadorian and Bolivian indigenous organizations (Andolina 2001; pers. comm., 2002).

5. Macas uses the hybrid term "llacta-ayllu" because "ayllu" is less often heard in Ecuador than in Bolivia today; however, his local listeners are familiar with another term for community, "llacta." Conceptually, these two terms are closely linked, with "llacta" referring more to the physical space occupied by a living community, while "ayllu" emphasizes the principle of descent that links the living to one another through the dead. "Ayllu" is the term of preference for writers in the southern Andes because it carries more of the affective weight that Raymond Williams (1976) ascribes to the term community (see the introduction to this volume).

6. My own ethnographic work in rural highland Ecuador (1989a, 1989b, 1995), some of it written when I was studying with Enrique Mayer, offers a similar picture of the local social structure.

7. Also very significant were the provocative publications of Peruvian historian María Rostworowski (e.g., 1977), who tested Murra's hypothesis against documentary evidence on coastal societies and argued that these polities were organized quite differently from their highland counterparts.

8. See, for example, Earls and Silverblatt (1978); Allen (1988:205–207); and Abercrombie (1998:66–301).

9. A specialist in Bolivia might well disagree with their recounting of regional history, however, which may be motivated by the desire to make certain territorial claims against their Aymara neighbors, as well as to fight for the collective advancement of all Aymara people.

10. The year 1952 witnessed the Bolivian revolution and the writing of Bolivia's constitution, which created "peasant unions" as the means by which indigenous communities could gain political access. The ongoing conflict between the peasant union movement and the ayllu movement is beyond my scope here.

11. Their vision of their own history begins with an imagined preconquest whole, Suyu Pakajaqi, which they describe as a regional state that underwent a

long and painful process of fragmentation under a succession of colonial, republican, and liberal regimes. The other side of this history, which they document through their archival work and the collection of testimonial histories from community elders, is that of resistance on the part of "empowered leaders," whose efforts succeeded in braking the most destructive historical processes and ensuring the indigenous community's survival, albeit in weakened and impoverished form.

12. See, for example, Mariátegui (1971, 1991); Valcárcel (1927); Zevallos Aguilar (2002); and de la Cadena (2000).

13. The colonial legal system acknowledged the ayllu but "tended to convert the 'community' into a cog in the administrative and fiscal machinery," he writes, while the liberal legislation put in place by the new republic that followed "attacked" and "destroyed" it (Mariátegui 1971:42–57). Indian communities had responded to these challenges by "modifying forms of cooperation and association"; in many places, rather than a fully functioning ayllu, what survives are simply "hardy and stubborn habits of cooperation and solidarity" (57–58).

14. As well as the Macas and Andolina papers previously cited.

15. This is of course a simplification; a longer discussion would detail the important bridge between the two intellectual communities provided by the work of scholars from the Andes who study, work, and/or live in the United States, such as Enrique Mayer or Marisol de la Cadena (2000), whose recently published book about Peruvian anthropology in the twentieth century has been very influential.

16. For example, see the description of the ayllu on the Web page of a French NGO devoted to developing water systems: http://www.agualtiplano.net/pueblos/perspectives.htm.

17. See the discussion in Weismantel (2001:xxxv–xxxvi).

18. See my own argument in this regard (Weismantel 2001:136–175).

19. Also relevant—and hotly debated—is the question of leadership structure. In Bolivia the ayllu movement has reintroduced traditional categories such as *mallku* and *jilakata* (and a national indigenous politician is known throughout Bolivia by the nickname El Mallku).

5

The Sinister Political Life of Community

Economies of Violence and Governable Spaces in the Niger Delta, Nigeria

Michael Watts

We seek to recover the...life of the community, as neither the "before" nor the "after" picture of any great human transformation....We see "communities" as creatures with an extraordinary and actually...quite sinister political life in the ground of real history.

Kelly and Kaplan (2001:199)

Community is an archetypal "keyword" in the sense deployed by Raymond Williams (1976). A "binding" word, suturing certain activities and their interpretation, community is also "indicative" (Williams's term once again) in certain forms of thought. Deployed in the language for at least five hundred years, the word community has carried a range of senses denoting actual groups (for example, "commoners" or "workers") and connoting specific qualities of social relationship (as in *communitas*). By the nineteenth century, community was, of course, invoked as a way of talking about much larger issues, about modernity itself. Community—and its sister concepts of tradition and custom— now stood in sharp contrast to the more abstract, instrumental, individuated, and formal properties of state or society in the modern sense. A related shift in usage subsequently occurred in the twentieth century, when community came to refer to a form or style of politics distinct from the formal repertoires of national or local politics. Here the reference was direct politics, community participation and organization, often but not always populist in orientation, typically working with and for "the people." At this historical moment we are awash in communities of this kind; in fact the "self-governing community" is one of the defining formulations of neoliberal rule (Schofield 2002). Nikolas Rose (1999) suggests that in the transatlantic economies, this new generation of communities—from community gardening to community partnerships—has arisen from the ashes of state withdrawal and socialist crisis, speaking the powerful language of civic renewal and self-improvement.

Across the modern history of community, there has always been a proclivity to read the concept positively, as an unalloyed "good"—to highlight, to the exclusion of all else, the purportedly ethical, moral, and social virtues of the community as such. Not unexpectedly, the "warmly persuasive" qualities of community (Williams 1976:76) have an echo in the related notion of a civil society—understood as a complex and dynamic ensemble of legally protected, self-organizing, and self-reflexive nongovernmental organizations in tension with one another and the state (Keane 1998:6–7)—that too is posited in roseate terms, as a realm of freedom, pluralism, participation, and reflexivity. Civil society and community both suffer from a sort of Manicheanism: the state is afflicted with the powers of coercion, while society is the home of freedom, "good living, warm and whole" (Foucault 2000:168).

Community stands, then, as a common currency connecting the differing expressions of modern justice as Nancy Fraser (Fraser and Honneth 2003) sees them: the *redistributive* sense of justice on the one side (communities of class or social strata) and the politics of *recognition* or recognitive justice on the other (communities of identity and difference). Community, not just the modern imagined nation (B. Anderson 1983) but community claims-making of a much more heterogeneous sort, must be understood as "political" (Pandey, this volume) and as "represented" (Kelly and Kaplan 2001), always read against the history of the modern state. Communities demand visibility, legibility, and enumeration as preconditions for claims-making and thereby for their entry into the modern universe of the political. Whether, as Pandey (this volume) suggests, defining and stabilizing such claims will at some point see a shedding of community's carapace as it reaches nationhood is perhaps an open question—for the simple reason that not all modern communities have national aspirations (for example, al-Qaida).

And whether and how such political communities can become some-thing genuinely subversive—what Foucault (1982) called movements of subjugated knowledge—depends in part on how deeply the state and capital have penetrated the trenches of civil society.

My account pays fidelity to community's modern political usage but at the same time locates community explicitly with respect to con-temporary forms of capitalism. Community is both in the business of modern rule (political actors claim community as a precondition for their claims on the state) and simultaneously, as Miranda Joseph (2002) puts it, a "supplement to capital" (it is *in* business). To put the matter slightly differently, communities are as tightly bound up with capitalism and the operations of the marketplace as they are with rule and governance. David Harvey (1987) has made much of the ways in which invented urban communities predicated on lifestyle, culture, or ethnicity produce built environments (and hence are sources of value) that simultaneously work against class antagonisms and absorb some of the surplus production generated by the circuits of urban capitalism. Miranda Joseph sees communities as shoring up the flows of capital in effect by legitimating and creating forms of hierarchy and difference that are "implicitly required but disavowed by capitalism" (2002:xxxii). These forms of analysis conjure up the spirit of Karl Polanyi (1945), who famously pointed out that markets cannot create social order; indeed they can colonize and ultimately destroy it. The market destroys the social character of three foundational yet "fictitious" commodities (land, labor, and money); its corrosive effects underwrite class-based communities such as such Chartism, the cooperative movement, and Owenism, each a reaction to the destructive process of commodifica-tion (see Burawoy 2003). Re-embedding of markets, or the reactions to disembedding to put it more positively, produces forms of association (the modern political community) that serve to maintain capitalist accumulation (that is to say, civil society as a counterweight to the anar-chy of the market).

Over the last two centuries, many First and Third World utopian populisms—often draped in nostalgia for a community lost—can be grasped as a reaction to the ruptures and costs of industrialization and development (Kitching 1980). Working-class communities, peasant sys-tems of common property management, the moral economy of Islamic schools, and so on are crushed by the unfettered powers of the market, and yet these selfsame conditions of destruction provide a fertile soil in which the ceaseless search for alternative communities can take root and flourish. The construction of collective identities arises from the broader practices of defining and delimiting communities, but at a cost:

> As a rule...these dissolve internal differentiations within any given collectivity in favor of a common external demarcation....The spread of such claims is only possible in communities where religious (or traditional) norms and affiliations have become shaky or uncertain. Surrogate constructions then offer magical formulae that suggest hidden ways of belonging, delimiting and persisting....Formulaic constructions of collective identity have become a symptomatic signature of the present. They are ubiquitous wherever societies, regardless of their actual differentiation, are transfigured into seamless communities, and assured of continuity by symbolic demarcation and fabrication of meaning. (Niethammer 2003:80–83)

In the unmaking and remaking of modern communitas, whatever its cultural, social, or historical circumstances, the new community must always address questions of representation (how it represents itself and what forms of political representation it endorses), forms of rule, means of internal discipline, membership and "purity," styles of imagination, and the relation between the community and the economy.

Within the maelstrom of capitalist modernity, the possibilities for community are almost endless. Yet paradoxically, community is an exemplar of what Ernesto Laclau (1996) calls an "empty signifier"— something that no political actor can monopolize the truth of over the long term. In this light, I seek to emphasize three relatively unexplored facets of community, capitalism, and modern rule: first, the fact that community-making can fail (often dramatically), by which I mean that its social imaginary disintegrates (fails to maintain its social appeal, its ideological function, and its social cohesiveness) and erodes to the point where a base unity dissolves. Community can fail to be defined and stabilized (Jensen 2004). Second, communities typically contain

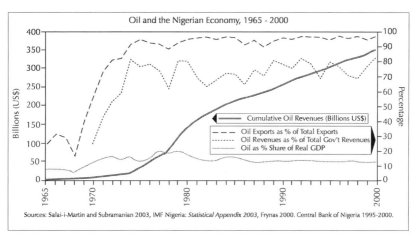

FIGURE 5.1

Oil and the Nigerian economy, 1965–2000.

both reactionary (despotic or disciplinary) and emancipatory (liberatory) expressions that are, as it were, in perpetual struggle with one
another; communities are not always warm and fuzzy. And third, communities (with their attendant forms of identity, rule, and terrritorial-
ization) can be produced simultaneously at rather different spatial
levels and within different social force fields, and to this extent they
may work with and against one another in complex ways. In short, people belong to multiple communities, navigating among them in a way
that works against the communitarian presumption that individuals
hold fidelity to only one community. These three antinomies have sinister qualities, to which my title refers.

My central task is to explore the antinomies of community in a
rather particular postcolonial state, namely the oil nation called
Nigeria (figure 5.1). Oil states—sometime called petro-states (Karl
1997)—encompass considerable variability, ranging from sparsely populated surplus producers in the Gulf states to industrial semiperiph-
eries such as Venezuela or Russia. But each stands in relation to a
particular sort of capitalism (which I shall call petro-capitalism), in
which a key resource (oil) and a logic of extraction figure centrally in
the making and breaking of community. I wish to focus on the *simultaneous* production of three differing, territorially based communities (or

governable spaces). Each community is imagined, so to say, through and with oil—the communities are "naturalized"—but they produce forms of rule and identity that are fragmented, unruly, and often violent, thereby threatening the very idea of community itself. And standing at the heart of each community is a double movement (a central antinomy) that, as I hope to show, provides a friction between these communities, making them operate at cross purposes, I think with rather devastating consequences.[1]

My argument runs something like this: Modern petro-capitalism operates through a particular "oil complex" (an institutional configuration of firms, state apparatuses, and oil communities) that constitutes a radical—and multifaceted—challenge to customary forms of community authority, systems of ethnic identity, and the functioning of local state institutions. These challenges are generated principally by mechanisms of property and land disputes and by forms of popular mobilization to gain access to first, company rents and compensation revenues, and second, the petro-revenues of the Nigerian state (largely by demanding and instituting new regional and/or local state institutions). The oil complex generates differing sorts of governable spaces in which identity, territory, and rule are in play. In some cases, generational forces (youth in particular) are predominant; in others the clan, the kingdom (chieftainship), or the ethnic minority (indigenous peoples). Local government councils or authorities, or radical (sometimes secessionist) insurgent movements, can also provide the setting in which new political communities are incubated. My empirical research in the Niger Delta—the oil-producing region in Nigeria—explicates these particular and local dynamics—that is, the ways in which these forces and powers singly, or in complex concatenations, produce different sorts of community and rule (and unruliness), differing styles of imagining (and unimagining), and contrasting forms of making and breaking community—all the while retaining a common structural relation to what I call the oil complex. The three communities I focus on are chieftainship, ethnicity (or indigeneity), and the nation.

A NOTE ON COMMUNITY AND GOVERNABLE SPACES

The idea of communities as governable spaces is derived from Michel Foucault via the brilliant work of Nikolas Rose (1999). For

Foucault (2000, 1982; see also Barry, Osborne, and Rose 1993; C. Gordon 1980), the notion of governmentality implies an expansive way of thinking about governing and rule in relation to the exercise of modern power. Government for Foucault referred famously to the "conduct of conduct," a more or less calculated and rational set of ways of shaping conduct and securing rule through a multiplicity of authorities and agencies in and outside of the state and at a variety of spatial levels. Modern governmentality was rendered distinctive by the specific forms in which the population and the economy were administered, and specifically by a deepening of the "governmentalization of the state" (that is to say, how sovereignty comes to be articulated through the populations and the processes that constitute the administered population). The new practices of the state, as Mitchell Dean (1999:16) says, shape human conduct by "working through our desire, aspirations, interests and beliefs for definite but shifting ends." It was the task of Foucault to reveal the genealogy of government, the origins of modern power, and the fabrication of a modern identity.

Governing—that is, what authorities wanted to happen in relation to what problems, objectives, and tactics—can be assessed by reference to the "analytics of government" (N. Rose 1999:21; Dean 1999). For Rose, these analytics of government constitute "governable spaces," and the spatializations of government are the "modalities in which a real and material governable world is composed, *terraformed*, and populated" (1999:32; see also Murdoch and Ward 1997; Hart 2003; Mitchell 2002). The scales at which government is "territorialized"—the word "territory" is derived from *terra*, "land," but also from *terrere*, "to frighten"—are myriad: the factory, the neighborhood, the commune, the region, the nation. Each of these governable spaces has its own topology and is, as Rose (1999:37) puts it, modeled in such a way through thought and practice that they become territorialized in various ways (the nation, the city, the village, or the factory). Governable spaces necessitate the territorializing of governmental thought and practice, but they are simultaneously produced at differing scales by the "cold laws of political economy" (39). The map has been central to the process of objectification, marking and inscribing community, serving as "a little machine for producing conviction in others" (37).

Governable spaces are produced at differing scales (what Peck and

Brenner [2002] call "politicized scalar narratives" and Neil Smith [1992] calls "scale politics"), and they are populated by political subjects and their enunciative modalities (M. Clifford 2001).[2] Perhaps the most compelling way in which territory, rule, and identity are currently constituted is, as Rose himself notes, through the idea of community. I want to think about the genesis of differing sorts of governable spaces/communities in Nigeria in relation to the "cold laws" of petrocapitalist development and nation-building that provide the forcing houses within which communities are constantly made and unmade. There is no presumption that the category of governable space or community implies in practice stable forms of government, or the successful definition or stabilization of community as such, or indeed the achievement of rule (Joyce 2003). Quite the reverse, the forms of hegemony in these spaces are typically weak and contested, violent and conflicted, and the communities are subject to different constellations of force and consent—much of which, in the final analysis, looks like *un*governability. As Alan Smart puts it: "[W]e need to pay more attention to areas in which control seems to be conspicuously absent, where neglect is more apparent than surveillance" (2001:31). Neglect, but also incapacity and incompetence.

ECONOMIES AND COMMUNITIES OF VIOLENCE

> The "normal" exercise of hegemony is characterized by the combination of force and consent, in variable equilibrium, without force predominating too much over consent... [But] between force and consent stands corruption-fraud, that is the enervation and paralyzing of the antagonist or antagonists. (Gramsci 1975, cited in P. Anderson 2001)

The strategic significance of Nigeria is incontestable. One of every five Africans is a Nigerian (the country's population is 137 million), and it is the world's seventh largest exporter of petroleum (providing the U.S. market with roughly 8 percent of its imports). A longtime member of OPEC, in the last three decades it has emerged as an archetypical "oil nation." With reserves estimated at close to forty billion barrels, Nigerian oil provides 80 percent of government revenues, 90 percent of foreign exchange earnings, 96 percent of export revenues and half of the gross domestic product. Nigerian oil is prized for its "lightness" and "sweetness," yielding more gasoline and diesel than "sour" Middle Eastern crudes. Crude oil production runs currently at more than 2.1 million barrels per day (a value of more than $20 billion at 2004 prices). Mostly lifted onshore from about 250 fields in the Niger Delta, Nigeria's oil now represents a vast domestic industrial infrastructure: more than three hundred oil fields, 5,284 wells, 7,000 kilometers of pipelines, ten export terminals, 275 flow stations, ten gas plants, four refineries (Warri, Port Harcourt I and II, and Kaduna), and a massive liquefied natural gas project (in Bonny and Brass).

Nigeria is a multiethnic state and was a British colony until 1960. Colonial indirect rule imposed a "decentralized despotism" (Mamdani 1996) orchestrated through regional rule by powerful ethnic (and regional) majorities. The backbone of each region was an export commodity and a government marketing board that financed party politics by taxing peasant producers. At independence, Muslim northerners sustained a fragile hegemony over a highly charged multiethnic polity, and it was into this weak federal system that commercial oil production was inserted. The breakup of the federation in 1967 (following a succession of military coups), the secession of Biafra (the former Eastern Region), and the civil war (1967–1970) that followed were in no small measure a reflection of the new saliency of oil in Nigerian economic and political life. In the wake of the oil boom of 1973, a huge influx of petro-dollars launched an ambitious (and autocratic) state-led modernization program. In short order, Nigeria became an oil nation. But what began as a boom with untempered ambition in the 1970s ended in the mid-1980s as a bust, compounded by the austerity of World Bank adjustment programs. In 1999, after a terrifying period of military authoritarianism under Sani Abacha, Olesegun Obasanjo became the first democratically elected president in two decades, inheriting an economy in shambles, vast political and economic resentments by oil minorities, and the prospect of building a democracy on the backs of long-standing regional, ethnic, and religious animosities.

Commercial petroleum production, which began in 1956 in Oloibiri in Baylesa State, seemed to offer a rather different prospect to the awful realities of the new civilian dispensation, not least for the largely neglected ethnic minorities (some 60 groups) of the southeastern region. But black gold ushered in instead massive environmental despoliation,[3] a crisis in forms of traditional livelihood, staggering corruption, deepening social inequalities, and growing local resentments across the Niger Delta, driven by the siphoning off of oil wealth from the oil-producing states to the coffers of other regions (especially the Muslim north). By the late 1970s and early 1980s, the beginning of popular resistance (and the call for "resource control") was already evident, but it was the charismatic leadership of Ken Saro-Wiwa and the 1990 Ogoni Bill of Rights, promoted by the Movement for the Survival of the Ogoni People (MOSOP), that marked a watershed in the popular agitation against the consequences of oil development in the Niger Delta. Saro-Wiwa and eight others from the MOSOP leadership were ultimately hanged at the hands of a military tribunal in 1995, but their murders ignited a prairie fire of struggles by other oil-producing communities (the Adoni, the Itsekiri, the Isoko, the Urhobo, and the Ijaw, for example),[4] a growing clamor for compensation across the nine oil-producing delta states, and the development of wide-ranging pan-ethnic political movements (such as CHICOCO, UND, and TROPCON)[5] calling for "true federalism" (Okonta and Douglas 2001; ERA 2000; Osaghae 1995; Obi 2001, 2004; Ikelegbe 2001). The broadening of civil society in the mid-1980s permitted oil-related grievances to be projected onto the larger screen of what Ikelegbe calls "participatory, highly mobilized, and coordinated platforms of civil groups in a struggle for self-determination, equity and civil rights" (2001:465).

Since the late 1990s, there has been a very substantial escalation of violence across the delta oil fields, accompanied by major attacks on oil facilities (it is estimated that more than one thousand people die each year from oil-related violence). The delta has indisputably emerged as "a region of insurrection" (Ikelegbe 2001:463). A report prepared for the Nigerian National Petroleum Company (NNPC) and published in 2003 was entitled *Back from the Brink* and painted a gloomy "risk audit" for the delta (ClearWater 2003). NNPC estimated that between 1998 and 2003, there were four hundred "vandalizations" on company facilities each year (581 between January and September 2004), and oil losses amounted to $1 billion annually (NNPC 2004). The tactics and repertoires deployed against the companies have been various: demonstrations and blockades against oil facilities; occupations of flow stations and platforms; sabotage of pipelines; oil "bunkering," or theft (from hot-tapping fuel lines to large-scale appropriation of crude from flow stations); litigation against companies; hostage taking; and strikes. A large group of Ijaw women that occupied Chevron oil refineries near Warri in 2002, demanding company investments and jobs for indigenes (*New York Times*, August 13, 2002), reflected the tip of a vast political iceberg. Mounting communal violence in the following year resulted in many mortalities and widespread community destruction and dislocation around the Warri petroleum complex. Seven oil company employees were killed in March 2003, prompting all the major oil companies to withdraw staff, close down operations, and reduce output by more than 750,000 barrels per day (40 percent of national output). This situation in turn provoked President Obasanjo to dispatch large troop deployments to oil-producing creeks. Ijaw militants, struggling to get a cut of the illegal oil "bunkering" trade—some estimates suggest that this innovative form of oil theft siphons a staggering 15 percent of production (WAC/SPDC 2004; see also www.legaloil.com)—threatened to destroy eleven captured oil installations. In April 2004, another wave of violence erupted around oil installations (at the end of April, Shell lost production of up to 370,000 barrels per day, largely in the western delta), this time amid the presence of armed insurgencies, specifically two ethnic militias led by Ateke Tom (the Niger Delta Vigilante) and Alhaji Asari (the Niger Delta People's Volunteer Force), each driven, and partly funded, by oil monies.[6] The periodicity and character of this militancy have certainly been shaped by the conjuncture of recent forces, including local and national elections, the emergence of ethnic militias and armed struggle as a political program for restive youth, and the growing militarization of the oil fields and oil installations throughout the 1990s. However, nobody seriously expects the endemic problems within the oil sector to dissipate any time soon.

The crisis in the Niger Delta must be located on a wider landscape of ethnic and linguistic complexity and deep-seated economic and political resentments across the region. There are five major linguistic categories (Ijoid, Yoruboid, Edoid, Igboid, and Delta Cross), but each embraces a profusion of ethno-linguistic heterogeneity. The history of the delta captures this cultural complexity, since precolonial trade patterns across the region reflected a rich and complex social division of labor rooted in occupation, ethnicity, and micro-ecology. These commercial and exchange relations were radically compromised by the Portuguese in the fifteenth century, however, and subsequently by French, Dutch, and British slavers. The advent of a so-called legitimate trade in rubber and cocoa under British auspices in the nineteenth century (to replace slavery after abolition) gave rise to an Oil Rivers Protectorate in which a vital commercial life flourished. The establishment of the Nigerian colony and the imposition of indirect rule in the early 1900s marked an end to the brief period of commercial expansion. For most of the first half of the twentieth century, the delta was an economic and political backwater. In the gradual transition to independence in the 1950s, the ethnic minorities voiced concerns to the departing British administration that their interests were virtually invisible in a Nigerian federation dominated by three ethnic majorities (the Hausa, the Yoruba, and the Ibo). What was true at the moment of imperial departure only became more so in the post-colony.

Let me make three fundamental points concerning the political economy of oil in Nigeria (see Watts 2000; Forrest 1995; Frynas 2000; S. Khan 1994; Obi 2001). The first is that oil capitalism operates through what I call an oil complex, with a broadly similar structure in, say, Venezuela, Gabon, or Indonesia (see figure 5.2). It is composed of several key elements including a statutory monopoly over mineral exploitation (the 1969 petroleum law; Revenue Allocation Decree 13 in 1970; the Land Use Decree of 1978),[7] a nationalized oil company (the NNPC) that has majority holding in its production arrangements with foreign companies,[8] the security apparatuses of the state along with the private security forces of the companies (to ensure that costly investments are secured), the oil-producing communities themselves (within whose customary jurisdiction the wells are located), and a political mechanism by which federal oil revenues are distributed to government and the states (see figure 5.3). The latter is effected by four means: a federal account (rents appropriated directly by the federal state), a state derivation principle (the right of each state to a proportion of the taxes that its inhabitants are assumed to have contributed to the federal exchequer), the Federation Account or States Joint Account (which allocates revenue to the states on the basis of need, population, and other criteria), and a Special Grants Account (which

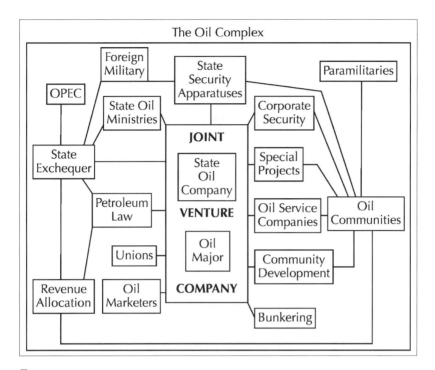

FIGURE 5.2

The oil complex.

includes monies designated directly for the Niger Delta).[9] Over time, the derivation revenues have fallen (and thereby revenues directly controlled by the oil states have shriveled),[10] while the States Joint Account has grown vastly (the nine oil-producing states received ₦886 billion from the Federation Account in 2003). In short, there has been a process of radical fiscal centralism (Furro 1992; Suberu 2004; Toyo 2002; Okilo 1980; Ikporukpo 1996; Ebeku 2003).

The second point is that the dynamics of the oil complex shape the character and dynamics of Nigerian development. Oil is of course a biophysical resource; it is also a commodity that enters the market with its price tag, and as such it is the bearer of particular relations of production and quite specific fetishistic qualities. Oil is "black gold," the bearer of powers, hopes, and expectations of unimaginable power. Oil is a constant reference point in the popular Nigerian imagination, in films, soap operas, and popular theater.

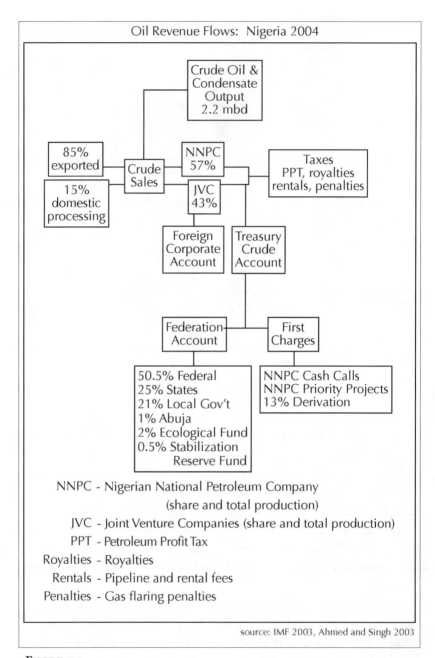

FIGURE 5.3

Oil revenue flows, Nigeria, 2004.

The third point is that Nigerian petro-capitalism contains a sort of double movement, a contradictory unity of capitalism and modernity. On the one hand, oil has been a *centralizing force* that has rendered the (oil) state more visible and globalized, underwriting a process of state-building and national community imagining. On the other hand, oil-led development, driven by an unremitting political logic of ethnic claims-making and staggering corruption by the political classes, has become a force of *fragmentation* and *illegitimacy*, radically discrediting the state and its forms of governance. It produced a set of conditions/communities that have compromised, indeed undermined, the very tenets of the modern nation-state. In short, one might encapsulate this double movement as the tension between fiscal centralism and regional/local dispersion. Fernando Coronil (1997) refers to this conundrum as "the Faustian trade of money for modernity," which in Venezuela brought "the illusion of development." In Nigeria, too, the double movement brought spectacle and illusion (Apter 2005): an explosive growth of modern infrastructure and a (brief) consumption boom for the middle classes, while 85 percent of oil revenues went to 1 percent of the population (and $100 billion of $400 billion simply went "missing"). But it also produced forms of governable spaces (the product of what I call political dispersion) that sit uneasily with the very idea of Nigeria—spaces that generated forms of rule, conduct, and imagining at cross-purposes with one another, antithetical to the very idea of a coherent modern nation-state that oil, in the mythos of the West at least, represented. How, then, can one grasp the imagination and creation of communities in and through the oil complex and petro-capitalism?

COMMUNITY AS THE GOVERNABLE SPACE OF CHIEFTAINSHIP[11]

Nembe community[12] in Bayelsa State is a center of Nigerian oil production. In the 1950s, the Tennessee Oil Company (a U.S. company) began oil explorations, but oil was not located in commercial quantities until much later, when Shell D'Arcy unearthed the nearby Oloibiri oil field in Ogbia. Subsequent explorations led to the opening of the large and rich Nembe oil fields near the coast along the Okpoama and Twon-Brass axis. Currently, the four Nembe oil fields produce approximately

150,000 barrels of high-quality petroleum through joint operating agreements between the NNPC and Agip and Shell. Nembe, however, is in crisis (and has been for close to a decade): it is a major theater of violence and intra-community conflict, largely ungovernable, and pulled apart by intense competition over political turf and the control of benefits from the oil industry. The violence can be traced back to the late 1980s, when the Nembe Council of Chiefs acquired power from the king (*amayanabo*), Justice Alagoa Mingi IX, to negotiate royalties and other benefits with the oil companies. The combination of youth-driven violence and intense political competition has transformed Nembe's customary system of governance and set the stage for further challenges to the traditional authority of chieftainship (see Kemedi 2002; HRW 2003).[13]

There is also a deeper history. Colonial indirect rule certainly left much of the Niger Delta marginalized and isolated, but it also, in the name of ruling through tradition, built upon and frequently expanded (or invented) chiefly powers of local rule. In Nembe, colonial structures were grafted onto a deep and complex structure of kingship and gerontocratic rule, though in comparison to its commercial and political vitality in the nineteenth-century palm-oil protectorate, the town had fallen into disrepair and economic ruin. At independence in 1960, Nembe was the chief city of Brass, a division of Yenagoa Province in the Eastern Region. An amayanabo (Ogbolomabiri) reigned in Nembe, but unlike the famous King Koko and his illustrious forebears, he had neither power nor authority (Okonta 2001). Rather, it was the district officer resident in Twon, representing the regional government in Enugu, who exercised effective power over Nembe. The Niger Delta Development Board, founded in 1961 to address the region's problems, and the Niger Delta Congress (the party representative for the division), offered little assistance before the entire oil-producing zone (Nembe included) slid into civil war and tragic violence. By the war's end in 1970, Nembe was a sad backwater mired in desperate poverty and stagnation. It was in this setting that commercial oil production proved to be so decisive.

To understand the dynamics of contemporary Nembe as a sort of oil community, recall that practical matters concerning access to and control over land lay in the hands of customary authorities (notwithstanding the fact that the 1969 petroleum law granted the state the power to nationalize all oil resources). Land rights, and claims on oil royalties, were from the outset rooted in the amayanabo, and derivatively the subordinate powers, namely the Council of Chiefs and the Executive Council. Historically, Nembe community was structured around a rigid political hierarchy consisting of the amayanabo presiding over a descending order of chiefs (or heads of the war canoe houses)[14] elected by all the war canoe houses. Although the chiefs were subservient to the amayanabo, they acted as his closest advisers, supported the amayanabo in the event of military threat, and in turn were responsible for electing the amayanabo from the Mingi group of houses—that is, from the royal line. The current Nembe Council of Chiefs is an assemblage of the recognized chiefs of Nembe "chalked" by the king (Kemedi 2002).

By the late 1980s, a widespread sense of malaise and frustration colored Mingi rule. In particular, the Nembe monarch's ineffectiveness in dealing with the oil companies led in 1991 to a radical decentralization of his powers to the Council of Chiefs, headed by one Chief Egi Adukpo Ikata. Insofar as the council now dealt directly with Shell and the other oil companies, and handled large quantities of money paid as rent and contributions to "community assistance," competition for election to the council intensified as various political factions (and families) struggled for office. By 2000 the council had grown from twenty-six to ninety persons. Coeval with the evisceration of kingly powers, an expansion of the council mandate, and the expansion of the council membership was a subtle process of "youth mobilization"—a social phenomenon that extends far beyond Nembe and is transforming the entire delta. In an age-graded society like the Nembe Ijaw, "youth" refers to persons typically between their teens and early forties, who, whatever achievements they may have obtained (university degrees, fatherhood, and so on), remain subservient to their elders. Central to the emergence of militant youth movements in Nembe Town was the catalytic role of Nimi B. P. Barigha-Amage, a Nembe indigene and former engineer at the ELF oil company. He deployed his knowledge of the oil industry to organize youths of the Nembe community into a force capable of extracting concessions from the oil companies, in essence by converting preexisting cultural organizations into the providers of protection services. In turn, Chief Ikata was quick to take advantage of youth restiveness (attributable to a lack of employment, limited educational opportunities, subservience in a hierarchic and stratified gerontocratic system, corporate neglect and irresponsibility, and the absence of anything like meaningful or participatory oil-funded social development) to pressure Shell into granting community entitlements (called cash payments). Chief Ikata and the young engineer in effect manufactured a new social pact: the engineer supplied the youths with information regarding community entitlements, and the chief deployed his knowledge of military logistics to organize the shutting down of flow stations, the seizure of equipment, and sabotage (Alagoa 2001; HRW 2005). In 1994 the military went into Nembe to attempt to control the disruption of oil production by militant youth groups aligned with differing local political factions.

Armed with insider knowledge of the companies and an understanding of a loosely defined set of rules regarding company compensation for infringements on community property, Barigha-Amage pushed further for the creation of youth "cultural groups," which gradually, with the support of some members of the Council of Chiefs, intermediated with oil companies and their liaison officers and manipulated the system of compensation in the context of considerable juridical and legal ambiguity over land ownership and compensation rates. Company liaison officers (CLOs), colluding with community representatives, invented ritual or cultural sites that had ostensibly been compromised or damaged by oil operations in order to defraud the oil companies (the CLOs took a percentage of the cash compensation). As the opportunities for appropriating company resources in the name of compensation proved successful (indeed lucrative), other sections of the youth community (often distinguished by differing familial or political affiliations) began to competitively organize to gain access to company rents—often through extortion, sabotage, intimidation, and sometimes hostage taking associated with occupations of flow stations on the Nembe oil fields.

By 1994 new political actors had emerged to lead youth factions, and the situation began to spiral out of control. Former university lecturer Lionel Jonathan formed a group called Isongoforo (House of Lords), and a year later Mrs. Ituro-Garuba, wife of a well-placed military officer, established Agbara-foro. With much at stake financially, and control of the space between community and company in the balance, conflicts within and among youth groups inevitably proliferated and deepened (Alagoa 2001). In turn, growing community militancy spilled over into often-violent altercations with the much-detested mobile police ("Mopos," locally known as "kill and go") and local government authorities. The regional state and governor attempted to intervene as conditions deteriorated, but a government report was never released for political reasons. As a result, a subsequent banning of youth groups had no practical effect (HRW 2002, 2005).

Slowly, the subversion of royal authority, the strategic alliances between youths and chiefs, and the growing (and armed) conflict between youth groups for access to Shell resulted in a ferocious struggle for power and the ascendancy of a heavily armed Isongoforo. In an environment of rampant insecurity, tension, and lawlessness, including the occupation and closure of flow stations, the companies provided Isongoforo forces with "standby" payments; in effect, the companies were hiring protection services. Isongoforo occupied the center of a new governable space, which it ruled through organized violence and terror in effect funded by the large quantities of monies commanded from the companies. In the run-up to the 1999 elections, the youth groups were further armed and funded by competing political candidates and political parties, since many of the youth leaders had political aspirations or were well connected to the statehouse.

This volatile state of affairs collapsed dramatically in 2000 as local resentments, conflicts, and disorder proliferated. In February a "Peoples Revolution"—ostensibly precipitated by the humiliation of the Council of Chiefs at the hands of Shell (backed by Isongoforo)—overthrew Isongoforo. The chiefs now became more actively engaged in newly emerging power struggles for access to the oil companies, orchestrating the occupation of flow stations and undermining the powers of Isongoforo by recruiting and supporting other youth groups. By May 2000, Isongoforo had been sent into exile, but it was promptly replaced when Barigha-Amage returned as high chief of Nembe and promoted his own "cultural group," Isenasawo/Teme. Teme instituted a rule of terror and chaos far worse than that of its predecessors. It, too, proved unstable and split into two factions, staging countercoups with much bloodshed. A government Peace Commission was established in January 2001 in a desperate effort to bring peace to one of the jewels in the oil-producing crown (Alagoa 2001). The governor of Baylesa State appointed a special adviser to the town to facilitate peace and a return to normalcy. While efforts have been made to negotiate the return of some of the influential youths banished from the town, as it currently stands Nembe is ungovernable; many chiefly notables are no longer resident in Nembe itself.

The slide into violence and armed struggle was stimulated by gubernatorial politics and competition among political parties because of its concurrence with the 1999 elections, in which some of the key youth leaders were expected to deliver votes for the incumbent gubernatorial candidate. In the creation of a sort of vigilante rule, there were complex complicities between chiefs, local youth groups, political parties, the state political classes, and the companies. The occupations of oil flow stations (for purposes of extortion) were often known in advance and involved collaboration with local company engineers and community development officers. Youths were de facto company employees providing protection services, while local compensation and community officers of Shell and Agip produced fraudulent compensation cases and entitlements. Nembe, a town with its own long and illustrious history and politics, had become a sort of company town in which authority had shifted from the king to warring factions of youths working for and against the companies. The Council of Chiefs stood in a contradictory position, seeking to maintain control over revenues from the companies, as a legitimate source of authority, while being intimidated and undermined by the militant youth groups on whom it partly depended.

What I have described is a case of the radical displacement of a specific form of customary authority (chieftainship) through the creation of a governable space of civic vigilantism, a sort of "thickening" of civil society but not of the sort that Robert Putnam (2000) might endorse. These sorts of intra-community struggles can be multiplied many times over across the oil-producing communities of the Niger Delta. Indeed, one of the most important transformations of the last two decades is the extent to which youths have now confronted and often overturned chiefly powers (Ojo 2002).[15] As I write, three recent stories in the Nigerian press signal the depth and extent of these insurrectional youth politics: King Agari of Mbiama was dethroned by youths who caned him publicly with sixty strokes (*Weekly Trust*, January 24, 2004); in the Irri community in Isoko South, Chief Ovuse Eba Ogeme was abducted by youths (*Vanguard*, March 22, 2004); and the *oba* of Benin is under threat from so-called youth rebels over oil corruption (*This Day*, March 15, 2004). Youth militancy is not always directed inward to the ruling dynasty—it might primarily target the oil companies (for example, when youth militants in Elelenwo or Agalabiri occupy company installations) (Ojo 2002). But the most striking commonality is the extent to which a generation of youths—"restive youths" as the press and the politicians dub them—have channeled their right and proper anger into a variety of well-organized and sometimes armed political movements. The Niger Delta Volunteer Force, discussed below, is the paradigmatic case. Against this background one can begin to understand the constellation of forces by which in so many oil-producing communities restive youths have directly challenged chiefly rule, often in a dramatic and public way. The case of Nembe is compelling because youth mobilization—whose political affiliations and ambitions in any case were complex, reflecting an unstable amalgam of clan, family, and local electoral loyalties—has thrown up the figure of the youth militant, representing a tense alliance between civic organizations (presenting themselves as cultural youth organizations) and private oil companies. Rule in Nembe now took on a vigilante form. In the context of a weak and corrupt local state and powerful local class forces (the companies and chieftainship), the character of this power nexus bears striking resemblances to the genesis of the Mafia in nineteenth-century Sicily (Blok 1974). It is youth—communities of youths as political actors— that is in full-blown insurrection, detonated by oil but inserted into a variety of political situations and assuming a panoply of organizational forms—from well-organized ethnic youth movements such as the Ijaw Youth Council to mobile parliaments to rebel insurgents and local "mafias" such as Teme in Nembe. As a consequence, oil-producing communities as the locus of chiefly rule have been turned upside down.

COMMUNITY AS THE GOVERNABLE SPACE OF ETHNICITY AND RESOURCE CONTROL

The Niger Delta is a region of considerable, perhaps one should say bewildering, ethno-linguistic complexity. The Eastern Region, of which the Niger Delta is part, is dominated statistically by the Ibo majority, and this fact speaks to a long history of excluded ethnic delta minorities dating back to the Willink Commission's (1959) observations on the simmering political resentments in the region. Throughout the colonial period and prior to the onset of commercial oil production, some minorities, anxious to remove the shackles of what they saw as Ibo domination, endeavored to establish political entities (native authorities) of their own. All this work amounted to very little, however. In fact, it was a measure of the deep disenchantment of the minorities, and of the Ijaw in particular, that shortly after the January 1966 military coup, in which young military officers led by Major Chukwuma Kaduna Nzeogwu attempted to take over the central government, a group of young Ijaw militants led by Isaac Adaka Boro, Nottingham Dick, and Samuel Owonaro formed a paramilitary organization, the Niger Delta Volunteer Force, and proclaimed a Niger Delta Republic (based on a desire to secede from the Nigerian Federation). The revolt was crushed within a couple of weeks (hence the name Twelve Day Republic), and its leaders subsequently joined the federal side when civil war broke out in the country in July 1967. But Boro's short-lived revolution dramatized the widespread feeling of powerlessness of the delta communities "reduced to 'divisions' in 'provinces' in a 'region' where previously they had been masters of all that they surveyed" (Okonta 2004:3). Boro proved to be a forerunner of the resource control movement that came three decades later.

The ill-fated republic proved prescient. General Gowon's creation of twelve new states in the federation—three for the ethnic minority groups in the Niger Delta—in May 1967, and the commercialization of oil production after the civil war ended in January 1970, moved Boro's struggle toward the invention of "oil minorities." The bulk of the oil fields were located in three new states—Midwest, Rivers, and South-Eastern—and the political elites quickly appreciated the strategic significance of oil to the federal exchequer (Okonta 2001). The origins of communities' self-definition as ethnically defined "oil minorities" lay on a wider field of what I described previously as deepening fiscal centralism and the demise of derivation beginning in the 1970s. But the oil minorities drew sustenance from two further developments in the following decade. The first was the devastating consequences of structural adjustment in the mid-1980s, when the hardships imposed by the Babangida government and the World Bank further deepened resentments in the delta among communities that had, after all, missed out on the oil "boom" and were compelled to swallow the bitter pill of austerity. The second development occurred at roughly the same time (in 1986), when Babangida inaugurated a "Political Bureau" tasked with, among other things, instigating a national political debate and providing "an objective and in-depth critique of our past political experience in order to serve as background information for the debate" (Nigerian Federal Government 1987:226). The Babangida regime's attempt to "mobilize" Nigerians for a new political culture as part of its transition program deployed such agencies as the Directorate of Social Mobilization (DSM) for mass mobilization for self-reliance, economic recovery, and social justice (MAMSER). In practice, all were co-opted, as Okonta has shown, in ways unanticipated by the military junta, by an angry citizenry that used DSM to nurture autonomous social forces opposed to the state (Okonta 2001).

The political career of Ken Saro-Wiwa and the famous Ogoni movement were a product of this conjuncture of forces. Saro-Wiwa brilliantly built upon the confluence of ethnic exclusion, oil minority politics, and the flourishing of civil society to construct the ethno-nationalist community in search of resource control. He was in fact a director of DSM at its inception but resigned after a year and went on to found MOSOP, along with similarly aggrieved Ogoni notables, in 1990. By Saro-Wiwa's own account (1989), his short stint in MAMSER opened his eyes to the possibilities of mobilizing the Ogoni to demand a better dispensation within the Nigerian political arena. A number of other minority groups followed MOSOP's lead. The Movement for the Survival of the Izon (Ijaw) Ethnic Nationality in the Niger Delta (MOSIEND) presented the Izon Peoples Charter, modeled on the Ogoni Bill of Rights, to the press in October 1992; the Ogbia Charter, drafted by members of the Movement for Reparation to Ogbia (MORETO), an Ijo clan, made its appearance a month later; the Ikwerre, an oil-producing group neighboring the Ogoni, established the Council for Ikwerre Nationality in 1993.[16] Out of this firmament emerged the clamor for a Sovereign National Conference and the delta-wide movement—now central to the so-called South-South Alliance of oil-producing states—for "resource control" and "true federalism"[17] (Ukeje 2001). I shall concentrate here on the Ogoni case because its political trajectory reveals the making and ultimate unmaking of an ethno-nationalist political community—in fact an oil minority that politically fell to pieces. At its core was a profound tension between community qua ethnic identity and community qua civic populism that proved (among other things) to be its downfall.

The Ogoni are typically seen as a distinct ethnic group, consisting of three subgroups and six clans dotted over 404 square miles of creeks, waterways, and tropical forest in the northeastern fringes of the Niger Delta. Located administratively in Rivers State, Ogoniland is one of the most heavily populated zones in all Africa. The most densely settled areas of Ogoniland—with more than 1,500 persons per square kilometer—are the sites of the largest wells. Its customary productive base was provided by fishing and agriculture until the discovery of petroleum, including the huge Bomu field, immediately prior to independence. Part of an enormously complex regional ethnic mosaic, the Ogoni were drawn into internecine conflicts within the delta region, largely as a consequence of the slave trade and its aftermath, in the period prior to arrival of colonial forces at Kono in 1901. The Ogoni resisted the British until 1908 (Naanen 1995) but thereafter were left to stagnate as part of the Opopo Division within Calabar Province.

As Ogoniland was gradually incorporated during the 1930s, the clamor for a separate political division grew at the hands of the first pan-Ogoni organization, the Ogoni Central Union, which bore fruit with the establishment of the Ogoni Native Authority in 1947. In 1951, however, the authority was forcibly integrated into the Eastern Region. Marked by tremendous neglect and discrimination, integration raised long-standing fears of Ibo domination among the Ogoni.[18] Ogoni antipathy to what they saw as a sort of internal colonialism at the hands of the Ibo continued in their support of federal forces during the civil war. While Rivers State was established in 1967—which compensated in some measure for enormous Ogoni losses during the war—the new state recapitulated in microcosm the larger "national question." The new Rivers State was multiethnic but was presided over by the locally dominant Ijaw; this situation did nothing to allay the fears of the minorities.[19]

During the first oil boom of the 1970s, Ogoniland's fifty-six wells accounted for almost 15 percent of Nigerian oil production,[20] and up until the withdrawal of Shell in 1994, an estimated $30 billion in petroleum revenues has flowed from this Lilliputian territory. It was, as local opinion had it, "Nigeria's Kuwait." Yet Rivers State as a whole saw its federal allocation fall dramatically in absolute and relative terms. At the height of the oil boom, 60 percent of oil production came from Rivers State, but it received only 5 percent of the statutory allocation (roughly half of that received by the Kano and Northern states and the Ibo heartland states). Between 1970 and 1980 it received in revenues one-fiftieth of the value of the oil it produced. Few Ogoni households have electricity, there is one doctor per 100,000 people, and child mortality rates are some of the highest in the nation. According to official statistics, 80 percent of the population is illiterate, unemployment is 85 percent, and close to half of Ogoni youths have left the region in search of work. Life expectancy is barely fifty years, substantially below the national average.

If Ogoniland failed to see the material benefits from oil, what it *did* experience was something the European Parliament referred to as "an environmental nightmare." The heart of ecological harm stems from gas flaring and oil spills. Three-quarters of natural gas in the oil-producing areas is flared (compared to 0.6 percent in the United States). As an environmentalist visiting the delta in 1993 noted, "[S]ome children have never known a dark night even though they have no electricity" (*Village Voice*, November 21, 1995). Burning twenty-four hours per day at temperatures of 13,000 to 14,000 degrees Celsius, Nigerian natural gas produces 35 million tons of carbon dioxide and 12 million tons of methane per annum, more than any other country in the world, making Nigeria probably the biggest single cause of global warming. The oil spillage record is even worse. There are roughly three hundred spills per year in the delta, either from the pipelines that crisscross Ogoniland (often passing directly through villages) or from blowouts at wellheads. Ogoniland itself suffered 111 spills between 1985 and 1994 (Hammer 1996:61). Figures provided by the NNPC document 2,676 spills between 1976 and 1990, 59 percent of which occurred in Rivers State (Ikein 1990:171) and 38 percent of which were due to equipment malfunction.[21] The consequences of flaring, spillage, and waste for Ogoni fisheries and farms have been devastating. Two independent studies completed in 1997 revealed total petroleum hydrocarbons in Ogoni streams at 360 and 680 times the European Union's permissible levels (HRW 1995).

The November 1995 hanging of Ken Saro-Wiwa and the Ogoni nine—accused of murdering four prominent Ogoni leaders—and the subsequent arrest of nineteen others on treason charges represented the summit of a process of mass mobilization around the environmental, political, and economic costs of oil development. It began after the civil war with a "supreme cultural organization" called Kagote, which consisted largely of traditional rulers and high-ranking functionaries and laid the foundations for the establishment of MOSOP. A new strategic initiative began in the late 1980s with a program of mass action and passive resistance on the one hand, and on the other a renewed effort to focus on the environmental consequences of oil (Shell's role in particular) and group rights within the federal structure. Animating the entire struggle was, in the words of an Ogoni leader, the "genocide being committed in the dying years of the twentieth century by multinational companies under the supervision of the Government" (Naanen 1995:66). A watershed moment in MOSOP's history was the drafting in 1990 of an Ogoni Bill of Rights (Saro-Wiwa 1992), documenting a history of neglect and local misery. The bill took on the question of Nigerian federalism and minority rights, calling for Ogoni participation in the affairs of the republic as "a distinct and separate entity," and outlined a plan for autonomy and self-determination in which there would be guaranteed "political control of Ogoni affairs by Ogoni people...the right to control and use a fair proportion of Ogoni economic resources...[and] adequate representation as of right in all Nigerian national institutions" (Saro-Wiwa 1995:11). In short, the bill of rights addressed the question of the *unit* to which revenues should be allocated—and derivatively the rights of minorities (HRW 1995; Okonta 2001). If the Ogoni could not have direct control of oil, at the very least they deserved their own state. It was a casebook example of claims-making by a modern political community.

In spite of the remarkable rise of MOSOP between 1990 and 1996, its ability to represent itself as a unified pan-Ogoni organization—as a political community—proved to be contentious. There is no pan-Ogoni myth of origin (characteristic of some delta minorities), and a number of Ogoni subgroups engender stronger local loyalties than any affiliation to Ogoni nationalism. The Eleme subgroup has even argued on occasion that it is not Ogoni. Furthermore, the MOSOP leaders were actively opposed by elements of the traditional clan leadership, by prominent leaders and civil servants in state government, and by some critics who felt that Saro-Wiwa was out to gain "cheap popularity" (Osgahae 1995:334); relations between the movement, the leadership, and the youth always proved to be fraught. Saro-Wiwa nevertheless was able to build upon more than fifty years of Ogoni organizing and upon three decades of resentment against the oil companies, providing a mass base and a youth-driven radicalism—and it must be said an international visibility after he refigured the Ogoni struggle in largely environmental terms for a number of European constituencies such as Greenpeace—capable of challenging state power. Yet at its core, the oil-producing ethnic minority proved internally contentious and intractable. Ike Okonta (2001) has brilliantly showed how the very idea of the Ogoni community ultimately unraveled into fragments of class, clan, generation, and gender. Community was made and unmade in the course of Saro-Wiwa's short political life. While the 2001 Oputa Commission (Nigeria's truth and reconciliation commission) marked a public "healing" of the differing Ogoni factions, as it now stands there is much acrimony and division within the Ogoni, compounded by the divisive role of the companies and the state. MOSOP, despite its ability to keep Shell from returning to its oil operations in Ogoniland, is something of a spent political force.

What sort of articulation of community, then, did Saro-Wiwa pose? What sort of governable space did the Ogoni political project represent? It was clearly one in which territory and oil were the building blocks upon which ethnic difference and minority rights were constructed. And yet it was an unstable and contradictory sort of articulation, as Okonta (2001) has shown. As we have seen, there was no simple sense of "Ogoniness," no unproblematic unity, and no singular form of political subject (despite Saro-Wiwa's claim that 98 percent of Ogonis supported him). MOSOP itself had at least five somewhat independent internal strands embracing youth, women, traditional rulers, teachers, and churches. It represented a fractious and increasingly divided "we," as the open splits and conflicts between Saro-Wiwa and other elite Ogoni confirm (Nigerian Federal Government 1996; Obi 2004).[22]

Second, Saro-Wiwa's political vision invoked Ogoni culture and tradition, yet he also argued that war and internecine conflict had virtually destroyed the fabric of Ogoni society by 1900 (Saro-Wiwa 1992:14). His own utopia was *restorative*, demanding a sort of restitution of Ogoni culture based on a quasi-mythic invocation of the past, and yet this definition proved difficult to stabilize and often hard to control. Finally, ethnicity was for Saro-Wiwa the central problem of postcolonial Nigeria—organized corruption as a way of life—yet it was also a panacea, the means for the multiplication of minority power. Invoking the history of minority exclusion and the need for more than simple inclusion as the basis for federalism led Saro-Wiwa to ignore the histories and geographies of conflict and struggle among and between ethnic minorities.

What, then, does the Ogoni case disclose about the construction of oil and community? Its most powerful message is how a particular set of circumstances (the oil complex) is used by a charismatic and entrepreneurial leader to provide an explicit political program for a preexisting ethnic group reinvented as an oil minority. Its language was resource control and true federalism, and it launched, or helped launch, a raft of other such political communities including the powerful Ijaw movements (the Ijaw National Council and the Ijaw Youth Congress). Paradoxically, MOSOP surfaced as a founding minority and resource control community even though its strategic significance as an oil-producing region was diminishing. But within a decade it had catastrophically fallen apart as a movement and intra-group struggles deprived it of much of its previous momentum and visibility. Ogoni community was not exactly a case of what Laclau calls an "empty signifier," but it did prove beyond the means of Saro-Wiwa and the leadership that followed to fully stabilize and imagine its political character. What was at work in this failure was a tension between a national democratic project and narrow ethno-nationalist claims-making—both united in some way by the common concern to control "our oil." In the case of the Ogoni, this tension ultimately compromised a certain sense of political community and made the imagined community in some respects unimaginable:

> The Ogoni evidence suggests that MOSOP and the Ogoni
> Bill of Rights were, at inception, driven by a civic language.

The goals were democracy and development. But the demands of nation-building, and competing alternatives with regard to how this project might be realized within a wider and more powerful Nigeria-wide political arena that exerted its own pressures on the nation builders, triggered shifts in positions, and with it a bloody Ogoni civil war. Shell, in aiding federal troops deployed to the area to protect the oil fields, ensured that what began life as a non-violent social movement quickly became drenched in blood. Personality clashes, rooted in the politics of the Nigerian civil war, also played a role in shaping the denouement of the Ogoni drama. (Okonta 2004:7)

Within a decade of Saro-Wiwa's death there was outright hostility and conflict between Ogoni villages, clans, and ruling elites. Indeed, it is not clear in what sense one can now talk of the Ogoni as a political community even if MOSOP continues to function.

Since the return to civilian rule in 1999, there has been a proliferation of such oil-minority movements—in part the "demonstration effect" of MOSOP—spanning the entire delta and speaking the political language of "resource control," "true federalism," and a call for a National Sovereign Conference.[23] Some communities have slid into conflicts with other oil-producing minorities (often over territory and access to company revenues) or have lost political ground as southern governors and political classes have captured the weapon of resource control. What has transpired is not a reconfiguration of federalism or more effective control of oil by the communities but a rush of windfall oil profits to the states associated with increased derivation and the vast flows of company and state monies to the new regional development organization, the Niger Delta Development Commission (NDDC). More corruption, more contracts, and more venality: in sum, business as usual. Not surprisingly, the ethnic communities have turned their frustrations to militancy (Alhaji Asari and Ateke Tom are the two most public militias[24]), their fires stoked further by the sorts of intra-community conflicts I described for Nembe. The delta has become ever more engulfed in civil strife: militant occupations of oil flow stations, pipeline sabotage, intra-urban ethnic violence, and of course the near anarchy of state security operating in tandem with company security forces. The making and unmaking of these sorts of governable spaces—compounded by corrupt police and security forces and by a large and violent military—has produced a situation in which it is not clear whether the oil industry can continue to operate (WAC/SPDC 2004). The massive dislocations of oil supply in 2002, 2003, and 2004 suggest it's a close call. In a desperate effort to keep the oil flowing amid this contentiousness and conflict, Shell has spent hundreds of millions of dollars as "cash payments" each year in the hope that youths and elders alike could be rendered pliant and quiescent. The payments have instead produced ungovernable spaces.

I have documented the multiplication of modern political communities that stand in some tension, or even contradiction, with each other. Only in this way can one understand the explosion of intra- and interethnic tensions in the delta, even if each has been aided and abetted by the state and other political forces. It is the relation between ethnicity, oil minorities, and Nigeria as a modern nation (the imagined community par excellence) to which I finally turn.

COMMUNITY AS THE GOVERNABLE SPACE OF THE NATION

One striking aspect of the oil-minority communities as they emerged in the delta is that they become vehicles for political claims, typically articulated as the need for political institutionalization: sometimes as local government councils (one of the struggles under way in Warri as I write), other times as a new state within the federation (such as the Ogoni). The demand for new local governments and states necessarily raises the question of a third community—that of the nation and the postcolonial nation-state, an entity that preexisted oil and came to fruition in 1960 at independence. Oil came to constitute, after the civil war, the basic means for the nation-building process—the making of an "oil nation" (Coronil 1999; Apter 2005). Nature and nationalism, one might say, become inextricably linked. But how did petro-capitalism stand in relation to the creation of the governable space called modern Nigeria? Or to put the matter more directly, what are the consequences for Nigeria as a nation of the multiplication of (oil-fueled) state and local governments as the vehicles for community aspirations?

Here one can usefully begin with the work of Mahmood Mamdani (1996) and his observations on postcolonial African politics. Colonial rule and decentralized despotism were synonymous says Mamdani. The native authorities consolidated local class power in the name of tradition (ethnicity) and sustained a racialized view of civic rights. The nationalist movement had two wings, radical and mainstream. Both wished to deracialize civic rights, but the latter won out and reproduced the dual legacy of colonialism. They provided civic rights for all Nigerians but bonus "customary rights" for indigenes. The country had to decide which ethnic groups were indigenous and which were not as a basis for political representation, a process that became constitutionally mandated in Nigeria. Federal institutions are quota driven for each state, but only those indigenous to the state may apply for a quota. As Mamdani (1998:7) puts it, "The effective elements of the federation are neither territorial units called states nor ethnic groups but ethnic groups with their own states....Given this federal character every ethnic group [is] compelled to seek its own home, its own state. With each new political entity the non-indigenes continues to grow." Once law enshrines cultural identity as the basis for political identity, it necessarily converts ethnicity into a political force. As a consequence, postcolonial political struggles came to be ethnic not racial, and such ethnic clashes, which have dominated the political landscape in the last three decades, are always at root about customary rights to land, and derivatively to a political machinery—local government or a state—capable of empowering those on the ground as ethnically indigenous.

Into this firmament enters oil, a valuable, centralized (state-owned) resource. It is a *national* resource—this is the juridical claim of the laws I glossed earlier, which established a statutory monopoly—upon which citizenship claims could be constructed. As much as the state uses oil to build a nation and to develop, so communities use oil wealth (or the possibility of future discoveries) to activate community claims (typically predicated on territorial claims over the oil fields themselves) animated by what is seen popularly as the unimaginable wealth conferred by black gold (for example, mega-construction projects such as a new capital city in Abuja or a massive new iron and steel industry near Abeokuta). The governable space of Nigeria is as a consequence "reterritorialized" by the newly enfranchised oil minorities.

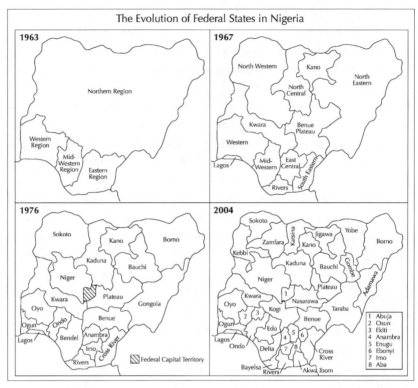

FIGURE 5.4

Evolution of federal states in Nigeria.

Access to oil revenues in turn amplifies what I call subnational political institution making; politics becomes a *massive state-making machine.* Only in this way can one understand how, between 1970 and the present, the number of local government areas grew from 100 to 774 (and is still growing) and the number of states grew from four to thirty-six (figure 5.4). Nigeria as a modern oil nation-state has become a machine for the production of ever more local political institutions, and this process is endless. The logic is ineluctable and of course terrifying.

What sort of national governable space emerges from such multi-plication, in which incidentally the political entities called states or LGAs (local government areas) become vehicles for the disposal of oil revenues? The answer is that the process works precisely against the creation of an imagined community of the sort that Benedict

Anderson (1983) saw as synonymous with the modern nation-state. Nation-building, whatever its imaginary properties, whatever its style of imaging, rests in its modern form on a sort of calculation, social integration, and state/bureaucratic rationality, which the logic of rent seeking, petro-corruption, ethnic-spoils politics, and institutional multiplication (of states and LGAs) works systematically to undermine. Lauren Berlant has said that every national community—and hence every national governable space—requires a "national symbolic": a national fantasy that "designates how national culture becomes local through images, narratives and movements which circulate in the personal and collective unconsciousness" (1991:61). But the manufacture of communities through the oil complex suggests that the Nigerian National Symbolic grew weaker and more attenuated. There was no sense of the national fantasy at the local level; it was simply a big lie (or a big pocket of oil monies to be raided in the name of ethnic possession). Forms of identity that mattered were irreducibly local.

The logic of political dispersion, coupled with the growing competition for an ever more centralized pot of black gold, deepened the process of politics as community-based claims-making, which demanded a more robust sense of subnational identification at a moment when the process of nation-building (through schools, institutions of national integration) was less capable of achieving its nationalist aspirations. Structural adjustment pulverized the state in a way that further compromised the federal state's capacity to nation-build, at the same time the flowering of civic organizations in the 1980s provided a political space in which identitarian politics could flourish. Not only did petro-development fail to deliver, but so did petro-nation-building and petro-nationalism. The measure of this sort of national evisceration— or nationalist "unimagining"—was the shocking extent to which ethnic xenophobia in Nigeria, largely suppressed in the wake of the civil war, has flourished in the most public of ways (carried forth violently by the proliferation of ethnic militias) since the return to civilian rule in 1999.

At independence, Obafemi Awolowo, the great western Nigerian politician, said that Nigeria was not a nation but a "mere geographical expression"; forty years later, this statement remained true but more so. Any construction of a robust, meaningful, national identity requires, as M. Clifford (2001:114) says, a "rigorous survey of the social body" to determine its makeup and nature. A petro-state of the Nigerian sort, wracked by corruption-fraud in the Gramscian sense referred to earlier, is the very antithesis of surveillance, or indeed of rigor. It is at best, as Nigerian novelist Chinua Achebe called it in *Anthills of the Savannas*, a big crummy family.

What is on offer is not the imagined community of Nigeria as a modern nation but perhaps its reverse: the *unimagining* or withering of a particular sense of national community. Nicos Poulantzas (1978) said that national or modern unity requires a historicity of a territory and a territorialization of a history. Oil capitalism and its associated complex have achieved neither of these requirements. The governable space called Nigeria was always something of a "public secret" (Taussig 1993): everyone fully understood that Nigeria as a community was something of a fiction never to be fully aired in public. Forty years of postcolonial rule have made this secret more public as ethnic segregation and local particularisms have continued unabated, undermining the very idea of the production of governable subjects. The double movement of petro-capitalism within the frame of a modern nation-state has worked against a robust sense of Nigeria as an imagined national community. This is certainly the case across the Niger Delta, but the same might be said of the impact of oil on the Muslim communities of Nigeria (Watts 1998, 2000). The dreadful operations of the oil complex have produced an increasingly *unimaginable* national community on which the question of Nigeria's future now hangs.

OIL, COMMUNITY, AND THE CRISIS OF SECULAR NATIONALISM

> Oil creates the illusion of a completely changed life, life without work, life for free....The concept of oil expresses perfectly the eternal human dream of wealth achieved through lucky accident....In this sense oil is a fairy tale and like every fairy tale a bit of a lie. (Kapucinski 1982:35)

Petro-capitalism in Nigeria functions through a particular sort of oil complex that is strongly territorial, operating through local oil concessions. Like oil complexes everywhere, it is a militarized and violent center of economic calculation. It is an instance of what Michael Klare

(2001) calls "economization" of security, of which Colombia is perhaps the paradigmatic case. Oil presents itself as a challenge to forms of community authority, interethnic relations, and state institutions. The oil complex generates differing sorts of communities—contrasting forms of governable spaces—in which the dialectics of order and disorder play themselves out with calamitous consequences.

A striking aspect of contemporary oil development in Nigeria is the *simultaneous* production of differing "scalar" forms of community. The styles of imagining in my three cases are inseparable from oil, but their forms of identification and the robustness of their spaces are often incompatible, indeed maybe antagonistic, with one another. Furthermore, standing at the center of each governable space is a community *contradiction*. For the local oil-producing community, the overthrow of gerontocratic authority has generated a "restive youth" that sometimes exercises a Mafia-style violent rule. At the level of the ethnic community, it is the tension between civic nationalism and a sort of exclusivist, militant particularism expressed through resource control ("our oil"). And at the level of the nation, one sees the contradiction between the oil-based state and fiscal centralization on the one hand, and radical state fragmentation characterized by an "unimagining" of Nigeria as a basis for full citizenship and national identity on the other. I have tried to root these contradictions in imperial oil, which serves as a forcing house for the production of unstable, contradictory, and contested communities. To understand, as Achille Mbembe (2000:282) puts it, why "regions at the epicenter of oil production are torn apart by repeated conflicts" is in my view to unravel the complex and unstable geographies of "communities of violence" in contemporary Nigeria...or Iraq.

At the heart of my oil and community story is the deception that Kapucinski refers to: that is to say, the terrifying and catastrophic failure of secular nationalist development. It is sometimes hard to gasp the full consequences and depth of such a claim. Between 1970 and 2000 in Nigeria, the number of people subsisting on less than one dollar a day grew from 36 percent to more than 70 percent, from 19 million to a staggering 90 million. All the oil revenues ($400 billion), according to the IMF, "did not seem to add to the standard of living" and "could have contributed to a decline in the standard of living" (Martin and Subramanian 2003:4). The average life expectancy has fallen since the oil boom began. From the vantage point of the Niger Delta—but no less from the vast slum world of Kano or Lagos—development and oil wealth are a cruel joke. But perhaps it is something more: bankrupt and to be abandoned altogether?

It is here that my story of oil, community, and a secular nationalism in crisis in Nigeria meets up with September 11, the occupation of Iraq, and the "new imperialism," as Harvey (2003) calls it. It provides the ether within which Islamism of various sorts draws its enormous political energy. "Petro-Islam" said al-Azmeh, describing the oil-rich Gulf states, "has broken the secularist and nationalist cultural, mediatic and, to a lesser extent, the educational monopoly of the modern Arab state" (2002:32). Oil, empire, neoliberal capitalism, and the Cold War made for a ferocious assault on, and radical destabilization of, a number of postcolonial states. Out of this maelstrom of failed secular nationalist development have emerged powerful communities of opposition and dissent articulated against both failed local states and American hegemony. From the ashes of failed secular nationalism can emerge all manner of communitarian alternatives: drug-fueled child militias and warlords in Sierra Leone, the most retrograde forms of Muslim orthodoxy among the Afghan Taliban, and ferocious ethnic xenophobia in the Balkans.

Nothing in the failure of secular nationalism can justify the tactics of the ethnic cleanser or the violent delta militant. These are exemplars of cold and unlovable communities. But they are not simply premodern excrescences either. They are modern political communities for whom there is, at best, a cool skepticism about the secular national development project. For al-Qaida it is outright rejection. This is not the case in the Niger Delta—even if the Pentecostal movement has drawn enormous strength during the oil period—but the communitarian responses did not necessarily fit comfortably with secular nationalism either. Communities growing out of the ashes of what are blithely termed "rogue" or "failed" states can be radical and oppositional, and indeed may be bulwarks against empire (the companies are uniformly detested in the delta); some retain a secular or nationalist thrust, others may propose a religio-political project only loosely anchored in the community of the nation-state. But radical community movements are not necessarily democratic any more than cosmopolitan movements are involved in the business of social justice (Buck-Morse 2003).

Running through my story of community in Nigeria is precisely this struggle between a rickety secular nationalism and the ceaseless search for alternatives, all forged within the crucible of an imperial oil complex.

Notes

This project would not have been possible without the advice, assistance, expertise, and research acumen of Von Kemedi, Patterson Ogon, Oronto Douglas, Sofiri Peterside, and Ike Okonta, and without the generosity of the Institute of International Studies at Berkeley, the National Geographic Committee for Research, the John Simon Guggenheim Foundation, the Harry Frank Guggenheim Foundation, and the Center for the Advanced Study of the Behavioral Sciences, Stanford.

1. The relations between oil (indeed natural resources in general), governance, democracy, and violence have emerged as an object of substantial scholarly attention, not least by economists and political scientists. Paul Collier (2000, 2003) of the World Bank, using resource dependency as a way of thinking about rebellion, especially in Africa, sees oil as central to the economics of civil war. It permits, indeed encourages, extortion and looting through resource predation (at least up to the point where 26 percent of GDP is dependent on resource extraction). It is the feasibility of predation (by states or rebel groups) that determines the risk of conflict. Rebels are predatory through secession. For Michael Ross (2001), oil is a "resource curse" and "authoritarian" due to its rentier effect (low taxes and high patronage dampen pressures for democracy), its repression effect conferred by direct state control over sufficient revenues to bankroll excessive military expenditures and expanded internal security apparatuses, and a modernization effect, namely that the "move into industrial and service sector jobs render them less likely to push for democracy" (2001:357). But if oil "hinders democracy" (as though copper might encourage parliamentary democracy?), one needs to surely appreciate the contradictory centralizing and dispersive effects of oil in relation to nation-building on the larger canvas of a segmented political economy that predates oil (see Watts 2004).

2. "The subjectivity of individuals, the so-called speakers and hearers of political discourse, who actually, or even ideally, populate a state, needs to be understood in terms of enunciative modalities—the statuses, sites, and positions—of their existence as political subjects. Enunciative modalities refer to the ways a discursive practice is attached to bodies in space" (M. Clifford 2001:56).

3. According to the conservative estimates of NNPC, between 1976 and 1996 there were more than 4,800 spills, accounting for 2.4 million barrels (the entirely daily output of Nigeria)—that is, each 100-square-meter plot within the Niger Delta received roughly two gallons of spilled crude oil over the period. Nigeria is also the largest flarer of gas in the world (historically, more than 80 percent of locally produced gas has been flared), accounting for a staggering 12 percent of world flaring (down from more than 20 percent in the late 1990s).

4. The Southern Minorities Movement (SMM), comprising twenty-eight ethnic groups from Rivers, Delta, Cross River, Akwa Ibom, and Edo states, was founded in 1993.

5. The Union of Niger Delta and the Traditional Rulers of Oil Producing States.

6. In the last six months, in the context of a deepening political crisis in the delta (a fragile truce was signed in October 2004), at least five hundred people died in the Port Harcourt area alone.

7. The civil war and an impending federal government victory over Biafra provided the military regime of Yakubu Gowon with the opportunity to pass the Petroleum Act of 1969, placing all minerals in the domain of the federal military government. This act provides in Section 1 that "the entire ownership and control of all petroleum in, under, or upon any land to which this section applies (i.e., land in Nigeria, under the territorial waters of Nigeria or forming part of the continental shelf) shall be vested in the state." The spirit and intent of the Petroleum Act was further consolidated in 1978, when the government enacted the Land Use Decree, removing land from the control of local communities to be held in trust for the central government by the state governors, and was extended in 2003 by the inclusion of deepwater offshore oil reserves (S. Khan 1994).

8. The Nigerian national oil company (NNPC) is Nigeria's largest company, with a turnover of more than ₦200 billion. It operates through five joint ventures with oil supermajors (accounting for 95 percent of total output) that are granted territorial concessions (or blocs). The largest joint venture (JV), accounting for half of Nigerian output, is between Shell and NNPC. Its full title is the Shell Petroleum Development Company/SPDC, in which the latter has a 55 percent holding. Historically NNPC has owed substantial monies—cash calls—to its partners (Shell, Chevron/Texaco, Exxon/Mobil, ENI/Agip, Total/Fina/Elf) as part of its obligations to the JV. NNPC's commitment to its partners for 2004 was $7 billion. Since the mid-1980s, the Nigerian oil industry has been under pressure to privatize, and in 1988 NNPC created eleven subsidiaries with the expectation of

sale. In 1991 new memoranda of understanding were offered to the oil companies, but calls to sell off NNPC, as of 2004, had been unheeded.

9. The state has created a number of special revenue accounts deploying oil
revenues for specific development purposes for the Niger Delta: the Petroleum
Fund (set up in the late 1990s), OMPADEC (Oil Mineral Producing Areas
Development Commission, established in 1992), and now the Niger Delta
Development Commission (NDDC), established by Obasanjo in 2002 and funded
in part by the oil companies. All have been the source of spectacular corruption
and waste, deployed to buy consent among increasingly angry delta constituencies. In the pre-oil period, in 1960, these agencies were preceded by the Niger
Delta Development Board, which suffered from an equally checkered history.

10. The principle of derivation was the pivot of fiscal federalism in the
country until May 1967. In that year, General Yakubu Gowon created new states in
a setting in which oil was assuming greater economic significance. Derivation was
then complemented by a distributable pool account (DPA)—subsequently named
the States Joint Account/Federation Account—wherein the federal government
raised and retained certain revenues to be distributed to the regions. Based on
financial need, population size, contribution to revenue, and balanced development, 42 percent of the DPA was allocated to the Northern Region, 30 percent to
the East, 20 percent to the West, and 8 percent to the Midwest. In practice, the
derivation formula favored oil-producing states (50 percent of mining rents and
royalties was allocated to the state of derivation), which in turn made these states
the envy of the more populous ethnic majority states in central and northern
Nigeria (each largely dependent upon declining primary commodity earnings)
(Adebayo 1993). The complaints of these "disadvantaged" states led the federal
military government to devise a new revenue allocation formula, Decree Number
13, in 1970. Previously, 50 percent of mining rents and royalties had been allocated to the state of derivation, 15 percent to the federal government, and 35 percent to the DPA; they were now shared in a 45:5:50 percent arrangement. The
allocation principle for the DPA was also revised; one-half was divided equally
among the states, and the other half was divided on the basis of population size.
In effect, this change began the slide toward fiscal centralism and the diminution
of derivation. By 1979 derivation had fallen to 3 percent, and it was 1.5 percent in
the early 1980s. Obasanjo increased derivation to 13 percent in April 2000 (see
Okonta 2004; Suberu 2004).

11. I am especially indebted in this discussion to the work of Von Kemedi,
who also assisted me in understanding the case and in setting up interviews. This

work is ongoing in a project involving Kemedi, Ike Okonta, and myself. In addition, the Nembe Peace Commission provided an exemplary account (Alagoa 2001). The special commissioner for Nembe appointed by Bayelsa State also provided much insight.

12. Nembe in its macro usage refers to six towns (Bassimbiri, Ogbolomabiri, Okpoama, Odioma, Akassa, and Nembe Town), which are part of the sixteen towns that comprise Nembe Kingdom. For the purposes of this paper, however, Nembe Town refers to Ogbolomabiri only.

13. The data for the case study were collected during a visit to the Niger Delta in January and February 2001 and July and August 2004. I also relied on the assistance of Von Kemedi and his work (Kemedi 2002) and the Nembe Peace Commission (Alagoa 2001).

14. The war canoe houses were the units of the kingdom's defense forces. A war canoe house consisted of the head of the house and a formidable number of able-bodied men who were responsible for defending the house and the king.

15. Ojo describes two similar cases. In the Ogbogoro War, the arrival of two oil service companies in Ogbogoro Town (15 kilometers southwest of Port Harcourt) in 1993 led to a dynastic struggle over the rightful accession to the stool (Eze Oha) in the context of the ruler's superintendent role over disbursements of monies, contracts, and employment. A ferocious struggle ensued (seven lawsuits are pending) between four rival ruling families; differing youth groups took up arms for their candidates. A bloodbath occurred in late 1998, and a government commission of inquiry was established. In the Urhobo community of Evwreni near Port Harcourt, youths killed the traditional ruler (*ovie*) in the context of accusations over the use of community funds provided by the oil companies. Between 2000 and 2002, the regicide unleashed a war between differing factions of youths similar to the situation in Nembe.

16. I am focusing here on what one might call social movements from below. But at the formal political level there was a parallel movement from above in which well-placed delta nationalists such as Alex Ibru, Chief Essien, Professor Isoun, and others established organizations such as the Association of Mineral Oil States in the early 1990s, the Southern Minorities Movement in Eku in 1994, and later the South-South People's Conference.

17. Curiously, there is no formal or official definition of resource control; the southern governors (who appropriated the term from the social movements of the minorities) imply three things: the power and right to raise funds within their territory, the executive right of ownership of resources within their territory,

and the right to customs and excise on trade to and from their territory. MOSIEND and MORETO, for example, both rejected constitutional provisions granting a statutory monopoly over minerals to the Nigerian states. The Izon Peoples Charter, drafted by MOSIEND in October 1992, called for "political autonomy, exclusive control over Ijaw natural resources and restitution for the harmful effects of oil exploration." The Ogbia Charter demanded the repeal of legislation granting the federal government authority over revenue allocation and sought 50 percent of the profits from oil taken from the Ogbia area, as well as greater representation in national institutions. According to the Kaiama Declaration of Ijaw Youth in December 1998: "All land and natural resources (including mineral resources) within the Ijaw territory belong to Ijaw communities and are the basis of our survival." True federalism, then, is a reframing of the revenue allocation process.

18. As constitutional preparations were made for the transition to home rule, non-Igbo minorities throughout the Eastern Region appealed to the colonial government for a separate Rivers State. Ogoni representatives lobbied the Willink Commission in 1958 to avert the threat of exclusion within an Ibo-dominated regional government that had assumed self-governing status in 1957, but minority claims were ignored (Okpu 1977; Okilo 1980).

19. The Ogoni and other minorities petitioned in 1974 for the creation of a new Port Harcourt State within the Rivers State boundary (Naanen 1995:63).

20. According to the Nigerian government, in 1995 Ogoniland produced about 2 percent of Nigerian oil output and was the fifth largest oil-producing community in Rivers State. Shell maintains that total Ogoni oil output is valued at $5.2 billion before costs!

21. The oil companies claim that sabotage accounts for a large proportion (60 percent) of the spills; in this view, communities gain from corporate compensation. Shell claims that 77 of 111 spills in Ogoniland between 1985 and 1994 were due to sabotage. According to the government commission, however, sabotage accounts for 30 percent of the incidents but only 3 percent of the quantity spilled. Furthermore, all oil-producing communities claim that compensation from the companies for spills has been almost nonexistent.

22. Saro-Wiwa (a Bane) was often chastised by Gokana, since most of the Ogoni oil was in fact located below Gokana soil. In other words, on occasion, the key territorial unit became the clan rather than pan-Ogoni territory (Saro-Wiwa 1989, 1995).

23. For the inhabitants of the Niger Delta, the legal case for "resource

control" has a colonial reference point, the Colonial Minerals Ordinance of 1916, which provided that "the entire property and control of all minerals, and mineral oils in, under, or upon any lands in Nigeria, and of all rivers, streams, and watercourses throughout Nigeria, is and shall be vested in the Crown." Resource control and true federalism proper emerged seventy years later as the product of social movements across the oil fields. In the wake of the election of civilian governors in the oil-producing states in 1999, however, the center of gravity of the resource control struggle shifted from youth-led social movements to the states and their political apparatchiks. The governors' populist aspirations were enhanced by jumping onto the resource control bandwagon; yet they simultaneously hoped to use but also dampen the flames of youth groups as a potent political force. At stake was the prospect of an increase in the oil states' share of the Federation Account. In 2001 the governors led agitation against the dichotomy between onshore and offshore oil, which claimed offshore revenues for the central government (in February 2003 a compromise was reached in which all deepwater oil accrued to the state). A bitter 1999–2001 struggle between the oil-producing states over a definition of the Niger Delta, as a basis for determining which states would benefit from NNDC funds, was part of the same political struggle (see Okonta 2004).

24. Both Asari and Ateke began their political careers grounded in ethnic youth politics and were promoted by politicians in the 1999 and 2003 elections. Asari's struggle took the form of a fight against the state, but each fought over access to territory and oil bunkering, which funded their arms supply.

6

Caribbean "Community"?

Deciphering a Regional Cipher

Aisha Khan

In what would become part of a more broadly influential approach in anthropological theory, Anthony Cohen, in his book *The Symbolic Construction of Community*, argued for an emphasis on culture rather than on structure. Highlighting the study of communities, he proposed that they should not be viewed "morphologically," as "a structure of institutions capable of objective definition and description" (1985:19); instead, a community is best understood by "trying to capture members' experience of it, its meaning...the view from within" (19). The "reality of community," then, "lies in its members' perception of the vitality of its culture" (118).

At the same time, our conceptual tools (or interpretive categories) are necessarily implicated in certain ideologies and modes of valuation (Williams 1976). Both interior and exterior views of community necessarily contend with more encompassing, hegemonic hierarchies of societies, ideas about their social organization and cultural practices, real and imagined. If the concept of community always has a positive connotation, as Raymond Williams (1976:76) suggests, then an inquiry into the concept's historical and contemporary utility and limitations might begin by asking which groups, past and present, are deemed to possess this positive characteristic, which others not, and what difference it makes for local groups themselves?

Given the historical foundation of the Caribbean region as a Euro-colonial capitalist venture, and the interpretation of its peoples as culturally uprooted, dispersed, and created anew (artificially in parts rather than organically in wholes), it should not come as a surprise that unlike in other areas of the world, the term community has not been a key analytical framework in much scholarly and other work on the region. For most of the history of scholarship on the Caribbean, community—based as it is on certain premises that I will consider below—has functioned as a cipher, expressing in a disguised way premises that are evident in, or that can be inferred from, certain academic and social policy models and literary metaphors, which have provided the defining principles of the region. The most notable among these discourses have concerned the family/household, "plural" societies, and a focus on absences (of culture, of history, of institutions). Central to these characterizations are broader questions about how epistemologies and relations of power are produced and sustained.

I intend to show in the following discussion that whether construed with optimism or doubt, "culture" and "history" spell community in the Caribbean, and so beg the question of the desirability and redemptive mission of that ostensibly favorable descriptor. What will also become apparent is the influence that different characterizations of race and culture among Caribbean peoples at different moments (and interpretations) of global migrations have on the representation of, and utility of, community. Focus here will be on Afro- and Indo-Caribbean peoples, whose diasporas and subjectivities have had the most sustained attention, in both academic scholarship and popular culture alike.

The discourse of community (culture/history) emerges out of encounters between social practices and their interpretation. Yet, as Ana Maria Alonso notes about historical discourses, "the meanings embedded in practice may not be clearly or fully evident to the consciousness of actors" (1988:34). These encounters largely occur retrospectively because the moments of the past are limned from present perspectives. This presentation is what masks interpretation, instilling within community, as metaphor and as object, a veracity derived from authenticity and timelessness, one that putatively transcends conscious action. As Alonso points out in her own discussion, political projects and memory are, therefore, inherently and necessarily interpellated. Indeed, the "view from within" community (A. Cohen 1985:19) may, in anticipated intentions as well as unpredictable consequences, conform to the very notions of culture and its presumed nature that keep the Caribbean and its peoples an academic, intellectual, and social policy problem.

Here I examine what the community concept resonates during the historical moments when such models are used. In a nutshell, has the Caribbean tended to not be spoken about in terms of community because of an abiding presumption of its lacking "culture"? Or because "plural societies" are presumed inimical to the (cultural) wholeness that community conventionally implies? And are such revisionist designators as "diaspora" what bring a new notion of culture to the Caribbean, thus recuperating community there; and do they do so, at least for certain such racially or ethno-culturally distinguished peoples as Indo-Caribbeans, because they continue to rest in part on geographic moorings located in notions of homeland?

CULTURE AND THE AFRO-CARIBBEAN COMMUNITY

A "warmly persuasive" term (Williams 1976:76), community assumes cohesiveness, if you will, a social glue that emanates in part from cultural contents. By the nineteenth century, the (reified) idea of culture comes to commonly signal a particular way of life (Williams 1976:90); this, in turn, implies coherence, structure, stability, and foundations based on tradition. These latter qualities imply boundaries that create distinct entities or groups. As Gerald Creed (chapter 2, this volume) suggests, anthropology's move into the study of "complex societies" coincided with the focus on communities (be they peasant villages or urban neighborhoods) as the places amid large-scale, heterogeneous, and colonial societies where the cultural uniformity and harmony of purported "simple societies" still pertained. The absurdity of such expectations was quickly apparent, fueling a retroactive skepticism of the simple models (and models of simplicity) upon which these assumptions were based. Eventually (by the late 1980s), scholars would question the value of "localizing strategies" (J. Clifford 1994:303) that both anticipated and affirmed apparently stable and uniform boundaries distinguishing cultural and other groups (see, among others, Lutz and Abu-Lughod 1990), but the relationship between culture and community is hardly abrogated, as I attempt to show here.

Models of social organization that posed a contrast between indigenous, homogeneous societies with their traditional cultures, and aggregated heterogeneous moderns with their cultures-in-transition, contended in the Caribbean with a central trope of Caribbean identity: the question of the region's quantity and quality of local culture—how much was lost by diasporic populations and, connected to this, what was/is the quality of the culture each population possessed? Quantity and quality of culture is arguably the most resonant of Caribbean cultural themes. At issue, then, is the way culture has been defined and allocated in the region (see, for example, A. Khan 2004). According to British colonial ideology, Africans lacked culture, and Indians and Chinese exhibited an inferior one. Britons in the Caribbean who had too much exposure to these peoples were alleged to have lost the purity and authenticity of their metropolitan counterparts. The relationship between culture and community in this region, therefore, has two dimensions. As I indicated above, the Western-colonial idea of community presupposes a foundation of culture that legitimates what otherwise might be random aggregations of people by conceptualizing them as a reasonable and recognizable centripetal, socializing force. Aggregated bodies are not labeled communities when they have an association with disorganization, especially if it derives from presupposed (cultural) loss. The doubt about, or denial of, community in the Caribbean, then, is linked to the doubt about, or denial of, culture there; these two signifiers are virtually inseparable in terms of their uses and meanings.

The culture that presumably makes community possible, and the communities that presumably rest on culture, conjure to a significant degree an implicit assumption about morality. The underpinning of morality in community is among its most problematic associations because morality is treated as an absolute litmus test rather than relative to the specific conditions in which it is in play. This "romantic doppelgänger," as Creed (chapter 1, this volume) characterizes it, is in the Caribbean more haunting than sentimental.

In mid-eighteenth-century Britain, the rising middle class was engaged in various efforts to impose its norms, particularly about marriage, on British society; its "first step" in these struggles was the Marriage Act of 1753. By the end of the century, elites had adopted middle-class marriage norms and soon thereafter combined forces with the middle class to impose these norms on the lower classes (Altink 2004:81). The significance of this situation, for our purposes, is the idea that acceptance of this particular marriage ideal (fully legal, indissoluble, cohabiting, monogamous, with distinct gender roles) would result in a more stable society. This result would come about, the logic continued, because put into practice, this middle-class ideal of marriage would produce "a drastic reduction in those lower class vices which upset the stability of society" (Altink 2004:81).

As Henrice Altink points out, this "discourse about marriage gradually found its way to the periphery," where British colonial subjects were expected to conform to metropolitan ideals (2004:81). In the British Caribbean, enslaved Africans could legally marry if the marriage was performed by an Anglican minister. Strange bedfellows in this context, abolitionists and absentee planters both supported slave marriage: abolitionists felt that marriage "would improve the slaves' moral behavior" as well as prepare them for freedom, and absentee planters believed that marriage (without necessary coresidence, however) would both increase the slave population and transform it into more docile and productive captives (82). Even as resident planters tended to be against slave marriage, their position "was largely informed by the connotation of marriage with freedom and equality" (82). Hence, while rejecting slave marriage, resident planters also imbued marriage with a moral imperative, making it synonymous with such principled and socially sought goals as equality and liberty.

The issue of morality, then, also inflects family and household, which are necessarily related aspects of social organization in the region that suggests (or denies) community. As Christine Barrow points out, "more than any other social institution in the Caribbean, the family has been the focus of research, debate and policy" (1996:458). Yet it is in the British Caribbean where family studies have predominated (Price 1971:24–25), arguably due in part to two kinds of emphases on the part of observers, one theoretical and one applied.

Early in the twentieth century, study of the family emerges from the debate about how the "New World Negro" family had developed over time and achieved its contemporary form. The two most important protagonists at the time were Melville Herskovits and E. Franklin Frazier. Neither relied on the notion of community in his arguments, although they both oriented their positions toward an African past. In Herskovits's (1958 [1941]) perspective, Afro-Americans were in essence Africans, possessing a partially surviving ancestral past that lent them cultural distinctiveness and challenged contemporary assumptions about cultural lacunae or inadequacies in Afro-America. As far as Frazier (1966 [1939]) was concerned, Afro-Americans were Americans, whose oppression, particularly through enslavement and associated erasures of cultural heritage, had prevented their full acculturation and assimilation. The theoretical emphasis of Herskovits's interest in ethnographically tracing cultural continuities contrasted sharply (in most cases) with Frazier's application of his ideas to current social problems.

It is Frazier's legacy of what might be called applied research that influenced Caribbean studies for many decades. In particular, as Richard Price rightly points out, advocates of Frazier's point of view assumed a relationship between "matrifocality"—that is, the female-centered family and household forms common to the region—and socioeconomic deprivation there (Price 1971:28). At the same time, social scientists studying the Caribbean in the first several decades of the twentieth century encountered the classificatory challenge of many coexisting forms of mating and cohabitation, from legal marriage to extra-residential unions with a whole range of conjugal arrangements in between, along with a great variety of both male-headed and female-headed households (Price 1971:24). Furthermore, it was understood that local individuals generally experienced more than one of these forms during their lifetimes. One consequence of this variation among social scientists was a sustained and energetic effort to categorize Caribbean family and household organization. Ironically, as they struggled with generalizing from the particular, "not only have diverse terms been applied to identical phenomena, but the same terms have been used to label different ones—often by the same author" (Price 1971:24). While most anthropologists sought to avoid making moral judgments about Caribbean extralegal arrangements, family and household remained fulcra of what would long be interpreted as "loose" social organization. Richard Price (1971) and Sidney Mintz (1966) were two among many scholars who voiced the opinion that "in contrast to many societies, those in the Caribbean exhibit a widespread absence of both community-based activities (centered around churches, schools, etc.) and activities structured around kinship groups" (Price 1971:49), and that the salient feature of rural Caribbean social structure may be "its heavy emphasis on individual dyadic ties, as opposed to membership in social groups having some corporate institutional or kin basis" (Mintz 1966:936). Although these were insights that argued against the idea of superimposing inappropriate, a priori interpretive categories (for example, Euro-bourgeois values and ideals) onto Caribbean peoples, a corollary image of shallow and unstable social institutions contributed to other observers' assumptions about Caribbean culture and its incapacity to form and sustain communities.

This model of social organization—the confluence of Frazerian ideas about the connection between socioeconomic deprivation and the family, the unexpectedly (to social scientists) fluid constitution of Caribbean social institutions (of which the family/household was seen as foundational), and the very real poverty and underdevelopment of many parts of the region—lent credence to pre-independence colonial governing strategies. Thus, while Nikolas Rose (1999) in another context suggests that community has recently become a means of governance, its purported absence seems to have been a basis for government intervention for some time.

Beginning about the time of the Great Depression, the Caribbean, particularly the British territories, was rife with labor unrest. In 1938 this situation prompted the British Colonial Office to establish a Social Services Department to investigate the causes of the disturbances. The authorities' unequivocal acknowledgment of economic and infrastructural underdevelopment was couched in terms of Caribbean social and cultural deficiencies and deviance. Adopting a model of what Christine Barrow (1988:157) calls the "social pathology" approach to studying Caribbean families, colonial observers such as Thomas Simey (1946) and Lord Moyne (1945) published, respectively, *Welfare and Planning in the West Indies* and the *West India Royal Commission Report* (known more commonly as the *Moyne Commission Report*). Simey, explicitly relying on

Frazier's perspective, argued that in aspects of their daily life other than religion, "West Indians are primarily influenced by European traditions," in particular the family, "which after all may be regarded as the basic social institution [and] has been moulded almost entirely by social and economic forces operating during and since the days of slavery" (1946:41). West Indian morals and manners were largely those of the slave master and "only continued repression of freedom has kept the Negro family from merging with that of the more fortunate whites" (Price 1971:27). Middle-class European family and household forms constituted the touchstone against which Caribbean families were deemed "deformed and malfunctioning" (due to the dissolution effected by slavery and the plantation), thus constituting a "threat to the social order" (Barrow 1996:459). Both Simey and Moyne emphasized "loose family organization": high rates of illegitimacy, marital instability, female-centered households, marginal males, juvenile delinquency, and sexual promiscuity (Putnam 2002; Mohammed 1988; Gregg 2001; Barrow 1996). For both Simey and Moyne (and many others; see, for example, Price 1971), "West Indian family life existed in a state of 'disorganization'" (Mohammed 1988:172). Indeed, this presumption is underscored by other regional contrasts in the Americas. Laura Putnam, for example, observes that very different notions of kinship and values gave rise to explanatory models that presented Latin American families as having too much hierarchy and too much male power—and Caribbean families as not having enough of either of them (2002:140).

While these debilitations were attributed by observers to the deprivations and lack of opportunity in colonial and postcolonial Caribbean society (resulting in a number of welfare policy recommendations and social programs), because the family has been regarded as a, or perhaps *the*, fundamental social institution, lacking it, continuing the logic, does not augur well for the formation of community. In fact, for Simey and many others, the family, "even when quite ephemeral," is the "outstandingly important social institution of the West Indies" (Simey 1946:79), and if the Caribbean family, particularly among the middle classes, could not meet the standards of Western, Christian society, then the whole fabric of Caribbean society would suffer the consequences (Simey 1946). Assured by social workers and church representatives that "promiscuity is on the upgrade," the *Moyne Commission Report* admonished that it is "the promiscuous union which creates a grave danger to the social stability of the West Indies" (West India Royal Commission 1945:220). In general cultural terms, states Gordon Lewis, the report saw Caribbean societies as "basically embryonic" (1968:84), where "'the whole West Indies'...are practically devoid of all the multifarious institutions, official and unofficial, which characterize British public life" (84). The Caribbean, instead, can be characterized by "low cultural attainment" due to "gross poverty" (86) and "the regrettable absence of those factors and traditions which elsewhere *make for social cohesiveness and a sense of membership of a community*" (West India Royal Commission 1945, quoted in Lewis 1968:84, italics added).

Exacerbating this focus on loss/lack, deviance (especially moral failings), and social disorganization in early Caribbean family studies was a concomitant scholarly "fixation" with lower-class Afro-Caribbean culture (Barrow 1996:23). With the middle class (European) as theoretical litmus test, along with the demographic predominance of working-class populations relative to middle-class populations, Caribbean research produced a largely ignored tautology: working class became the synecdoche for Afro-Caribbean culture, and Afro-Caribbean culture became the synecdoche for the Afro-Caribbean working class. One result of this situation was "a glut of research and writing on deviancy in the West Indian family...apart from very few exceptions, all looked at 'deviancy' primarily within lower class families" (Mohammed 1988: 171). While women, especially mothers, were viewed by postwar scholars (for example, Scheele 1956; Henriques 1949; Matthews 1971 [1953]; Y. Cohen 1956) as exerting an undue influence on family and household forms—where undue spelled aberrance—this scholarly look askance involved not only women's gender issues but men's as well. What would become a growing literature on deviancy, expressed in terms of Caribbean gender roles, household composition, and family organization, projected the image of an unhealthy, and dangerous, absence of Afro-Caribbean men from their family and household responsibilities (and thus lack of leadership therein), resulting in a broader social marginality.

Reaction against this point of view grew during the subsequent decades. Taking male "crews" and their performance of reputation and respectability (for example, P. Wilson 1973) and men's street life (for example, Rodman 1971; Brana-Schute 1979; Lieber 1981; Rubenstein 1987; compare Chevannes 2003) as serious analytical arenas, discussion shifted against the presumption of social marginality. Instead, these scholars interpreted men's crews and other such public sphere practices as, among other things, gender-specific communities of men who were socially integral (rather than marginal) to the various kinds of communal groupings that constituted their societies. Still tenaciously carrying the day, however, was the overarching model of Euro-Western norms and Afro-Caribbean family forms—forms never understood on their own terms, as Rhoda Reddock (2004:xvii) points out—deviating from them.

If family, or the absence thereof, is the fulcrum of community (at least in the Caribbean), then emanating from its specter is the issue of the roles of women and men within the family. As we saw above, researchers have traditionally approached Caribbean gender roles in terms of ideal and real responsibilities entailed in domestic arrangements. While the (Euro-bourgeois) model of femininity has long implied the inadequate femininity of women who historically, and necessarily, have been active—and *recognized* as such—in the public sphere, primarily as laborers, and in the private sphere, primarily as "matrifocal" females, these issues of femininity are greatly under-researched (see Douglass 1992; C. Freeman 2000; L. Lewis 2003, for notable exceptions).

Following suit is the paucity of study of masculinity in the Caribbean. Gaining momentum are studies that more closely consider the symbolic dimensions of gender roles, including the question of femininity and masculinity, surpassing the male crew and street culture studies of three decades earlier that were still moored to the family/household as a key unit of analysis. Deriving significantly from debates among academics about the emasculating effects of disempowering enslaved African men with regard to the abuse of their wives by European masters (for example, Altink 2004), the sociological consequences asserted by E. Franklin Frazier received fortification from other arenas. Among these was the psychological perspective of Erik Erikson. Erikson's claim was that enslaved African women lent the only "super-identity" available after African men became enslaved, and that

Caribbean men's motivational impetus was negatively affected by the "pervasive maternalism" that came with the value of simply being born, which also predominantly shaped Caribbean identity (Erikson 1964: 602, 606, quoted in Price 1971:27–28).

Currently being redressed with vigor by new scholarship, these kinds of approaches have begun to lose some of their currency in Caribbean research. At least two possible reasons come to mind. One is that psychological analyses were not as extensively applied to Caribbean studies as sociological frameworks have been. The other is that, for all the probable good intentions, the conclusions still hint at deviance and dysfunction as their organizing principles. That said, however, that these sociological and psychological approaches remain significant interlocutors in current research confirms a staying power that, at least indirectly, still shapes the discourse on gender, family, and household in the Caribbean. While current studies tend to approach masculinity as necessarily linked to unequal power relations, as possessing multiple layers of meaning, as mutually constitutive with femininity, and as always in flux and negotiated (for example, L. Lewis 2003), their most resonant interlocutor continues to be (variations on the theme of) marginality. Still remaining are shadows of certain abiding themes that demand engagement.

If working-class Afro-Caribbean women have been portrayed as exerting too much "matriarchy," this predominance has not been typically represented as posing a noteworthy problem for social processes beyond contributing to dysfunctional families—as aiding and abetting rather than causing social instability, per se. This is probably in part because of the long-assumed ancillary importance of women's activities to society building and social cohesion. At the same time, the reasoning has presumed, men's inadequate assumption of domestic obligations allegedly renders working-class Afro-Caribbean men as, among other things, not fully matured into responsible adults and therefore not reliable citizen-leaders of functioning social formations at various levels—community, civil society, nation-state, and so on.

Linked to the idea of a slippery or, worse, nonexistent family system that ostensibly undergirds the social building blocks of society were models of Caribbean social organization whose point of departure was another expression of community-building material: the ethnic group.

Problematic for researchers in their own right, ethnic groups (and their communal tendencies), viewed as haphazardly concentrated in the region, also failed, like Afro-Caribbean families, to be the right stuff for durable communities.

By the mid-twentieth century, while theories of racial hierarchy were losing their credibility in light of, among other things, paradigm shifts in the sciences and reaction to the tenets of Nazism, there arose new sociological theories about presumed deviance, justifying the separation and unequal treatment of colonial subjects and retaining conventional assumptions about the relationship between community and locality. European colonial ideology assumed that when people were dislodged from the ancestral (primordial) homeland that had generated the cultures that formed their communities, social fabric unraveled. Without locality, or place, the thinking went, cultures had no moorings and communities could not form, or they formed in precarious or dysfunctional ways. Academic models and colonial policy worked in tandem to explain the tensions—both real and imagined—in societies unnaturally created from the aggregation of fundamentally different peoples taken out of their respective places and brought together in service of various phases of international capitalism—not the least of which were sugar plantations.

Paramount among these new sociological approaches was the notion of the "plural society." Proposing it as a justification of Dutch colonial policy in Southeast Asia, J. S. Furnivall (1956 [1939]) first hypothesized about the plural society, choosing Burma as his case in point. In the plural society model, "Western societies were seen as organic and unified, consensual, normative systems in the words of Talcott Parsons, with highly developed institutions of civil and political society and a common value system" (Bates 2001:5–6). In regions like the Caribbean, the model of the "plural society" generated a veritable industry of vigorous engagement among several decades of Caribbeanists, either relying on it or critiquing it. (This work would include the also influential and contrasting "creole society" model [see, for example, R. T. Smith 1967].)

Among the major academic proponents of the Caribbean region as comprised of "plural societies" is Jamaican social anthropologist M. G. Smith (for example, 1965). Building on the work of Furnivall, Smith advanced his interpretation of this model as it applied to the

Caribbean (revisiting it over time). The plural society, he said, was a "unit of disparate parts," lacking "a common social will" (1965:vii), without the historically rooted "moral consensus" that undergirds the social integration of "normal" societies (xii). Groups, or ethno-cultural segments, that comprise a plural society each possess deep-seated cultural differences rooted in norms and values; an organic consensus among segments will not, therefore, emerge. These segments, mutually exclusive and inherently incompatible, coexist with each other through the imposition of authority by a foreign and dominant minority population that keeps things, including the population itself, cohesive and in order.

Even more recent scholarship, critical of the plural society model and seeking cultural and other *presences* (including that of place, in the form of "routes" and "roots" [Gilroy 1993]) rather than presuming *absences*, grapples with the legacy of dislocation. Representative examples include Kenneth Bilby's image of the

> social landscape confronting a typical immigrant to a Caribbean plantation society...during the era of slavery. Torn from the local community into which he was born, not to mention any larger political or religious groupings with which he has come to identify, the newly arrived African finds himself in an entirely unprecedented state of social suspension...new communities...had to be formed through a process of near total reinvention...the new setting would have been devoid of preexisting units of social structure— even of the most basic familial kind—to which some sense of primary community would normally attach. These, like other aspects of social and cultural life, had to be created anew. (1999:312–313)

Exemplifying the present day, Donald Robotham describes Caribbean societies as "conceived of by the colonizers as 'plantations' rather than as potential nations, even less so as nation-states. As very small island states that are almost exclusively populated by transplanted peoples, there is very little autochthonous tradition for present-day ruling groups to draw on in order to construct a 'thick' nationalist imaginary" (2000:8–9).

The impact of this history and ideology is not limited to ruling

groups. The notion of absence is also pervasive (perhaps still hegemonic) in wider social arenas. In rural Barbados, for example, "when
villagers are asked to describe Bajan [Barbadian] 'culture,' most people are hard put to think of anything to say....It is fairly common to
hear Barbadians claim that 'Barbados has no culture.' The suspicion
that Bajans may be 'mimic men,' versions of someone else rather than
truly themselves, is a recurring theme in the former colonies of the
Caribbean" (Gmelch and Gmelch 1997:190). Finally, in Southall,
England, most Afro-Caribbeans, asserts Gerd Baumann, see themselves
as not possessing "a culture," having been stripped of it through the
depredations of four centuries of enslavement (Baumann 1996:
126–127). As Jamaican economist Gordon K. Lewis saw it, "leadership
from the top and middling ranks" of West Indian society was not forth-
coming because these groups "had little to do but to endure the ennui
of colonial existence...leadership from the bottom...was frustrated, in
part, by the fact that the West Indian masses, of all ethnic strains, exhibited throughout a diffuse sense of immigrant mentality," where, for
example, East Indians looked back to "Mother India" and the Jamaican
Maroons "retreated in upon themselves, turning their back on movements of national unification" (G. Lewis 1968:83). Lewis's conclusion
was that the pronouncement made by Lord Harris in 1838 that "a race
had been freed but a society had not yet been formed" was still true one
hundred years later (83).

One hopes that before the 200th anniversary of Lord Harris's declaration, assumptions, both implicit and explicit, about the absence of
society, or the dubious construction of the building blocks of society in
the Caribbean, will be relegated to a historical footnote. But we have
some conceptual distance to travel until then. By considering two key
themes in the study of Caribbean social organization, the family and
the plural society, we can see that while the hegemonic assumption
about community has been that it is impossible or at least implausible
in the region, this negation paradoxically raises other, related issues
about what conditions are required—ideologically and theoretically—
to produce the state of community. In this way the conceptual baggage,
rather than the neutrality of community, is underscored, revealing that
this notion is not generically sanguine but specifically antagonistic.
Perhaps we can refine Raymond Williams's (1976:76) suggestion that

the concept of community is never employed as anything but favorable and positive, to never *deliberately* so. Yet even optimism has its relational pessimism. That is to say, from the Afro-Caribbean case it would seem that community, like all ideological concepts, is more prescriptive of what ought to be than descriptive of what is. And paradoxically, these prescriptions reiterate what (allegedly) cannot be, as well as what should be.

CULTURE AND THE INDO-CARIBBEAN COMMUNITY

In part because of the mutually constitutive relationship between Afro-Caribbean culture and the Afro-Caribbean masses, class is a familiar unit of analysis among these populations. Another reason is that when places, particularly colonial territories, are deemed not indigenous, or cohesive, or stable enough to produce the cultural requirements for community and society, culture becomes an ancillary or irrelevant unit of analysis. As I have discussed elsewhere (for example, A. Khan 1994, 2004), in contrast to long-entrenched ideas about the loss of culture endured by enslaved Africans on New World plantations, for more than a century the dominant approach to Indo-Caribbean cultural patterns—both scholarly and popular—anticipated the whole-cloth (or near whole-cloth) preservation of Indian culture. Indians initially came to the Caribbean as replacement labor—indentured servants, "bound coolies"—for sugar plantations recently divested of slave labor after 1838, when emancipation in the British Caribbean colonies was ratified. The conviction was that across the Atlantic and onto the plantations, the obdurate persistence of tradition and custom was re-creating, inevitably, key aspects of Indian social organization (for example, caste hierarchy, extended and joint families, clothing and cuisine styles) and belief systems (for example, pollution rules that supposedly translated into racial aversion, and other such supposed cultural essences as acquisitiveness, determination, and shrewdness). These propensities were popularized—as negative or positive attributes—by scholars, politicians, travelers, the media, and Indo-Caribbeans themselves, as reestablishing "village India" throughout the region. Yet as David Lowenthal reminds us, "history and memory are distinguishable less as types of knowledge than in attitudes toward that knowledge" (1985:213). Clear in this conviction about cultural tenacity was the propensity to focus both on an idealized Indian culture belonging to the subcontinent and an idealized diasporic memory, and thus an imaginary, among immigrant indentured laborers.

This idealization, in emphasizing certain, selected traditions and practices as representative of Indian culture-in-diaspora, necessarily involved the homogenization of cultures in the plural into an increasingly unitary Culture in the singular (see, for example, A. Khan 2004; Vertovec 1996). Yet South Asian regional, cultural, religious, and phenotypic identification was uneven, not only among Caribbean societies but from estate to estate. Indians on overseas plantations "were simply not one people from one place...they spoke different languages and had different perceptions of propriety in marriage, food, and almost every other practicality of life" (Kelly 2001:51). This diversity challenged ideological constructions of Indian cultural uniformity but lost the battle of representation. Rather than an iconography of heterogeneity, through the persuasions of post-independence communal politics in the Caribbean (and other Indian diaspora localities, from Mauritius to Manchester), and until recently through the abiding legacy of academic scholarship, portraits of Indian culture-in-diaspora as homogeneous India propelled overseas still prevail (but see Khan 2004:ch. 2).

A related consideration in understanding the ideological significance of how groups of people are represented is that conferring the designation community is a way to enable containment through establishing normativity; that is, it is a way of fitting particular populations into hegemonic social structures. In Fiji, for example, Indo-Fijians have, from the time they were indentured "coolies" to their formation into peasants and workers, conformed to a standard of living established by sugar interests and the Fijian government based on a self-serving preconception of what the "Indian community" is and what it needs. As John Kelly explains, "the 'Indian community' was offered a highly normativized place in Fiji. Institutions were designed to maintain that (basically very low) place" (2001:57). Homogeneity and normativity are not necessarily synonymous ideological strategies, yet they contain similar processes of political containment, inasmuch as each advances images of conformity (social fit) and cooperation (social harmony).

In addition to scholarly and popular assumptions about the purportedly "intact" religious beliefs and practices enduring among indentured Indians and their progeny, family, household, and gender roles have been the most commonly emphasized elements of traditional Indian heritage. Claimed by Indo-Caribbeans, foreign and local scholars, and some Afro-Caribbeans to be virtually the opposite of Afro-Caribbean forms (again, when implicitly synonymous with the working class), Indian kinship is typically portrayed as rigidly patriarchal (rather than unstably matrifocal); virtually absent of divorce, illegitimacy, and consensual unions; and fiercely moral and modest when it comes to matters of sexuality. Rarely culturally differentiated in the literature according to class divisions, Indo-Caribbeans ostensibly are comprised of these characteristics, ones that are said to constitute Indo-Caribbean communities.

Yet these neat portrayals required ideological work and the passage of time to become hegemonic. As Reddock (1998:31) points out, at the point of their entry into Trinidadian society, both Indian and African women arrived as workers, not wives. And both labored in "heavy work," notably on sugar plantations. Moreover, both contended with particular Victorian-colonial ideas about gender roles and domestic relations. While, as we saw above, eighteenth- and early-nineteenth-century enslaved Africans were interpreted in part through the moralizing lens of middle-class marriage ideals that were seen as fostering social stability, mid-nineteenth and early-twentieth-century indentured Indians were interpreted in part through Victorian-colonial and Indian notions of patriarchy and the distinctions between public and private spheres (Shepherd 1998; Reddock 1998). Speaking about Jamaica but applicable to the larger region, Verene Shepherd observes that "by the time of the Indians' arrival...attempts were already underway to adhere to a 'proper gender order' in the division of labour" (1998:90). This proper gender and class structuring was reinforced by British colonial governing in the region, which encouraged the image of indentured Indian women laborers as "protected housewives" in an effort to mollify Indian subjects on the subcontinent who promoted these images of (elite, respectable, idealized) Indian womanhood (Reddock 1998:33; see also Kelly 1991).

While Euro-colonial stereotypes presented Indian women as submissive, tractable, inherently controllable, and thus not strictly appropriate for or well-suited to "heavy work" or public sphere visibility, these qualities were lent credence on overseas plantations by the assumption that, in contrast to enslaved Africans, indentured Indians could rely on a cultural repertoire unimpaired by dislocation from its origins in India. But in addition to this idea of culture transported intact (subscribed to by European and Indian alike) was indentured Indians' increasing practice, beginning in the early twentieth century, of concentrating men into formal, wage labor occupations and women into informal labor and domestic work at home. The dominant narrative that explained this shift was that Indian women were more naturally inclined to be keepers of the hearth (and thus bearers of tradition); hence their official definition as (non-earning) "housewives" (Reddock 1998:37). Also subscribed to by both Europeans and Indians alike, this emphasis on Indian women as wives and mothers rather than as laborers met the needs both of a labor system and a sociocultural system in transition.

By the turn of the twentieth century, indenture policy began to encourage permanent or at least long-term settlement of indentured laborers, heretofore avoided by regulating a greatly uneven ratio of men to women on Caribbean plantations. A population of settled sugar workers called for the reconstitution of Indian families, which required the formation of morally respectable nuclear households, monogamous couples (whose marriages—if Hindu or Muslim—would not, however, be legally sanctioned until the mid-twentieth century), and distinctly gendered public and private spheres. Planters gained by the increase in laborers' investment of time and energy as sugar workers, and by paying no wages to supposed non-earning housewives, who nonetheless still participated in cane farming, subsistence agriculture, animal husbandry, and other "heavy work" (see, for example, Reddock 1998; A. Khan 2004:ch. 3). Their interests dovetailing with those of colonial and religious authorities, as Rhoda Reddock (1998:42) notes, indentured Indian men gained by the increase in opportunities for *sanscritization*, or upward mobility in class or caste terms. A key indicator of elite or near-elite status was emulating family organization among the upper classes in India: a secluded, non-earning wife and a patriarchal husband (Reddock 1998:42). The Western, bourgeois model of the ideal, modern, socially as well as biologically reproductive unit was also one entailing a dependent (and implicitly nonauthoritative) mother and an in-charge father. As Bridget Brereton observes, having a wife was an important symbol of masculinity and status on the plantation (1979:182). Because the needs, organization, and historical moment of indenture so differed from those of slavery, and because Indians at home and abroad could make their voices heard, at least to some extent and on some issues, the result was almost the reverse of characterizations of Afro-Caribbeans. Whereas a working-class metonym represented Afro-Caribbeans, who allegedly possessed weak men and strong women, and thus fragile families, communities, and societies, an ideal culture metonym represented Indo-Caribbeans, who allegedly possessed weak women and strong men, and thus stable families, communities, and... *not* societies.

The plural society model, along with models of the family, influenced the ideology about community and society among Indians. Putative schisms back in the motherland as well as disruptions in the new settings have been viewed as abrading the smooth and cohesive grain of intact culture. One centrifugal force was the presumed tendency toward factions in Indian culture and society. In 1957, for example, a special issue of the *British Journal of Sociology* focused on factions in India and overseas Indian communities. Issue editor Raymond Firth noted that "'faction' has now become almost a catchword in the study of village society in India," whose study leads to "the very heart of village life" (1957:292). This idea is intriguing, given the difference, in colonial ideology, between community and communalism (for example, Pandey 1990, this volume; Bates 2001). The solidarity of local communities is viewed by scholars as a major feature of Indian society since ancient times, whereas the idea of communalism belongs largely to the (British) colonial imaginary (Bates 2001). Given the social unrest in British colonial "plural societies" such as those in the Caribbean, animated by twentieth-century independence movements, trade union struggles, and protests over economic deprivation, and given the, as it were, mental exportation of "intact" cultural traditions among Indians in diaspora, it was no great leap to seek communal factions to study. According to John Kelly, "for more than a century, [Euro-colonialism's] communalisms have been exported out into the labour diaspora realms" (2001:63). Conflicts among factions, then, were accepted as inevitable or natural (Bates 2001:2; compare Furnivall 1956 [1939]; M. G. Smith 1965). In processes of decolonization, communities should emerge, according to modern Western thought, out of communal forms of representation. Rather than in "plural societies," where innate, essential differences dividing groups require overseeing by overarching, allegedly objective interests, or in faction-riven societies, where much of the same supposedly obtains, in truly modern, democratic, universalistic societies, many true communities should form and ultimately coalesce into one true Community.

It is important for studies of Indians overseas, Firth asserted, to pay special attention to factionalism and to discover its extent and significance in "the new systems" (1957:292), particularly in regard to "the behavior of political parties" (293). A perceptive anthropologist, Firth acknowledged that factions can have positive aspects, such as being more flexible than descent groups in mobilizing political and other forms of support. Yet this same flexibility can mean the instability of democratic forms of government; their "turbulence" and unscrupulous methods and "disregard of communal responsibility" makes factions an "expression of disruptive forces in the community" (293). The implicit assumption here is again that communities are cohesive, harmonious, and consensual. But Firth's hints that factions foster fanaticism ("total committal" [294]), being made up of impassioned slogans and tempestuous methods (293–294), means that this form of social institution makes for a cohesiveness that ultimately poses a danger to modern communities called democracies.

While Ashis Nandy is generally correct, at least with respect to the Caribbean, in his charge that diasporic South Asian communities "look to the mother country to redeem their self-respect whenever their dignity is threatened in their adopted country" (1990:102), his urging overseas Indian populations to let go of the mother country and enter "the political realm of their new country" (105), both misses the point and inadvertently reinforces local Caribbean theories about assimilation. Through the obdurateness of their cultural practices and traditions, regional ideology narrates, Indo populations will ever be a "recalcitrant minority," in the famous words of the Trinidadian post-independence republic's first prime minister, the late Dr. Eric Williams. Their historic marginality (political and economic) has been until quite recently rationalized as being due to their (implicitly inherent) cultural rigidity and psychological unwillingness to assimilate into the larger community of Trinidad's callaloo (heterogeneous yet harmonious) nation, with loyalties ultimately always pulled, centrifugally, back toward the subcontinent.

Along with Nandy, also inadvertently reinforcing this ideology is Arjun Appadurai's (1993:424) claim that when South Asian diasporic communities are no longer exposed to the "depredations of their home states," they become "doubly loyal to their nations of origin" and hence "ambivalent about their loyalties" to their country of residence (in this case, to the United States). And while presenting a different argument about diasporic peoples' relationship with the nation-state, one emphasizing counter-hegemony rather than liminality or ambivalence, James Clifford still bolsters this ideology: "Whether the national narrative is one of common origins or of gathered populations, it cannot assimilate groups that maintain important allegiances and practical connections to a homeland or a dispersed community located elsewhere" (1994:307). Certainly intending something quite different, the foregoing are, nonetheless, just what Caribbean nation-states such as Trinidad say when they want to justify exclusion. (One could also ask why allegiances cannot be multiple, just as "non-localizing strategies" are [J. Clifford 1994].) Clifford continues that "positive articulations of diaspora identity reach outside the normative territory and temporality (myth/history) of the nation-state" (307), where the "specific cosmo-politanisms articulated by diasporic discourses are in constitutive tension with nation-states/assimilationist ideologies" (308). But when looking at an empirical case, the contrary is evident: Indo-Trinidadians (and Indo-Caribbeans in general) use their diaspora discourses as a way of better grounding themselves *as* communities, *within* the nation-state and national narratives rather than unidimensionally in resistance to them.

As far as Nandy's polarized choice between either being *of* India or *of* an overseas locality, Indo-Trinidadians (and other Indo-Caribbeans) participate vigorously in the "political realm" of their not-so-new country (more than 160 years of settlement) precisely by maintaining ties, both symbolic and material, with their diasporic homes. They do this in large part through the reification of "we culture," as the local expression goes, what otherwise might be seen as an "internally coherent universe" that serves as a "useful fiction," to borrow from Renato Rosaldo (1989:217), in claims to the possession of community that are based on their abiding culture. As concept and experience, most diasporas, and the communities they are envisioned to contain, necessitate their being moored in place, even if implicitly, rather than transcending place. But the place is simultaneously here and there.

UNPACKING REVISIONIST CRITIQUES, CONVALESCING "COMMUNITY" IN DIASPORA

By the late 1980s, paradigmatic changes in the humanities and social sciences were emphasizing a turn toward approaching cultural and social phenomena in terms of constructions rather than essences, and dynamism rather than stasis. In the Caribbean, anthropology and literature in particular applied these new approaches to the region's cornerstone concept, creolization, challenging its conventional message of cultural loss. Especially emphasized were processes of contentious creativity in the development of new cultural forms out of preexisting, retrieved cultural materials as well as from entirely fresh ones. In the 1990s, both the historical fact of and scholarly attention to Caribbean migration became combined with a new focus on globalization: such terms as "transnationalism," "deterritorialization," "diaspora," "ethnoscapes," and "traveling cultures," for example, became coined or rediscovered. In the context of Caribbean migration history and creative creole-cultural adaptability in a newly global world, the concept of community can be safely assumed and put to use in describing the life and culture of Caribbean peoples, particularly Afro-Caribbean peoples (who comprise the demographic majority in the region, and with the most sustained academic attention). Thus, for example, based on her research among West Indian immigrants in New York City, Mary C. Waters suggests that Afro-Caribbeans are "perhaps the quintessential postmodern peoples" due to their engagement with capitalism, the preponderance of cultural mixing in the region's "created societies," and the importance of migration in their lives (2001:202). In a similar vein, George and Sharon Gmelch, ethnographers of Barbados, employ the phrase "relational communities" to represent the reality that community is "becoming increasingly detached from place" (Gmelch and Gmelch 1997:189). Now greatly "geographically dispersed," Barbadians live "outside the village and parish, in other parts of the island and in other countries in the Caribbean, North America, and Europe" (189), forming widely scattered yet cohesive communities linked by relationships based on kinship, remittances, politics, and so on (see also Glick Schiller and Fouron 2001).

Theorists of the entire region, such as Paul Gilroy, think of community as part of the political language of social movements that call for equality, justice, and opportunity (Gilroy 1987:234). Although community reflects "the concentration of black people," for Gilroy "the term refers to far more than mere place or population. It has a moral dimension…[signifying] a particular set of values and norms in everyday life: mutuality, cooperation, identification and symbiosis" (234)— images that reinscribe traditional community assumptions. Straddling the descriptive and theoretical realms is Kenneth Bilby's analysis of the "imagined communities" of religious practitioners in Jamaica, for example, Rastafari. Recapitulating the conventional Caribbean scenario, Bilby sees Rasta brethren and sistren as "forced to re-create themselves as social beings from the shreds of their individual pasts," yet where the "broadly shared creole culture" was not sufficient to build a "viable sense of community" (1999:323). At the same time, the spiritual communities that did form, Bilby argues, were particularly "open [and] adaptable" as well as "oppositional" (323) (against hegemonic authority in the form of Euro-colonialism), "loose-knit," "highly flexible," and without centralized authority (324). Consequently, Rasta have no conventional "home" situated on an actual expanse of land but rather have a state of mind (Zion, which is literally Africa/Ethiopia and metaphorically a moral and just universe). Rastafari, and the communities it comprises, are therefore "neither here nor there" (326) (rather than a simultaneous here and there), having escaped "original breeding grounds" and creating amorphous, diasporic, imagined communities (324) that span vast physical space and metaphysical territories.

Whether imagined through spiritual philosophy or constituted through shared moral commitments to resistance and justice or through de facto social constituencies resulting from globalization, community in the Caribbean is rarely explicitly represented as not a cultural/social possibility; it has become an accepted principle of social organization. It is, however, arguably still not the principal framework through which we view Caribbean peoples but a fortifying adjunct to more trendy academic foci: transnationalism, deterritorialization, and diaspora.

Interestingly, it is Afro-Caribbeans who are generally characterized as being engaged with modernity on a global scale; Indo-Caribbeans— with their allegedly intact traditions—have only more recently begun to be portrayed in this way. Today, however, especially in the rubric diaspora, we find a new, apparently more compelling application: a generic, rather than specified, South Asian diaspora. As some scholars have commented, Gilroy's (1993) massively influential conceptualization of diaspora and the Black Atlantic, for example, relies on a black/white binary that cannot fully recognize South Asian contributions to Black Atlantic cultural productions (see, for example, Gopinath 1995). Yet due significantly to the writings of South Asian academics, many from sites dislocated from their own points of origin, there is currently a veritable industry of musings about (primarily Western Hemisphere) diasporas, and certainly not only from South Asian authors. I will consider a few of the most influential of these contributors to diaspora theory and some of the consequences of their work for the concept of community and its application to Caribbean peoples.

Several terms and perspectives—"diaspora aesthetic" (Hall 1990), "discrepant temporalities" (Bhabha 1990), "changing same" (Gilroy 1993), "deterritorialization" (Appadurai 1996), and, from the vantage point of media, the "mediated engagement with 'distant' peoples" that "deterritorialize[s] the process of imagining communities" (Shohat and Stam 1996:145)—are these days immediately recognizable. In brief (and I hope without too much disservice to these authors), each phrase is an attempt to capture theoretically the continuities among dispersed people, which form a people, but outside of (Western/academic) hegemonic notions of ethnos, or peopleness, that assume a natural, necessary connection between identity and place, and between normative and alternative notions of progress through time. Among many of these authors, diaspora becomes a kind of curative antithesis of community, the freeing up of bounded and isolated, routed as opposed to rooted, peoples and identities. In other words, diaspora is the means of community or the reason for it. While Avtar Brah (1996:180) posits that the intense (academic) association between diaspora and displacement has meant that location can easily fade from view, I would suggest that rather than a disappearance of place in the concept of diaspora, the concept's reliance on community makes place/location ambiguous, and perhaps amorphous, if also an unavoidable predicate.

Thus Appadurai argues that the "nationalist genie" is "increasingly unrestrained by ideas of spatial boundary" (1993:413). Deterriorialized folks engage in the construction of locality as a "structure of feeling" (1996:199), since, in an atmosphere where "steady points of reference" are in extreme "cultural flux" and uncertainty, inventing identity markers (tradition, ethnicity, kinship) is today a "slippery" project (44). But even if ethnoscapes, rather than situated, bounded sites, now demarcate the world, the structures of feeling that build localities may well still re-create geographic moorings. Simply because nouns such as "narrative," "consciousness," and "discourse" presently have currency does not necessarily mean that communities only hang in the abstract or that their imagined condition can be disarticulated from the visceral cues of specific (and sometimes single) locations.

Hall defines "the diaspora experience" not "by essence" but by "a necessary heterogeneity and diversity," by hybridity (1990:235). Thinking in terms of what he calls hybridized religious universes, such as those of Rastafari (among other Caribbean religions), Hall sees communities existing within diasporas where the past continues to speak to "us" not as "facts" but post-experientially, "like the child's relation to the mother...always-already 'after the break,'" "always constructed through memory, fantasy, narrative and myth" (227). What is uniquely and "essentially" Caribbean is its "diaspora aesthetic": the mixes of pigmentation, physiognomic type, cuisine, "cut-and-mix," "cross-overs," and so on (235). So while space is conceived as transcending place, it (space) ultimately is place still, since Hall's diaspora aesthetic indexes "uniquely" (235) regional characteristics, not the least of which are "those islands of enchantment" that are "rising up out of that blue-green Caribbean" (236).

For Clifford, embedded within diaspora is the idea of community. Rather than eschew the concept as solely an emblem of place, Clifford sees communities (in diaspora) as spatially and temporally multidimensional and connected: "[D]iasporas...connect multiple communities] of a dispersed population...multi-locale diaspora cultures are not necessarily defined by a specific geopolitical boundary" (J. Clifford 1994: 304). Moreover, he argues that diaspora signifies people's "struggles to define the local, as a distinctive community, in historical contexts of displacement" (308). Acknowledging local actors and practices allows Clifford to interpret diasporic communities in terms of counter-hegemonic resistance, community members' awareness of separation, loss, and hope—the "defining tension" of "diaspora consciousness" (312). Homi Bhabha (1990) also proposes the potential subversion that is latent in diaspora (see also Mercer 1994). Bhabha sees diasporic unsettlements producing, among diasporic peoples, disruptions of the linear chronologies of the nation-state into which these people are unevenly incorporated. "Counter-narratives of the nation that continually evoke and erase its totalizing boundaries—both actual and conceptual—disturb those ideological manoeuvres through which 'imagined communities' are given essentialist identities" (Bhabha 1990:300). Since the political unity of the nation is represented, paradoxically, by a modern territoriality that rests on the "atavistic temporality" of traditionalism, "quite simply, the difference of space returns as the Sameness of time, turning Territory into Tradition, turning the People into One" (300). This claim raises the question of what subversion ("disruptions") means and the forms it takes, notably, nuancing our approach to the uses of atavism and the desirability of tradition and unity. In at least one context of displacement, diasporic Indo-Trinidadians seek to compensate for the rupture of their ancestors' subcontinental history and culture by entering, not rejecting, a Western, linear, progressivist narrative. That is, Indo-Trinidadians construe the linear chronologies of the Trinidadian nation-state, into which they have been unevenly incorporated, to serve their interests as particularly constituted political and cultural—*place*-based—communities.

If in the authors above we can see that etic treatments of community tend to be based in some fashion on spatial models, even if implicitly and against their intentions, in South Asian diaspora studies some scholars have also critiqued a similar focus on spatial models (places of origin, homelands) as constituting the basis of diasporic identities. This critique draws attention to what can be an overemphasis (*in scholarship*, as distinct from subjects' experience and interpretation) of the significance and coherence of foundational cultural elements, such as tradition, authenticity, or heteronormativity, that help anchor identity into a single, stationary place and produce ahistorical models of culture and its transformations.

Two generally overlooked yet important differences in emphasis obtain here. First is the distinction in scholarship on diasporas between what I call "coolie odyssey" and "deterritorialized routes" approaches.

The former, coolie odyssey, often focuses on colonial-historical dimensions of indentured peoples and processes that some contemporary critics claim are portrayed as being *completed*—that is, diasporic journeys indicative of foundational moments of diaspora that were (implicitly) somehow less nuanced and complex than those of postcolonial globalization, somehow contained within a past of more delineated, predictable contexts that labor immigrants eventually outgrew as they assimilated into their respective societies, or that the societies outgrew as they transformed over time. The latter distinction, deterritorialized routes, laud revisionist critics, tends to focus on present-day transnational transformations as continuously *open-ended* processes and practices, suggesting a striving for theoretical generalization rather than historical particularity (despite recent discussions of "vernacular modernities" [for example, Hall 1999]) yet emphasizing the probing of the implications of fluidity of culture, instability of place, and multiplicity of diasporic subjectivities.

This disjuncture between approaches leads to the second difference in emphasis, that between etic and emic perspectives. Theoretical intervention into the experience and character of diaspora is typically an exterior voice, emanating from the gaze of the observer rather than the sensibilities of such observed as today's living progeny of "coolie" laborers. Thus, promising suggestions for creative ways to reconceptualize community in diaspora, such as, for example, Gayatri Gopinath's (2005) framework of queer sexuality that decenters the primacy of blood, patrilineal descent, and family as biological and national reproduction to challenge conventional models of diaspora, still begs the question: "conventional" for whom?

Many emic conceptualizations, such as those among Indo-Trinidadian (Indo-Caribbean) people, memorialize family (in the form of lineage), homeland, place, and coherent foundational cultural elements as the core of their communities. They do so in ways that harness temporal models of change over time, even while freezing culture within static space/locality. In other words, Indo-Trinidadians characterize their communities in terms of an ancestral past represented by the cultural practices of both deceased forebears and living progeny moving progressively forward toward modernity or retrogressively backward toward tradition. But this movement to and fro through time does not represent a precise dichotomy between a *before* (traditional) place and an *after* (modern) place. Instead, place attains its meaning (and therefore its situatedness) through its variable association with (1) the authentic subcontinental traditions of so-called peasant labor culture or (2) the authentic subcontinental traditions of elite learned culture. Although learned culture involves edified proficients and experts (notably religious), it also can be disembodied from specific actors, thereby transcending temporal boundaries—that is, the past lives in the present as particular forms of knowledge that are simultaneously context-specific and context-universal.

Wishing to include emic perspectives of Indo-Trinidadians, while attending to the critique (generally toward "coolie odyssey" research) of overreliance on adynamic representations of place as the basis of diasporic identities, necessitates a move from diaspora studies in the strict sense toward other, applicable ways to think about time and the ways we might differentiate time and history. As noted above, Indo-Trinidadians imagine community progress as a linear timeline of tradition and modernity; place attains meaning in being potentially constituted by both "peasant" and elite forms of authenticity (at times disembodied from actors, thus transcending temporal boundaries and placing the past in the present as knowledge). Here, chronological time per se is not the problem. Rather, it is what chronological time contains: presuppositions and judgments about appropriate life courses and generationally appropriate practices—in other words, *anachronism* (Halberstam 2004). Judith Halberstam's examination of the concept of anachronism by "queering" chronological models of time allows exploring the role of anachronism in diaspora narratives. Identifying certain cultural practices as anachronistic conveys value judgments about things out of their proper place and time. But Indo-Trinidadians challenge prescriptive and uniform evaluations of what tradition or custom "belongs" where, and what does not, by taking the temporal specificity (and thus the factor of "appropriateness") out of what is traditional and what is modern, holding constant the location of the past and yet also rendering it outside of time through its being unceasingly relevant to present and future Indo-Trinidadian identities. Instead of anachronisms constituting the measure of modernity, Indo-Trinidadian diaspora narratives mark progress by what I distinguish as apocryphal time and lived-event historiography.

Apocryphal time commemorates consistency and continuity in *community viability*; lived-event historiography emphasizes great transformations and watershed moments in *community advancement*. Both are ways of asserting community in diaspora that allow movement and stability, tradition and modernity, to exist at the same time, because what is challenged is the notion of anachronism rather than the linear chronologies of the nation-state into which they are unevenly incorporated (compare Bhabha 1990). In doing so they reject the image of existential *de*territorialization from a timeless place (the Indian subcontinent of ancestral heritage), thereby holding time steady—and apocryphal. They also strategically promote the idea of their experiential *re*territorialization within the historical chronology of colonial indenture schemes and post-independence identity politics (the Trinidadian nation-state of descendant heritage), thereby being a part of, progressing within, Western trajectories of modernity.

Constructing communities as moving through linear time toward and away from a stationary and predictable ancestral place is in some respects, then, compensation, in the form of cultural capital, for precarious contemporary sociopolitical moorings. Engaging in the local (Western) discourse of modernity and tradition is a discourse of *rightful, incontrovertible* belonging whose justification lies in a cultural visibility required by the Trinidadian state's system of patronage: the distribution of resources and opportunities based on communally defined groups. In Trinidad's origins as a colonial society, a system of stratification based on a class-race-color hierarchy—beginning with slavery and continuing through emancipation and indenture—laid the foundations for a postcolonial society whose hallmark has been ethnic group competition fostered by class inequalities and state control of certain resources. The nature of colonial society is, in most cases, that economic and social boundaries are made to correspond with racial, ethnic, religious, and other communal groups, which are differently incorporated into the stratification system of the society (Hintzen 1989:6). Through this unequal incorporation, which fosters conflictual political and economic interests, adversarial relations often develop among communal groups. In Trinidad, the strength of communal politics derives from the implementation of voting, where the most important and visible dimension of political cleavage is race (Hintzen 1989:20). Reliant on communal politics, the state became synonymous with "black"; and opposition parties largely with "Indian." Indo-Trinidadians construe their diaspora as a seamless narrative, emphasizing their journey as a way of welding together putative fragments of heritage and practice into identities that establish and provide "proof" of communities, and thus social cohesion, stability, cultural continuity, and political clout.

At its most broad, the Indo-Trinidadian strategy of building and cementing communities by means of an ideological commitment to situated places—homeland as well as country of citizenship—underscores the need to appreciate the range of Indo-diasporic streams over the course of two centuries around the globe. These distinctions within diasporas, such as cross-cultural and multigenerational contrasts, complicate still-typical theoretical analyses of a monolithic South Asian diaspora. Hindu Panjabi migrants in London, for example, do not speak of "home" as a single, stable entity or point of reference, emphasizing instead multiple homes over time (Raj 2003). At the same time, the contemporary Hinduization of India (as a nationalist agenda) involves a concerted outreach to the "global Indian family"—the NRI (nonresident Indians) and PIO (people of Indian origin), or a "20 million strong Diaspora spread across 110 countries" (www.indiaday.org/ficci/about_us.asp). This government strategy relies on notions of filial piety, although only certain countries are deemed to possess "qualified" Indians (Raj 2003). As Dhooleka Raj observes, "the term 'NRI' is loaded with connotations of longing and belonging, albeit initiated because of the Indian government's need for foreign investments" (2003:177). Here we can see simultaneous instrumental processes at work: the identification of "communities" that comprise the Indian "family" worldwide and the grounding of a unitary and fixed homeland. Despite this effort, not every member of this big Indian family conforms to this imagery.

Not only has India been a very different political, social, and cultural place in these two historical moments, but almost two centuries has meant that Indian emigrants also have possessed quite different class identities, family organization, ideas about the known and unknown world, and relationships to the mother country. While the contemporary Indian nation-state courts NRIs and PIOs, and not coincidently as "true" Indians, colonized labor migrants, such as those indentureds headed for the Caribbean, were generally an enigma to those at home under the British Raj (although useful for political agendas as well [see, for example, Kelly 1991]) and, at worst, contemptible. Referring to Indians coming back to Calcutta from South Africa, even Mohandas Gandhi discredited them as being neither Indian nor colonial: "social lepers," they ostensibly lacked Indian culture except the partial and inadequate habits they learned from their "uncultured, half-dis-indianized," diasporic parents (Mohapatra 1996, quoted in Raj 2003:176).

Sounding, ironically, like the typical characterization of Afro-Caribbeans (who, as we saw above, often were not granted even partial and inadequate African cultural habits), this portrait of diasporic cultural loss helped stimulate Indo-Caribbeans' embrace of assumptions about their "intact" tradition in the New World and their construction of what became their identity in contrast to Afro-Caribbeans: a *whole*-cultured, fully Indianized community, defined by distinct boundaries of cultural pedigree based on a steady-state locality called Home and a linear, progressivist narrative of apocryphal time and lived-event historiography. We often think of diasporic communities as deterritorialized, thus as evidence of how scholarship has commendably shaken old community assumptions of boundedness and homogeneity. But this spatial element in the constitution of "diaspora" reinvigorates notions of homeland; there are continuities, not breaks, confirmed in these assumptions. Paradoxically, deterritorialized flux still generates anchored localities.

The promise of "redemptive return," Stuart Hall (1999:3–4) tells us, is an interpretation at the heart of the concept of diaspora among Caribbean peoples. In this metaphor, history heals original ruptures of displacement, "circling back to the restoration of its originary moment," constituting a hope "for Caribbean people, condensed into a sort of foundational myth" whose "redemptive power lies in the future, which is yet to come" (4). In diaspora imaginaries (the ideational contexts of diasporic identities) among Indo-Caribbeans—who are only implied in Hall's discussion—communities are always embedded in the future, always going to happen, always going to be present. As such, Indo-Caribbean communities are legitimated by foundational myths and by foundational futures, as they challenge notions of anachronism, interpret apocryphal time and lived-event historiography, and localize and reterritorialize place.

What should be evident at this point is that while the histories of Afro-Caribbean and Indo-Caribbean peoples have profound parallels and similarities, the historical and cultural interpretation of their histories has produced dramatically different portraits of them as communities. Rarely (if ever) always a deliberate term of approbation, the concept of community takes on, as all symbols do, the valences of the larger contexts in which it is couched. The "view from within" communities (A. Cohen 1985:19) consists of a dialectic between the emic view (what members experience and interpret, in all its variations) and the etic view (what interlocutors and analysts observe and interpret, in all its variations). In conjunction with the Afro-Caribbean, community has conventionally made its presence felt primarily as an absence, an inadequacy—even while today these scholarly and social policy biases are being challenged. Among Indo-Caribbeans, community has conventionally made its presence felt primarily as an inherence—either through the local ideologies of identity politics or through the lens of shifting trends in academic research. Contrasting ideas and presumptions about the nature of cultural transformation, and of culture itself, among diasporic Africans and diasporic South Asians; the nature of the world at different moments in time (for example, the nineteenth, twentieth, and twenty-first centuries); and the nature of academic discourse all offer a promise of future paths to take in the direction of a better understanding of local, regional, and global conflict, instability, and people's creative responses. Yet as we have seen, even our most favored and ostensibly reliable frame of reference, community, cannot serve us well as a point of departure, unless it is approached as that which reveals much more deeply embedded assumptions about human capability and desire, and whose narratives will prevail.

Acknowledgments
Many thanks to Carla Freeman for her thoughtful comments.

7

Conflicting Concepts of Community

Diversity and Diaspora
in American Suburbs

Susan H. Lees

TENAFLY, N.J., June 23—A legal fight over the placing of Orthodox Jewish boundary markers on public property seemingly came to a close today when the United States Supreme Court declined to hear the case, but the mayor here said that the town still had not decided whether to proceed with further action to have the markers removed.

The three-year fight is over a symbolic boundary known as an eruv, a zone that allows Orthodox Jews to carry objects outside the home on the Sabbath despite the overall prohibition against work. The eruv is marked by small black plastic strips placed on hundreds of telephone poles. The strips, along with the lines that connect the poles, allow Orthodox Jews to push a baby carriage or carry keys, for instance, as they walk within the eruv.

The Supreme Court's decision not to hear the case came after a unanimous decision in 2002 by three judges of the United States Court of Appeals for the Third Circuit that permitted the eruv to remain. A Federal District Court said in 2001 that the town could remove the eruv.

The fight has bitterly divided this town of 13,800—even among Jewish residents—and has brought sharp words from the mayor.
—*Jonathan Miller* (New York Times, *June 24, 2003*)

This struggle in a prosperous New Jersey suburb illustrates the conflicting constructions of community, in which a civil society, defining itself in terms of inclusive "diversity," finds the limits of its ability to incorporate diversity tested by a diasporic community, which defines itself in terms of an exclusive ethnic as well as religious heritage.[1] The fight is emotional, and it is in a way mysterious: it appears to revolve around an ancient ritual practice that would seem harmless and fairly irrelevant to the lives of modern suburbanites. What lies behind the passion with which this struggle has been fought? Why does the practice survive? Why does the Borough of Tenafly want to prohibit it? Why is the fight so bitter? To address these questions and others, we need to explore the many layers of meaning of community as it relates to diasporas.

Diasporas and diasporic identities have attracted increasing attention from scholars (and politicians) in recent decades (see Sheffer 2003). The diasporic community is virtually by definition a community whose membership is defined in some sense genetically (see J. Clifford 1994). This idea is inimical to notions of civil society and citizenship in the United States. As Jonathan Boyarin notes,

> [h]aving identified the notions of diaspora (in which territory is not a neutral ground for citizenship) and genealogy (in which identity is substantially determined by ancestry), it becomes possible to see how mainstream American notions of polity and identity depend on a subordination of ancestry and "foreign" geographical origin. Thus the individualist bent of American politics is tied to a historically grounded rejection of genealogy. The forms of genealogy involved in this Americanist rejection were primarily those determining hereditary social stigmas and privileges. (1997: 1548)

A similar genealogical rejection, albeit of different historical origins, might also apply in much of postwar Western Europe, which is dealing with major immigrant populations emanating from the Third World.

If the diaspora is by definition comprised of people who identify with a home "elsewhere" (compare Khan, this volume), what does it mean when they take possession of a neighborhood as their own, with its own distinctive identity? When diasporic groups produce communities in the segregated spaces they are assigned by their partial exclusion from the hegemonic culture they inhabit, we have diasporic neighborhoods. These moments of community *then challenge that cultural hege-*

mony. In the case of culturally identified blacks in the United Kingdom as well as African Americans in the United States, racial discrimination has resulted in a conspicuous ghettoization of minority communities and the production of a distinct black diaspora community with its own counter-hegemonic culture (which has become not only influential but even commodified in recent decades). This culture contains a distinct and clearly articulated element of critique of white hegemony—a critique of the racism that brought it into existence (Gilroy 1991; compare J. Brown 1998). Perhaps a similar process is occurring or will occur with respect to Muslim immigrants throughout Europe and the United Kingdom, though it takes a different form.

The Jewish diaspora is of course much older. It has exhibited some similarities, such as the population being forced (until recently) to reside in ghettos and exclusion from mainstream positions of economic, political, and social power. A combination of external political persecution and internal cultural coherence resulted in the persistence of Jewish diasporic identities over millennia. Unprecedented freedom, acceptance, and prosperity of Jews in the United States during the past century or so have radically altered the context of their identity. This paper will explore one aspect of how debates over the expression of diasporic identity play out "on the ground" of a relatively new frontier: the upscale American suburb. In this instance, the debate involves modern Orthodox Jews and more secularized Jews, as well as non-Jews, in an engagement with identity and expression that has surfaced over several different issues in contemporary America (see Heilman and Cohen [1989], Heilman [1976], and Freedman [2000] on conflicts among various modern Jewish groups over religious practice in the United States).

Modern Orthodox Jewish communities ideally reject certain values in the dominant culture, including certain aspects of modernity: a high value on change (rather than appreciation and preservation of tradition), the centrality of capitalism and capital accumulation (rather than learning), and individualism (rather than family and community life). But in many respects, this idealized community is not entirely different from that of the ideal suburban community, which also values tradition (historical "conservation" is highlighted among the values promoted by Tenafly), family, and learning. Why, then, does the possibility of an ethnic, diasporic enclave (a community within a community) pose such a threat? The key word here seems to be "ghetto," a term we associate with racism, violence, and lack of control. That the civil community represents itself as "diverse" and "inclusive" is important. This conceptualization provides critical opportunities for members of certain marked minorities who aspire to higher social mobility by means of *integration*. On the other hand, it demands some degree of assimilation: conformity to certain cultural ideals and practices, specifically that marked cultural and religious practice does not become too *conspicuously* "different" and that everyone accepts a certain homogeneity in conduct (this is the "social contract" described by Davina Cooper [2002]). It further demands that no one "ethnic group" conspicuously dominates the whole. It professes tolerance and respect, although it also covertly places a high value on the hegemonic (hence unmarked) ideal. For the modern American affluent suburb, the unmarked ideal has long been understood to be an upper-middle-class version of white Anglo-Saxon Protestant culture.

In the Tenafly *eruv* dispute, this ideal representation of diversity and inclusiveness is challenged by a diasporic religious community. Jewish identity is conventionally conceived at least in part in something like genealogical terms. Members (descended from common ancestors, sharing a common tribal history) identify with others with whom they share a genealogical past and present.

Despite a Christian tendency to categorize Jewish people in religious terms, most Jews have tended to experience themselves as a civilization. Although one could argue that Jews have always had a conception of themselves as "a people," this more expansive identity has been especially characteristic of Western Jews since their emancipation following the French Revolution. Since then, anti-Jewish hatred largely has been known as anti-Semitism, a racial/ethnic hatred that in this case includes a religious component (Brettschneider 1996:12).

This diasporic "community" demands conformity, too, and is fairly exclusive. Its very existence expresses both an implicit antagonism to the "other" community within which it finds itself and a dependence upon it for its own self-definition. The antagonism lies in its persistent refusal to be absorbed. The dependence lies in its own identity as "other."[2]

Because of the implications of "diversity" and "inclusiveness," the civil and diasporic communities appear to be conceptually incompatible (although not necessarily in practice—Jewish religious communities usually exist without conflict in both the urban and suburban United States). Nevertheless, members of the second are drawn to the first for certain of its benefits—the comfortable lifestyle, the opportunity to escape the oppression of urban enclaves, and even the opportunity to form new versions of old enclaves that are in many ways more modern yet more observant of traditions. In fact, the prosperity and safety (tolerance) of the suburbs allows for an elaboration of ethnic/religious tradition that was more difficult for an earlier urban generation to achieve.[3]

Religious and ethnic enclaves (Sivan 1995) (not to speak of "ghettos") challenge civil society in several different ways. Contemporary civil society promotes *diversity* as a value—the very emphasis placed on this term underscores a recent past and troubling present clouded by racist discrimination. Both government institutions and civil society see diversity as a way to redress and correct the injustice and harm done by past racist discrimination. Antidiscrimination laws in housing and employment presumably protect and promote diversity. However, a problem can arise when promoting "diversity" might entail government protection or sponsorship of a specific group's distinctive practices, practices that may exclude others or even offend them. The radical new consciousness of ethnic identity today, so evident among indigenous and sometimes migrant groups around the world, opens the door to demands that are seriously problematic. Specific cases, such as Native Alaskans' demand to suspend a ban on the hunting of whales for them alone, so they can practice traditional rites, challenge the U.S. government. The constant tension between civil society and other community identities does not offer an easy resolution. Where political control over the uses of public space (and resources) is at issue, the demands of distinct identity groups may be irreconcilable, raising the question of what "diversity" might legally and morally entail.

DEFINING COMMUNITY AND DEFINING SPACE: UNDERSTANDING THE ERUV

The eruv, the space enclosed by the symbolic boundary that prompted the Borough of Tenafly to appeal to the U.S. Supreme

Court, lends a spatial or territorial dimension to the community of Orthodox Jews who subscribe to the practice it represents. It forms the Orthodox community into a neighborhood of a special kind, and it may have a dynamic function of altering the composition and behavior of inhabitants of the existing neighborhood. The thirty-five to forty (media reports give varying numbers, up to seventy) Orthodox Jewish families who lived in Tenafly claimed at the time of the dispute that they would be the only ones directly affected by the eruv, which enclosed about one-third of the area of the town. But clearly, the borough council and many Tenafly citizens felt otherwise. To understand what this conflict was about, we need to begin with the meaning of the eruv itself.

Explaining the eruv starts with explaining the Sabbath, the day on which Jews, out of reverence for God, either in commemoration of the seventh day of creation on which God "rested," or in commemoration of the liberation of Jews from Egyptian slavery, are enjoined to desist from all labor. What constitutes labor came to be defined in Jewish law (*halacha*) as activities falling into one of thirty-nine categories of work prohibited on the Sabbath (prohibited because these forms of labor were involved in constructing and dismantling the portable tabernacle in the wilderness as the Jews followed Moses toward the promised land), and these categories have become refined through time and with changing circumstances by various rabbinic decisions. The folklorist Alan Dundes (2002), in a look at Sabbath prohibitions, has recounted many of the contemporary interpretive and practical means by which those who wish to observe traditional constraints adapt the prohibitions to the exigencies of contemporary life. For example, lighting or extinguishing a fire, and by extension turning electricity on or off—which involves lighting or extinguishing a spark—is prohibited on the Sabbath. Yet life in a world dependent on electricity may call for adjustments, such as using automated devices for turning lights on and off, or using elevators that stop on every floor, so that the observant Orthodox Jew need not actually press the switch.

Skeptics (like Dundes) feel that these adjustments are "subterfuges" employed to get around the prohibitions. Thus some critics of the eruv feel they should not endorse what amount to machinations for circumventing religious observance. For some participants in eruv conflicts, the theme of subterfuge is an important issue; more than one anti-eruv partisan declared: "I won't help Jews break their own laws." However, not everyone agrees that these "solutions" constitute subterfuges. The material abundance that provides the comforts of modern life has also provided the potential means to observe the Sabbath ever more rigorously. Elaboration of law—embellishment so to speak—is a sanctioned form of religious Jewish observance and is not regarded traditionally as "subterfuge" but instead is honored as a way of meditating on, exploring the meaning of, and showing and developing knowledge about the law. Filling out the meaning of the law is entirely permissible. Indeed, it is a revered activity, beginning with the Talmud, which is replete with both open debate and elaboration of meaning.

Among the proscribed forms of labor is that of carrying. An observant Jew may not carry objects from within one's house to a public place, or within a public place for any meaningful distance. This law means that on the Sabbath, an observant Jew should not carry a key in her pocket when she goes to the synagogue, carry a casserole to her mother's house for the Sabbath dinner, or push a stroller or wheelchair to the synagogue or the park, until the sun has set on Saturday night.

The prohibition against carrying is ancient and must have posed some hardships even in ancient times. The sages of antiquity apparently devised a means to retain the prohibition even while easing the hardships it would pose on women and men. The ancient sages were concerned that people would be strongly tempted to break the prohibition, often unintentionally—women had to carry their babies, for example, and some older people needed sticks to help them walk. To reduce the potential for such infractions, it would be "necessary" to redefine space, at least for the Sabbath.[4] The sages proposed the following:

> For people living in homes that share a common courtyard, one of the residents is to take "one entire loaf of his bread," and make the other residents shareholders in that loaf by reciting, "Take this loaf and acquire a share therein on behalf of all the Israelites dwelling in this court...." A representative of the other tenants then takes the loaf, raises it a handbreadth, whereupon the maker of the eruv takes it

back and recites some blessings, adding "By virtue of this eruv it shall be permissible for us to take out and to carry from the houses to the court and from the court to the houses, and from one house to another, for us and for all Israelites who dwell in the houses of this court." Since all the tenants have now acquired a share in this loaf, and at the beginning of the Sabbath it is in the house of the person who made the eruv, it is considered as if all of them had dwelt in this house, and therefore they are permitted to carry within the entire area as if they were in one house— that is, one domestic space. This ritual creates an eruv. (Ganzfried 1927)

This symbolic common household, a temporary domestic space, can be extended to interconnected courtyards if there is a doorway between them. If walls surround the courtyards, the *eruv hatzeirot*,[5] or "intercommunity of courts," can be extended to incorporate all of them, if their representatives all share in the loaf of bread and the loaf is stored in a place accessible to them (such as a synagogue).[6] If the loaf is in fact a board of matzo, which does not spoil, it can be stored from one week to the next and need be replaced only at Passover, once a year.

Eruvin (plural of eruv) date at least to the first century of the Common Era; the responsibilities of a Babylonian Jewish community's leader, according to a text cited by Jacob Neusner (1984), included setting the eruv for the town.[7] According to Rabbi Yosef Bechofer (1998), an authority on the urban eruv, through medieval times the walls of the town might serve as boundaries of the eruv; but once walled cities fell out of fashion, there was indeed a problem: how to define the enclosed space of the ritually shared domestic household. Around this time, according to Bechofer, rabbinic authorities devised additional means to demarcate the boundaries (although some laws regarding eruvin had been elaborated earlier in the Talmud): one could use existing walls or natural boundaries, but where there were none, one could put up strings or wires, punctuated by symbolic doorways, to demarcate invisible walls, as long as the symbolic constructions adhered to rabbinic strictures. Today, even these elaborations have been modified and adapted in various ways to both meet rabbinic requirements (and rabbis do differ in their interpretations) and adjust to local circumstances.

The eruv in Tenafly did not involve the erection of strings or wires but rather depended on existing lines to demarcate its borders, a common practice in contemporary times. The existing lines were communication cables already attached to utility poles used by phone and cable companies. Put up on these poles were some plastic strips, indistinguishable from other plastic strips running down the poles, which symbolically signified "doorways" in the "wall" demarcated by the cables that had been designated as markers of the boundaries of the eruv. These strips, called by the Orthodox *lechis*, were attached to the poles by the utility company as a public service, something it had done for other communities without any problem (the plastic strips were on hand and were normally used to cover lines going along the poles).

It should be clear from this description that an eruv defines more than a neighborhood but also a special kind of community, in which contiguous houses are joined as one household by the sharing of food ownership. In effect, for the purposes of the Sabbath rest, the joined households are as one household, and their common space is taken from the public realm into the realm of the "domestic," where food is shared. It is a special kind of domestic space in that it comes into ritual effect only for the twenty-five hours of the weekly Sabbath, and only for purposes of carrying; it is not meant to allow people to walk in the streets in their pajamas brushing their teeth, nor does it free them from other restrictions on labor, such as those that prohibit lighting fires, writing, or handling money.

Having an eruv is extremely important for modern Orthodox Jewish community life. Very important to that community life is family participation in group rituals, and the eruv is absolutely critical for this purpose. However modern the "modern Orthodox" may be, it is still primarily women who care for small children. As many proponents of eruvin everywhere point out, if there is an eruv, then Orthodox women who care for small children are free to leave the house (with all the paraphernalia needed for infant and child care, such as diaper bags and strollers) to join others in the synagogue services and social life outside their own homes on the Sabbath. While individuals can adhere to Orthodox practices as individuals, a community life of Orthodox Jews relies on family participation, and that requires an eruv.

THE TENAFLY ERUV CONFLICT

The facts of the eruv conflict in Tenafly are complex, and we need not go into every detail here. Essentially, the Tenafly Eruv Association, which had been formed to establish the eruv and arrange for the erection of its boundaries, approached the mayor of Tenafly, Ann Moscovitz, in 1999 to obtain permission from the borough to have an eruv in the town.[8] The lechis—symbolic doorways marked by plastic wire covers—had already been put on the public utility poles by CableVision, the cable company serving the town, as a public service. When Mayor Moscovitz brought the matter to the borough council, the council voted to deny permission, based on an existing borough ordinance that prohibited the use of the public thoroughfare for private purposes. Since the Eruv Association had already arranged for the markers to go up, the council required it to have the markers removed. The Eruv Association then brought suit against this injunction to a federal district court, requesting that the town be prohibited from enforcing the removal of the markers. The district court ruled in favor of the town on the grounds that the association was acting without permission from the borough in violation of the town's ordinance. The Eruv Association immediately appealed this ruling on various grounds, and the U.S. Court of Appeals for the Third Circuit overturned the district court's decision. Subsequent appeals by the borough were rejected by the courts.

The more explicit constitutional arguments made in the various courts hinged on the obvious issues: the "establishment" clause and the "free practice" clause. The town claimed that permitting and facilitating the establishment of the eruv would violate the constitutional prohibition against government establishment of religion (by favoring one religious group's demands) or, alternatively, open the door to equal demands by any group to use the public thoroughfares for religious or other ideological purposes. The Eruv Association claimed that the town was interfering with the free practice of its religious beliefs and discriminating against Orthodox Jews. The outcomes of the appeals indicate the opinion of the courts that the town was indeed acting discriminatorily, given evidence that in the past, the town had rarely enforced its ordinance banning the use of the public utility poles but had brought the ordinance into effect only to bar the eruv. This apparent bias undermined the town's constitutional claims. The judges dismissed Eruv Association claims that the town was engaging in housing discrimination by disallowing the eruv (thereby discouraging Orthodox Jews from living in Tenafly) and did not uphold any notion that the town should facilitate the practice of any religion. Rather, the court was clearly concerned that the town not discriminate against any one group.

The question remains: What motivated the town to try to bar the eruv? Motivations among borough council members and townsfolk in general surfaced not only in direct testimony in court but also at town hall meetings, where the public came forth to express opinions (transcripts were included among the legal briefs in the case). Interestingly, the arguments, discourse, and outcome resemble closely a twelve-year conflict over the establishment of an eruv in London, England, which appeared to end in 2003 with a victory for eruv proponents. Similar conflicts have emerged elsewhere over the past few years, notably in Palo Alto, California. Nevertheless, hundreds of eruvin have been established in the United States and elsewhere without any conflict; where conflict emerges, it does so in special circumstances that share similar components.

Conflicts over eruvin in the United States are among a number of different points of ignition in a continuing and perhaps growing struggle among modern Jews, and to a lesser extent between Jews and non-Jews, over how Jews should live in the modern world and how they should live among non-Jews (see Freedman 2000).[9] To a certain extent, the conflicts are about the legitimacy of changing Jewish practice, but are also about exclusivity, residential space, and Jewish communities. The discourse about eruvin, which contains frequent reference to freighted terms such as "ghettos" and "concentration camps," indicates the depth of emotion involved in the conflicts. What Jews who oppose eruvin often fear is the *marking* of Jews and the residential concentration of Jews in neighborhoods, which are viewed as a threat to their liberty and to the legitimacy and authenticity of the assimilated lives they have made for themselves in affluent suburbs. To Jews who favor eruvin, opposition threatens their freedom to practice their traditions, while at the same time being accepted as equal members of the larger community, and the freedom to create their own communities of like-minded coreligionists in which to live and raise their families in affluent suburbs. Both freedoms appear to be constitutionally guaranteed, but of course these freedoms can come into conflict with the constitutional prohibitions on governments establishing specific religious institutions or favoring one religious sect over another. The ambiguity of the constitutional guarantees and constraints regarding religion is what accounts for the plenitude of cases that come to the U.S. Supreme Court over religious matters. Yet the constitutional arguments of eruv opponents, in the end, can be undermined by the legacy of racial/ethnic discrimination in the United States. While regulations that make the establishment of an eruv difficult can be imposed, if a motive to discriminate against Jews is discovered, these regulations will be challenged and, most likely, eventually dismissed, as was the case in Tenafly.[10]

What we observe in the Tenafly case, as in the London case, is a conflict between two overlapping notions of community, both of them romanticized and idealized, and in the Tenafly case, both laying a claim to legitimacy of rights in courts of law. While the eruv is purported to reflect religious belief and practice, conflicts over the eruv reflect contested understandings of rights to public space that may have important practical implications far from the domain of Sabbath observance. Parties on either side of the conflict recognize these practical consequences. Some of the passions that emerge in the conflict, however, are driven by nonmaterial considerations, which cannot be lightly dismissed.

It is not clear from the decision of the U.S. Court of Appeals that the borough council of Tenafly discriminated against Orthodox Jews per se, but rather only that the council did not want an eruv. Yet questions of anti-Semitism, or discrimination against some kinds of Jews, were a subtext of the debate. The eruv supporters argued that prohibition of an eruv would make the town inhospitable to Orthodox Jews, while permitting an eruv would instead send a welcoming message. The rhetoric became bitter. As a letter to the *Bergen County Record* argued in 2002:

> After the court ruling on Thursday, a borough lawyer, Bruce
> S. Rosen, was quoted in *The New York Times* as saying, "My initial opinion is that it twisted and stretched some previous

decision of both the Third Circuit and U.S. Supreme Court beyond recognition."

Rosen's choice of verbs is appropriate.

Twisted and stretched is what happens to razor wire placed around concentration camps. Tenafly's legal assault against Orthodox Jews practicing their faith is anti-Semitism in full bloom. The flower stinks and so does a municipal government that attempts to hide behind needless litigation. If the borough council wants to hide behind something, it should be honest with itself and the rest of New Jersey and invest in some white sheets. (http://www.bergen.com/cgi-bin/page/pl?id=5434968, 2002)

Yet opponents of the eruv protested vehemently the implication that they were anti-Semitic (and this was an element of the outraged sensibilities of participants in eruv conflicts in North London and Palo Alto as well). The mayor of Tenafly is Jewish, as are many residents and apparently virtually all the lawyers involved on both sides of the case. Many Orthodox Jews of Tenafly had lived in the town without a problem for decades (but they had not broken the social contract by "imposing" their religious practices on the public). Some residents, despite the fact that the eruv is virtually invisible, and despite the fact that they are indifferent to the beliefs that establish the eruv or make it desirable, do not like the idea of what Calvin Trillin (1994), in a *New Yorker* article on the North London eruv, called a "magic schlepping circle" in their neighborhood.

Not every objection to the eruv was made explicit. A visit to this beautiful town, even a visit to its Web site, suggests that the visible face of the town is very important: the houses, the trees, the gardens, and the lawns. Tenafly's physical appearance expresses something about certain American values. It is interesting to consider Tenafly in light of Robert Ash's (2000) analysis of the case of the Hampstead Garden Suburb, the most hotly contested area in the North London eruv dispute.[11] The Hampstead Garden Suburb was deliberately planned and designed to have the appearance of an idealized British country village, in its architecture and its layout. Ash suggests that the suburb represents a "freighted legacy": "This crafted and managed landscape embodies values of stability, permanence, and that monstrous cliché, 'heritage'" (103). British nostalgia for the idealized virtues of country life was materialized in this place (compare Creed,chapter 2, this volume). Tenafly does not look like the Hampstead Garden Suburb, which is quintessentially British, but it is similarly neat and clean, with spacious and manicured lawns, all of which bespeak consideration for neighbors and appreciation of conformity.

The stereotypic image of the observant Jew, although politically incorrect these days, is certainly in the minds of some opponents of the eruv. Such stereotypes associate orthodoxy with ultra-Orthodox and Hassidic Jews, who are regarded as urban and foreign (sometimes "medieval")—men dressed in long black overcoats and wide black hats, with side curls hanging down, accompanied by their wives and large numbers of children, conspicuously "different" and conspicuously unconcerned to be so. This stereotypic Orthodox Jew is simply out of place among the genteel houses and gardens of the suburb.

In this vein (but rarely expressed openly in the Tenafly dispute), is an association between the image of Orthodox Jews and the stereotype of an unattractive, urban, lower-class lifestyle, including the bad manners and slovenly habits of the poor. In the United States, the existence of such an attitude is well exemplified in Stephen Bloom's *Postville* (2000). Bloom depicts a small town in Iowa virtually destroyed by an invasion of ultra-Orthodox Jews. These Jews (as described by Bloom) do not observe the conventions of social conduct of American small-town life: they neglect their lawns, are impolite and discourteous, have too many children, drive and park badly, and are even unsanitary in their personal hygiene. The latter is conveyed by the graphic image of a "greasy" surface of the town's *mikva* (ritual bath), on which Bloom discovers a "pubic hair." Bloom, like many opponents of the eruv, is a self-identified (and assimilated) Jew and is utterly repelled by the ultra-Orthodox Jews of Postville. He regards them as destroyers of an American idyll.

Like the Hampstead Garden Suburb, Tenafly's representation of itself on its Web site emphasizes its architectural past and its dedication to conservation of *this* past, a past that is not *visibly* ethnically diverse at all. The idealized suburb has no Jews; they don't fit in; to bring them in would "spoil the neighborhood." Anxiety about a threatened invasion of Orthodox Jews resembles "white flight" issues of the recent past in the United States. What we are talking about, then, is not simply a concern about people practicing their religion in public but a fear of changing the ethnic composition of a neighborhood and thereby ruining it for others.

It is hard to gauge how widespread these fears were, since they were rarely openly admitted. Instead, those who resisted the establishment of eruvin expressed concern about what would happen as a consequence—that is, that the town would become more attractive to Orthodox Jews, and more would then come to live within eruv boundaries. Many believed this trend would change the community in ways that were socially and *materially* undesirable.[12] The sorts of change they mentioned included rises in real estate values (most believed these would go up *within* the eruv's boundaries, which would be a problem only for those whose homes fell outside the eruv); threats to the viability of the public school system, because Orthodox Jews do not usually send their children to public schools; changes in the commercial centers, particularly fears that businesses that do not cater to Orthodox Jews would suffer; and especially a change in the town's demographic makeup, specifically ghettoization. All these issues were raised at town meetings, and references were made to other towns in New Jersey with eruvin, including neighboring Englewood and more distant Teaneck, which had, in opponents' views, suffered the negative outcomes they feared in Tenafly. A final consideration was the potential for dispute and contention over the eruv among Jews themselves, specifically the Reform and the Orthodox. Some town council members claimed, in explaining their votes against the eruv, that the potential for conflict was a major consideration for them.

The kind of discourse we find in the Tenafly eruv conflict appears to be a suburban rather than an urban phenomenon. Moreover, municipal–eruv association disputes (unlike disputes between ultra-Orthodox Jewish sects) are more likely to be found in wealthy suburbs. Tenafly's median income, according to the most recent census data, was $132,449.[13] These two facts—that eruv disputes are suburban and that they take place among the wealthy—are suggestive. Yet we must situate the conflict in historical time to gain insight into its nature. Very few eruvin were established in the United States before the 1970s, as one rabbi testified at a Tenafly town meeting, and those established were situated in urban locales, mainly in and near New York City, where there was already a substantial concentration of Orthodox Jews. Those that were established *subsequently* were a product not of the Jewish move to the suburbs in the post–World War II era but of civil rights laws that enhanced the self-esteem and assertiveness of many minority groups in the United States. Jews were already in the suburbs (Brodkin 1998; Katznelson 1991), but changes were taking place in the orientation of the younger generation of American Jews (Freedman 2000). Many were becoming interested in older traditions and increasing their religious observance as open ethnic identity became more desirable among the constellation of identity features that began to constitute the individual in the contemporary United States.

The mayor of Tenafly recounts that before the early 1970s, Tenafly was "restricted." Jews were prevented from purchasing homes in desirable parts of the town and were excluded from its principal private establishments, such as the country club. Today, a large proportion of Tenafly residents, including the mayor and some council members, are Jewish, and some might find it ironic that many of the eruv's most vocal opponents are Jews. But perhaps it is not so ironic. The Jews who moved to Tenafly when it first became open to them were looking for the sort of community they eventually found and helped develop there. Some Orthodox Jews who wish to establish an eruv also say they wish to benefit from the diversity of Tenafly.[14] The possibility that the eruv will result in an Orthodox Jewish enclave poses a threat to the very diversity that made Tenafly attractive in the first place.

The most frequently cited objection to the eruv at Tenafly town meetings was that it threatened to establish a "community within a community." Tenafly's citizens, like its public image, emphasize "diversity" as the town's primary and most desirable characteristic. A separation of subcommunities would threaten that ideal. Opponents of the eruv imagined the development of an exclusive community within the larger inclusive community. The community they defended was described most frequently as both diverse and inclusive; the one they feared was homogeneous and exclusive. While never made explicit, it was clear that most problematic was that membership in the latter did not depend on geographical residence, or simply on belief and practice, but that it did indeed have a genealogical component (as diasporic communities usually do; see J. Clifford 1994; Boyarin 1997; Boyarin and Boyarin 1993). Members identify not with the local geographically defined community but the nonlocal genetically defined community. As Davina Cooper points out in the case of the North London eruv:

> Opponents characterized orthodox Jews, during interviews, as intensely arrogant in their disregard for existing spatial meanings, and in their assumption that they could legitimately appropriate Christian designated space. Their association of orthodox neighbourhoods with cultural and social outsiderness highlights the embarrassment of the more assimilated Jews towards an orthodox "kin" who fail to understand the relationship between soil and belonging. Underlying such discomfort is a particular vision of orthodox Jews: that they are so absorbed in their own narrow "lost" world that they do not know where they are; more particularly, that they are somewhere else. Their vision always turned to the past, orthodox Jews remain forgetful of the ways in which diaspora territory and space is both meaningful, and already "taken." In other words, it is not vacant space that can be inscribed from scratch. (2002:99)

Similarly, some Tenafly residents shared the sentiments of one Ms. Klein, expressed on an episode of PBS's *Religion and Ethics Newsweekly* dealing with the Tenafly conflict (February 2001): "One of the things that has bothered me and has bothered other people in the town is that the eruv people have acted as if the desire or lack of desire for the eruv to be erected was immaterial. It was felt that the eruv proponents were not acting as good members of the community."

For the nonobservant Jews and non-Jews, geography was the antidote to inherited status/membership (see Boyarin 1997). The formation of a Jewish community within civil space would be inimical to their ideas about the openness of communities, the absolute test of which was diversity. To combine geography with inherited group membership would be a major threat to their idealization.[15] And this idealization was of immense importance to those who had immigrant backgrounds, particularly the Jews, who saw the American ideal as the converse of the oppressive past in which they were strangers. The entry of the "other" strangers, the Orthodox and possibly even the ultra-Orthodox Hasidim, could make strangers of *them* in what had now become their own community. The presence of more extreme Jews would force them to take sides. Herbert Danzger argues that:

> Mainstream Judaism—which is to say Reform and Conservative Judaism—had become so Americanized by the 1960's that when the counter-cultural movements of that period rejected the "establishment" and attacked its soft underbelly, education and organized religion, Reform and Conservative Judaism came to be rejected as well. A new ethnic consciousness paved the way for renewed interest in Orthodox Judaism. Jewish identity bifurcated: While many Jews simply lost interest in Judaism, some became more involved in religion...the middle did not hold. (1989:227)

Worse yet, their own legitimacy as members of the American suburban community might be called into question. As in the case of the North London suburb: "The refusal or inability of such Orthodox Jews to be accepted as part of the ethnocultural majority drew attention to assimilated Jews' own roots and precarious sense of belonging" (Cooper 2002:95).

"GHETTO" AND AUTHENTICITY IN TENAFLY COMMUNITY DISCOURSE

> "They are building their own ghetto," said a Holocaust survivor. At a public meeting, a man identifying himself as "a proud, practicing Jew" called the eruv an unwanted "line in the sand" with "members of the tribe on one side, members of the community on the other side." (Purdy 2001)

As this *New York Times* report reveals, the multilayered meanings of "ghetto," evocative of the brutality and danger of existence in a world of hatred and prejudice, of disenfranchisement and rejection, freight criticism of the eruv by those who associate its "walls" with these negative conditions. In the quotation, the authenticity and authority of the speaker is doubly freighted by reference to his history of suffering—he is identified as a Holocaust survivor.

Modern America ideally opposes "walls" that separate peoples, and at the same time it honors and encourages "difference"—this is the underlying message of the catchword "diversity." If after the Second World War the more assimilated secular and Reform Jews sought opportunities to join the American mainstream, after the fallout of the civil rights movement (which elevated "diversity" as a value), such Jews also realized that they could retain a modicum of ethnic and religious identity with pride (Katznelson 1991; Brettschneider 1996; Prell 1999). But for the Orthodox minority of American Jews, the new emphasis on ethnic identity and respect for diversity provided an opportunity to become more visibly and assertively different. A younger generation of Jews chose to assert their Jewish identity with the revival and elaboration of traditional practice, altering it in some ways to conform to modern times and modern values while not relinquishing a heritage of ritual practice. The result of this new interest by a younger generation in the revival and elaboration of practices that had been abandoned or rejected by an earlier generation of more assimilated American Jews led to schisms in many quarters, with arguments between practicing Jews of older and younger generations in particular.[16]

While the new value placed on American "diversity" (as opposed to the "melting pot") opened the door to aggressive expressions of ethnic "difference," many did not anticipate the bitter arguments that would ensue as members of various ethnic groups began to debate the meaning of ethnic identity in their own groups. The issue of "authenticity" emerged as a critical point of contention, and neither Americans nor Jews are unique in this respect (see, for example, J. Brown 1998). For more assimilated American Jews, as was the case in a number of other ethnically distinct groups in wider national contexts, specific public expressions of "traditional" practice challenged the authenticity of their own group membership and their own practices. For Jews, authenticity has been associated (rightly or wrongly) with knowledge about and adherence to a specific set of ritual practices (Heilman 1976).[17] For example, Jewish ritual and prayer are traditionally conducted in Hebrew. Jews who are ignorant of Hebrew are at a great disadvantage in Jewish contexts. Various Orthodox sects have indeed claimed that Reform Judaism (the most "assimilated" and dominant form of Judaism practiced in the United States) is not authentic

Judaism at all because of its failure to adhere to traditional practice. It is worth mentioning that Reform Judaism "declared [in 1846] as no longer binding the Talmudic concept of the eruv" (Seltzer 1980).

Many Jews who have chosen modern Reform Judaism have nevertheless internalized the value placed on knowledge and adherence to ancient practice despite "official" rejection of many traditional practices such as the eruv. Thus, while many Orthodox Jews reject Reform Judaism as inauthentic practice, many Reform Jews are alarmed and defensive about this accusation. They frequently express anxiety and resentment that Orthodox Jews look down on them and make them feel uncomfortable about their failure to observe traditional practices and about their ignorance of traditions. Internal divisions among the diasporic community are particularly alarming to those who hope to reconcile their diasporic and civil community memberships.

Most American Jews reject or ignore many if not most Sabbath prohibitions. Many anticipate criticism and rebuke before it has even occurred, citing instances where such confrontations have occurred elsewhere. A focus on Sabbath practices through the establishment of an eruv is particularly threatening with respect to this anxiety because of its public nature. Having an eruv in the town will not only presumably attract more Orthodox Jews but will guarantee that these more visible Jews (men wearing skullcaps and carrying prayer shawls, women dressed in fine clothes for worship, accompanied by large families of children) will be out in the streets on Saturday, when the secular Jews and non-Jews are going to sports events, shopping, cutting the grass, and generally engaging in secular life. Their presence threatens to render the unmarked secular Jew inauthentic and to define authenticity in part by the types of walled locations the secular Jew associates with a "ghetto."

"Diversity" as a value in the civil community has encouraged the Orthodox minority to assert its distinctiveness in a safe environment. Those who have become committed to living a more observant Jewish life are reinforced by opportunities afforded by diasporic community life in America. This, in turn, challenges the very foundation of a civil community, or perhaps more accurately reveals its grounding in ideas actually at odds with diversity and more in keeping with the harmonious and homogenous notion of community. The eruv, like certain symbolic practices among diasporic populations in many parts of Europe today (such as the French Muslim woman's wearing of a head-scarf), is often regarded as "foreign," hence inauthentic with regard to the larger civil community in which it finds itself. In these specific instances, these symbolic practices are used in a counter-hegemonic way, claiming space in a form that challenges the ideals of diversity. The eruv evokes an identity with a different past (not the past of America, New Jersey, or Tenafly, but the past of the Jewish nation) and a different space (the Holy Land). It superimposes a place on an existing place. Both are "imagined communities" (B. Anderson 1983) expressed in space. Secular Tenafly's community heritage, as represented by its eth-nically marked but visible historic houses, renders Tenafly's assimilated Jews "invisible" in a diverse community, because these houses have no ethnic designation, hence it denies the relevance of past origins for community membership. The establishment of an invisible structure, the eruv, however, renders Tenafly's Jews visible in that it draws atten-tion to the distinctiveness of Jewish practice—on the weekly Sabbath. The eruv pushes the limits of tolerance and diversity, revealing the fragility of a civil community just where civil society is most desirable—that is, where "cultural pluralism" is presumably the basis of the free-dom and openness that drew diverse peoples to the United States in earlier times and to its prosperous suburbs in the late twentieth cen-tury.

Notes

1. My account of the Tenafly eruv conflict is based primarily on legal docu-ments produced for the 2002 U.S. Court of Appeals for the Third Circuit hearing, and to a lesser extent on news media coverage and interviews with individual par-ticipants, whose identities I have not revealed, at their request. I have received helpful suggestions from Jonathan Boyarin and Samuel Heilman and a number of other readers, and assistance obtaining legal briefs from J. C. Salyer and others involved in the legal dispute. The opinions offered here, and any possible errors, are of course my own.

2. The importance of diaspora to Jewish identity has been the subject of many volumes of scholarly literature, much of it controversial. Jacob Neusner (1989) argues that Judaism as the religion of a people emerged during its first

codification under the direction of the returned Babylonian *exiles* (freed by Cyrus the Great and led by Ezra), whose interpretations came to dominate belief and practice; thus, from the start, it was characterized by a diasporic consciousness, as potentially competing beliefs and practices were suppressed. Repeated experiences of exile and diaspora reinforced this consciousness. Some today would argue that diaspora has become fundamental to Judaism and should be regarded as a positive trait—undertaken voluntarily rather than as something to be endured under duress—as a source of great moral and creative benefits (Boyarin and Boyarin 1993). But others, probably the majority even in the diaspora, would strongly reject this notion despite the great achievements of Jews in exile. Whatever one feels, it is undeniable that the theme of "otherness" is fundamental for Jews in their sacred texts, that being strangers among others is definitional, and that anxieties about the meaning of "home" are of great importance in Jewish lore, tradition, and cultural discourse.

3. Solomon Poll (1962) suggested that the elaboration of Jewish practice among Hasidim in Williamsburg, New York, an urban enclave, was the product of newfound prosperity in America.

4. This is a very common rationale for the existence of the eruv, but I have not been able to find any evidence to support the story, nor any documented history of the origins of the practice. The practice itself predates the Talmud and is elaborated in a tractate of the Talmud later on.

5. The word *eruv* is commonly translated as "mixture" or "amalgamation," referring to the amalgamation of public and "private," or domestic, space.

6. In this instance, the elaboration of the law leads to what Charlotte Fonrobert (2003) calls a rabbinic theory of neighborhood, in which the neighborhood becomes an extension of a household ("private space") and the household is defined specifically as a group of people who share food ownership and cohabit a space surrounded by walls.

7. Note that at this time, as in an earlier era, the Jews in Babylonia were clearly recognized by civil authorities as a diasporic enclave; this community preceded the cataclysmic Roman exile of the Jews, the emergence of rabbinic Judaism, and the process of written interpretation of Jewish law known as Talmud.

8. It is a requirement of Jewish law that if the eruv encloses non-Jews or nonpracticing Jews, their consent must be obtained and a nominal rent be paid to them for their part of the space within the eruv. The Tenafly Eruv Association had initially gone to the county for permission, which it obtained, which might have been sufficient for Jewish law, but the county had no authority over the public

thoroughfares within the borough itself. When the existence of the eruv plan was informally brought to the attention of the mayor, there began discussions that eventually led to more formal applications for permission and subsequent denials of permission, followed by a series of lawsuits.

9. There have been some conflicts, even some violent ones, among different sects of ultra-Orthodox Jews in the United States (specifically in New York) concerning eruvin, but I will not be concerned with these here.

10. In the case of Palo Alto, a well-publicized threat of a lawsuit against the town by an organized group of atheists also appeared to play a role in the reluctance of the town council to approve an eruv.

11. Had the London eruv been confined to the predominantly Jewish neighborhood of Golders Green, it seems unlikely that there would have been a quarrel. The eruv became a problem only when Orthodox Jews laid claim to territory outside the places customarily identified with Jews.

12. My colleague Jeff Osleeb (an urban geographer) and I researched, with three students, Lori Coppola, Wendy Ponte, and Nadine Brambilla, whether it is possible to detect, measure, and document such changes. Does the establishment of an eruv result in higher house or land prices within its borders? So far, we cannot document this fact in any straightforward way, although we have all heard anecdotally that higher real estate prices do occur after an eruv has been established. Local New Jersey newspapers carried alarming stories, such as one titled "Home Costs Soar in Clifton's Rosemawr," with a subheading "Enclave of Orthodox Jews Create Eruv, Spur Housing Demand" (*Herald News*, February 25, 2001). The article suggested that an influx of Orthodox Jews, attracted by the establishment of an eruv, accounted for an increase in housing prices. However, real estate prices soared everywhere in the region, perhaps across the entire country, at the same time, so it is hard to factor out an eruv as a primary or even minor cause.

13. According to the 2000 census, Palo Alto's median income was $98,447, although there was wide variation, ranging from $65,686 to $146,896; the upper ranges might predict conflict in Palo Alto, too.

14. The *New York Times* cites Chaim Book, the leader of the Tenafly Eruv Association, as saying, "We like the ability to socialize and interact with people other than us" (Purdy 2001:32).

15. It has been brought to my attention that some Americans resist the idea that in the contemporary United States, Jews are regarded as a "race" rather than simply a "religious group." Jews are not marked as "people of color," and unlike

"people of color," they have choices about whether and how much to adopt a "Jewish" identity. Nevertheless, the concept of Jewishness as an inherited trait is conspicuously evident in American public discourse. Public figures, such as former secretary of state Madeleine Albright, have discovered their genealogical Jewishness—yet one cannot be genealogically Methodist or Baptist. Further, one can be part Jewish, as one can be part Native American, but less easily part Catholic or part Muslim. Jewishness may or may not entail religious belief and practice, but it is, in American belief, an inherited trait.

16. Debates arose among Reform Jews over whether or not to revive certain ritual practices, such as the ritual bath (mikva); an older generation of Reform Jews saw the notion of revival of the abandoned practices as a betrayal of the basic principles of Reform Judaism. Younger Orthodox Jews also revived practices that their parents had abandoned. The split between the more traditionally observant and the rest appeared to widen during the 1990s.

17. Heilman (1976) suggests that contention over interpretation of authenticity and rigor of ritual practice has long been endemic among modern American Orthodox Jews and that it may be inherent in values that esteem ritual knowledge in an egalitarian social milieu.

8

A Debt to Society

Miranda Joseph

It is a commonplace to say that criminals pay a "debt to society" by spending time in prison. But this commonplace begs any number of questions: How is crime understood as a debt? Why is the debt to society (rather than, say, to a particular victim), and what is meant by society? How is responsibility for the debt assigned to a particular "criminal"? How has time become the general equivalent for crime?[1] The mode of accounting naturalized in this phrase has dire consequences: approximately two million people are currently incarcerated in the United States (a tenfold increase in the last thirty years), and those incarcerated include a disproportionate number of people of color, the poor, the uneducated.[2] In this essay, then, I want to begin to unpack this phrase and denaturalize the mode of accounting it presumes. And through a discussion of the accomplishments and limitations of the restorative justice movement, which accounts debts to *community* rather than *society*, I will also ask what other modes of accounting we might deploy.

We might take the use of the word "debt" in "a debt to society" to be a metaphor. But the link between debt and prison is by no means simply rhetorical. Or rather, the rhetorical link is not so simple. In the early modern period, defaulting on debt carried the threat of imprisonment or servitude (Mann 2002; Coleman 1974; Daniels 1995). And as I outline below, the abolition of debtors' prison was intimately related to the penal reforms that initiated the use of incarceration (rather than corporal punishment and execution) for criminals during the late eighteenth and early nineteenth centuries. Through an exploration of these related transformations, I suggest that both reforms depend on an emergent mode of accounting, which works to discipline subjects and constitute their creditworthiness (or lack thereof). The rhetorical link between debt and prison, between juridical and financial debt, lies in this mode of accounting, of representation, a mode that simultaneously constructs particularities and abstractions, writing particularizing facts and characteristics such that they form the basis for abstractions, for the reading of commonalities and equivalences.

In the final section, to begin to address the question of alternatives, I will examine the premises and goals of the restorative justice movement. Restorative justice is a diverse set of initiatives aimed at relocating criminal justice processes from "society" to "the community," recasting the debt of the "offender" as a debt to an individual victim rather than the state; I explore the extent to which this particularization of justice provides a useful intervention against the dominant mode of accounting.

In introducing the "provocations" that provide a common framework for this volume, Gerald Creed notes that the authors in this collection agreed that "while articulating discipline and accumulation, [community] nevertheless holds the promise of escape from the conditions of its own constitution" (chapter 1:12, this volume). In *Against the Romance of Community*, I put this idea somewhat differently, arguing that community has a "supplementary" relationship with capitalism: it both shores up capitalism and—this is where the "promise" might be— potentially supplants or displaces it. I also argued there that community has a hegemonic function, articulating the desire for that which is not capitalism with capitalism. That is, while one must take the desires driving deployments of community seriously as, at least in some cases, anticapitalist yearnings, the deployment of community generally co-opts those desires to create willing subjects of capital. My exploration of restorative justice will attempt to locate its moments of promise, even as my account suggests that those moments are rather quickly foreclosed.

DEBT AND THE DISCOURSE OF COMMUNITY

Both credit and incarceration have been written into what I have elsewhere identified as the romantic discourse of community, a discourse pervasive in the social science literature as well as in the popular imagination that situates community as the "other" of modernity and especially of capitalism, which is generally understood to destroy community. The development and expansion of credit and incarceration are explicitly seen to have participated in or at least to be symptomatic of the destruction of community, and community is often posited as a bulwark against the evils of indebtedness and incarceration. Mark Colvin, for instance, describes a decline of communal social control in the American colonial and early postcolonial periods as a precondition for the emergence of the penitentiary (1997:35–36); and David Garland argues that one aspect of "late modernity" that formed the context for the vast increases in incarceration of the late twentieth century was a loosening of "the grip of tradition, community, church and family upon the individual" (2001:89).

The inscription of credit into the romantic discourse of community turns on a story of a decline in interpersonal trust. Avram Taylor explicitly connects the history of credit with the discourse of community in his assessment of "the effect of credit on working class communities" and his attempt "to relate this to the debate about the decline of the working class community" in the post–World War II period in Britain (2002:2). He states that his theoretical perspective is based on "Weber's ideas about the rationalization of social life, Ferdinand Tönnies' notion of *Gemeinschaft* and *Gessellschaft*, as well as the more recent work of Anthony Giddens on the nature of modernity" (10), precisely the sociological tradition that elaborates the romantic narrative of community. While Taylor seeks to temper some of the starkest claims about the decline of community, he argues that forms of credit characteristic of prewar working-class communities, such as neighborly mutuality, corner store credit, and street lenders, which evidenced an "interpenetration of instrumental and affectual rationalities" (35), declined in the postwar period, replaced either by more impersonal forms of credit, demonstrating, he says, a decline in trust, or by forms of credit that instrumentalize affectual bonds.

However, precisely because credit requires (or in some accounts is) trust, and the story of the modern period is a story of nearly incredible increases in the sheer quantity of credit of all kinds, histories of credit necessarily become stories of the development of social formations as much as stories of the destruction of prior formations. Some versions of this story fit in quite well with the narrative of communal decline in that they describe a replacement of "interpersonal trust" with "system trust" (Luhmann 1979). Presuming that trust must be established on some basis beyond the transaction itself, they describe a shift in the location of that external basis from personal relationships to the state, corporations, and monetary systems. For instance, in *A Republic of Debtors*, a narrative of the emergence of bankruptcy law in the nineteenth-century United States, Bruce Mann attributes to economic expansion a rapid depersonalization of credit (through the invention of bills of exchange and other credit instruments that allowed owners of debt to be far removed from the original transaction and the original social relationship in which that transaction was embedded) and, in a sense, a destruction of social bonds as creditors turned to the courts and prisons to deal with debtors. In Mann's story, however, these social bonds are restored in a more depersonalized form through bankruptcy legislation, which allows debtors (of a certain class) to maintain, at least to some extent, their social position. Likewise, assessing the conditions that enable the development of "good" credit systems (through a comparative history of European nations), free market enthusiasts MacDonald and Gastman (2001:3) argue that the crucial factor is the development of third-party guarantors for impersonal credit relationships—that is, the ability of merchants to trust not each other but the rule of law and states as enforcers of contracts.

By contrast, in his history of credit in early modern England, Craig Muldrew takes issue with key pieces of Luhmann's argument. While Muldrew largely accepts Luhmann's contrast between preindustrial interpersonal trust and modern system trust, between what Muldrew calls "the early modern web of tangled interpersonal obligation" and "a utilitarian world in which a massive body of economic knowledge is used to operate systems which seek to reduce economic agency into predictable patterns of behavior" (1998:6), against Luhmann's functionalist presupposition that trust sustains credit relations, that it is a means for creating such structures, Muldrew argues instead that trust is the substance of social process itself, that it *is* credit (and vice versa). Where Luhmann argues that interpersonal trust is possible only in "simple" societies, Muldrew, noting the complexity of early modern English trade, suggests that interpersonal trust—precisely in the form of credit (which represents, indistinguishably, both reputation and economic ability)—is both possible and necessary even in relatively complex societies (1998:7).[3] In Muldrew's account, as the dramatic expansion of the economy extended social relations beyond their prior scope and thus required new management strategies, creditor-debtor relations were the medium—the language, the means of communication—through which social relations were negotiated and performed (5). In a recent essay on debt in contemporary Cameroon, Janet Roitman affirms this perspective. She argues that debt is not exterior to social relations, not something that is a "perversion or deviation" from normal social relations but a fundamental and constitutive social fact (2003:212). Thus she claims that attributions of credit and debt can be used to sustain or resist and transform social relations; she recognizes debt as a dynamic "mode of either affirming or denying sociability" (212). That is, while recognizing vast changes in social and economic relations, Muldrew's and Roitman's arguments point to the significance of interpersonal relations in modern, apparently depersonalized systems. Their arguments also suggest to me that we might see the "system trust" Luhmann describes not so much as abstract trust in a system but as a commitment to an "imagined community" (B. Anderson 1983).

MacDonald and Gastman acknowledge the centrality of the imagined community of the nation in their discussion of the creation of modern national credit systems:

> The process of nationalism, both the cause and the result of wars and imperial expansion, multiplied national debt and produced crises of public credit resolved through more nationalism and war, as well as the creation of a working public and private credit system capable of allowing the state to function and private enterprise to flourish. (2001:128)

In his discussion of "so-called Primitive Accumulation" in volume 1 of *Capital*, Marx likewise (though obviously from a very different perspective), notes the central role of nationalism:

> The only part of the so-called national wealth that actually enters into the collective possession of a modern nation is— the national debt....And with the rise of national debt-making, lack of faith in the national debt takes the place of the sin against the Holy Ghost, for which there is no forgiveness....The public debt becomes one of the most powerful levers of primitive accumulation. (1977 [1867]:919)

Rather than understanding the growth of credit as actually disintegrative of social bonds, we might understand the narrative of lost trust (of communal decline) as integral to the development of credit. To this effect, both Mary Poovey (1998:128) and Muldrew (1998:128) quote John Mellis (a sixteenth-century promoter of double-entry bookkeeping), who, according to Poovey:

> conjures a fictitious "time past" when a merchant's honesty could be signified by using a single phrase ["By the faith of a good faithfull merchant"] both to establish historical precedent for the prestige he now claims and to designate the present as a fallen or debased age, whose decay is signaled by the distrust now generally directed against merchants. (1998:41)

Poovey thus presents the narrative of lost trust and declining communality as a performance aimed at establishing creditworthiness. The deployment of this narrative to present a particular individual or group as an opportune site through which abstract capital might flow, simultaneously elides other transformative and constitutive social processes. It is not merely coincidental that this narrative is offered by a promoter of double-entry bookkeeping, which, as I will discuss below, Poovey describes as another crucial technique for performing creditworthiness. Despite, or rather precisely through, new modes of accounting— of knowing and constituting subjects—persons and their relations continue to play a crucial role in the circulation of credit.

As Marx's connection of national debt to "so-called primitive accumulation"—the "historical process of divorcing the producer from the means of production...written in the annals of mankind in letters of blood and fire" (1977 [1867]:875)—makes clear, the constitution of credit relations that are also social relations incorporates diverse subjects as unequal subjects of capitalism, of exploitation and domination. In her ethnographic study of midwestern farm loss in the 1980s and 1990s, Kate Dudley (2000) argues that while access to credit had everything to do with the reputation and family name of the recipient, with assessments of the farmer's character and work ethic, and while farm loss had everything to do with shifts in international markets and international relations, to a crash in the value of farmland and crop prices, farm losses were nonetheless accounted as a matter of personal responsibility by the farmer's friends and neighbors, who distanced themselves from the farm loser and bought up the farm loser's means of production (land, equipment, and so on) in the foreclosure auction. In his discussion of credit in early America, Mann similarly shows the central role of communal relations in constituting creditworthiness, while emphasizing the constitutive and transformative role of credit in communal relations:

> Not surprisingly, sureties [additional signatories to loans] almost invariably were friends or relatives of the debtors whose debts they warranted—suretyship rested on blood, affection and honor, not profit. Family ties not withstanding, by securing the express written promises that constituted commercial transactions, sureties were creatures of a commercial economy, not a traditional one. (2002:16)

When debtors failed, they put their families and friends at risk, often pulling them into insolvency: as Mann says, "Every suretyship was thus a potential creditor-debtor relationship, both between the original creditor and the surety, and between the surety and the original debtor" (2002:16). In both cases, foreclosure is not only an economic matter; communal relationships are likewise foreclosed. The moment of foreclosure, then, reveals that even while debt depends on communal relations it also constitutes the debtor as the individual liberal subject of capital and the state.

All the diverse strategies for what Spivak has called "credit-baiting"

(1994:237), at scales ranging from microcredit development programs to the proliferation of predatory mortgage lending, "payday" loans, and IMF lending to "developing" nations, might be said to depend upon or produce debtor-subjects whose racial, sexual, national, and class identities, and communal membership, are crucial to the transaction. That is, particular subjects and communities do not stand outside credit relations and thus do not provide protection from them. And insofar as debt constitutes debtors as liberal subjects, it functions as a lever for primitive accumulation. Rather than constructing romantic narratives of communal decline, in this view the urgent project is the assessment of particular regimes of accounting and the technologies, including communality, for constituting debtor and creditor subjects within such regimes. Such a project is a version of the one Nietzsche undertook when he investigated how man has been bred so as to have "*the right to make promises*," when he asked how man has become "*calculable, regular, necessary*, even in his own image of himself, [so as] to be able to stand security for his own future, which is what one who promises does!" (1989 [1887]:57–59).

As I undertake a critical examination of how man has been made creditworthy, or rather, subjected to debt as a dynamic "mode of affirming and denying sociability" (Roitman 2003:212), especially as it is deployed to create and sustain relations of exploitation and domination, the possibility of foreclosure gives me pause. While foreclosure might free the debtor from oppressive relations, if it entails the severing of social relations, a kind of social death or exile—and it certainly can entail such violence—then the objective of this critique cannot be to reject credit and debt per se, but rather, following Derrida, to ask:

> How to distinguish between two disadjustments, between the disjuncture of the unjust and the one that opens up the infinite asymmetry of the relation to the other, that is to say, the place of justice?…Not for law, for the calculation of restitution, the economy of vengeance and punishment…but for justice as incalculability of the gift and singularity of the an-economic ex-position to others. (1994:22–23)

To put this another way, if credit and debt are constitutive social facts, ways of affirming or denying sociability, then social relations turn on keeping the flow of credit open. But crucially, per Derrida, if this "credit," these social relations, is to be "ethical," meaning responsible to alterity, it cannot be accounted in a mode that aims at balance or could result in foreclosure. And thus my project must be to distinguish between modes of accounting rather than to reject accounting.

One answer to the lack (of knowledge of the future) produced in relation to credit in the early modern period was accounting. According to Poovey (1998:59), the newly invented double-entry book-keeping did not serve the function of actually rendering any sort of realistic account of one's assets. Rather it was a rhetorical strategy for demonstrating precision, accuracy, and balance (that is, a financial balance that made one appear creditworthy by eliding the crucial, unknowable element of whether one would be paid what one was owed). Poovey argues that double-entry bookkeeping created a precursor of what she calls "the modern fact"—a particular kind of particular that can stand as evidence for induced abstraction. That is, it required the subordination (and translation into numbers) of particulars (which seem to be privileged because they appeared to, but did not, refer to specific transactions in the world) to a formal system in which the particulars became meaningful (64). As a rhetorical strategy, "the balances produced by this system of writing proclaimed the credit-worthiness of the individual merchant; more generally, the system's formal coherence displayed the credibility of merchants as a group" (xvii). The argument was strengthened, Poovey suggests, by the fact that "for late sixteenth-century readers, the balance conjured up both the scales of justice and the symmetry of God's world" (54). But further, as a public and rule-bound system of writing, double-entry bookkeeping not only linked particular economic transactions to an abstract system, it also linked particular subjects to abstract subjectivity. Poovey argues that this system of accounting simultaneously disciplined those who participated in it and, by "making every writer who was willing to write to rule equivalent," anticipated, or began to create, "the universal human subject" (65).

The process of abstraction, the project of making particular things or people into bearers of abstract capital, is, as I've argued at length elsewhere, a difficult and ongoing one for capitalists (Joseph 2002:13–21). Here, I want to recognize (to learn from Poovey) that this process is in significant part an epistemological project. And as I will argue in the next section, the epistemological project of constituting particulars for the purpose of abstraction turns out to be a central technology for constituting subjects as differentially creditworthy bearers of not only abstract capital but also (and maybe indistinguishably) juridical credit and debt. That is, particularization differentially subjects (weds) various communal and individual subjects to the apparently abstract operations of criminal justice.

DEBT AND INCARCERATION

Starting in the 1790s in the United States, criminal justice reform movements instigated the replacement of corporal punishment with incarceration: these movements invented and built penitentiaries where criminals were imprisoned for "determinate sentences" (of time) and made to labor and pray on a highly regulated schedule, with the expectation that doing this time would uplift and reform the criminal (Colvin 1997; Meranze 1996; Beaumont and Tocqueville 1964 [1833]). These same movements worked for what we might call the decriminalization of debt—an end to imprisonment of debtors and ultimately the replacement of debtors' prison by bankruptcy law.

Foucault has argued that the shift in penal techniques can be described as a shift from the prioritization of sovereignty to the prioritization of discipline, a new governmentality that laid hold of the soul rather than the body (or rather, given the hard labor and physical brutality incorporated into the penitentiary, a new governmentality that laid hold of the soul in addition to the body). Discipline, according to Foucault, works through surveillance and examination, the constitution of the criminal as a text to be read and measured. Though the emergence of bankruptcy law in the United States came more than two hundred years after the invention of double-entry bookkeeping in England, I would nonetheless suggest that it was precisely submission to the disciplines of accounting and timeliness, to examination, that enabled debtors to separate their bodies from their debts. And in both cases, this examination was a double process of producing differentiating particulars, "facts," by constructing (writing) texts (such as the body of the criminal or the books of the debtor) and abstracting (is this reading or another writing?), such that the particulars articulated with general categories, general equivalents. The elaborations of these financial and juridical disciplines are, of course, not analogous but rather deeply intertwined processes, for as Foucault also points out, the new techniques of punishment were intertwined with a new "economy of illegalities," "restructured with the development of capitalism," such that the property crimes of the poor were subject to normal courts and punishments while the commercial crimes of the bourgeoisie were subject to "special legal institutions," "accommodations, reduced fines, etc." (1977:87), such as, we might add, bankruptcy law.

Penal reform movements in the United States were informed by what is retrospectively called classical criminology, and specifically by Cesare Beccaria's famous treatise *On Crimes and Punishments.* While the meaning of his text remains a matter of debate (Beirne 1994), he was and is a symbol for the "enlightenment" of criminal justice (Sherman 2003) and clearly articulates the procedure for subjecting particular individuals to abstract justice. Beccaria argues that society is established by social contract, that the laws embody that contract, and that punishment should exist only to dissuade people from usurping for private purposes the deposit of liberty that they and others have made in establishing the contract and thus the sovereignty of the state (1963 [1764]:11–12). He argues for "the rule of law," the establishment of general laws, applicable equally to all, by the legislature (14). He proposes that the role of judges is "to complete a perfect syllogism in which the major premise must be the general law; the minor, the action that conforms or does not conform to the law; and the conclusion, acquittal or punishment" (14–15), thus proposing precisely that particulars (particular crimes) are to be abstracted in order to be subject to the abstract law. While the role of the judge is to be limited to deduction, the process turns on the constitution of the minor premise of the syllogism (has the particular crime been committed?). Beccaria proposes an array of rules of evidence that interestingly seem not unlike the procedures for establishing creditworthiness through bookkeeping: he suggests the assembly of a variety of independent proofs or pieces of evidence that are adequate to persuade what has come to be called "the reasonable man" (20–21). In other words, like early double-entry bookkeeping, rather than providing an absolute accounting of assets or in this case facts, the accounting of evidence must perform a rhetorical function of persuasion.

However, with regard to certain crimes, accounting is not merely like evidence; it is evidence. Beccaria devotes a chapter of his text to debt, arguing that through "rigorous examination" "innocent bankrupts" should be distinguished from "fraudulent" ones. Those found to be innocent should not be punished but rather simply made to pay, or to work until they can pay. Meanwhile, he urges that frauds be prevented by laws that require "public and open registration of all contracts, and liberty for all citizens to consult the well-ordered documents, a public bank formed out of intelligently apportioned revenues...designed to provide timely financial assistance" (1963 [1764]: 78). For Beccaria, then, with regard to debt, the issue of criminality turns not on whether or not one is a debtor but rather on how one represents that debt.

In this context, it is interesting that, as Mann points out, the restoration of social bonds and social standing for debtors made possible by bankruptcy law was motivated by the incarceration of debtors who were also creditors—wealthy businessmen, not those who were indebted because they were poor. Meanwhile, the debtors argued against their imprisonment and tried to establish their social creditworthiness by distinguishing themselves from slaves and criminals. According to Mann, they mobilized "images of the absolute power of the creditor and of heartless creditors tearing families apart, images that require the reader only to substitute 'master' for 'creditor' to be transported into the world of plantation slavery" (2002:141); and further they claimed they were inappropriately treated as (or worse than) criminals. Mann quotes from *Forlorn Hope*, the prison newsletter published by Keteltas (1800):

> [W]hy should the state nourish and protect the violators of its institutions (*who are in that respect debtors to the public*) [by providing them food and clothing in penitentiaries, unlike debtors, who had to provide for themselves while incarcerated] and yet give up the necessitous man for a failure in a private contract? As the law now operates...it is a greater crime to run into debt, however fair the prospect of paying, than to rob a man on the highway, commit a rape or burn a house. (2002:105, italics added)

It appears that the distinction between criminal (fraudulent) debtors and innocent debtors turns not only on the representation of the debt through a financial accounting that can be subjected to "rigorous examination," as Beccaria suggests, but on a social accounting as well.

Meanwhile, just when bankruptcy law was finally and fully established for creditors (Mann's tale of the emergence of bankruptcy law concludes in the 1870s), the discipline of financial accounting and public contracts was applied to debtors of another sort with the aim of restoring their social position, but this time as slave labor. After the Civil War, freed slaves were subject to an array of laws that took advantage of the phrasing of the Thirteenth Amendment, which abolished slavery and involuntary servitude *"except as punishment for crime"* (Clarke 1998:110). Laws against vagrancy, which really criminalized unemployment, and against breaking labor contracts, which was a crime for blacks, a civil matter for whites, among others, reinscribed the obligation to labor under exploitative conditions (68–69, 178). Once found to be criminals for failing to fulfill these obligations, former slaves could be and were forced to labor (Colvin 1997). Direct leasing of convicts was one technique for putting convicts to work; another was criminal surety laws, which enabled whites to pay fines for convicted blacks, who then were obliged to work off their (involuntarily acquired) debts to those whites (Clarke 1998:112). And, of course, accounting was a means of re-enslavement not only through its deployment in criminal law but also in the context of sharecropping and tenant farming, which turned most black farmers into debt-peons (180–181). If, in the case of creditors, the "rigorous examination" associated with bankruptcy law enables the circulation of capital by staving off foreclosure (by determining that they are innocent bankrupts), in this case the circulation of capital is enabled precisely by foreclosure, of both the newly gained citizenship and the property rights of African Americans, who are, through the supplementation of financial accounting by social (racial) accounting, constituted as "fraudulent bankrupts."

Like Keteltas, Beccaria's understanding of crime more generally is that it involves a failure of social creditworthiness, that it is a violation of the social contract and social obligation, the reciprocity necessary to a healthy economy (Zeman 1981). It would seem that for Beccaria (and maybe for liberal criminal justice more generally), "a debt to society" is not incurred in the moment of a crime, but rather a crime is understood to have occurred when a failure, or active refusal, to maintain an ongoing debt, to fulfill obligations, is discerned, or when, as in the case of freed slaves, subjects are constituted as always already not credit-worthy.

Like Beccaria, Nietzsche diagnoses the modern social bond, the bond to the state, as a structure of permanent indebtedness:

> The feeling of guilt, of personal obligation, had its origin in the oldest and most primitive personal relationship, that between buyer and seller, creditor and debtor....The community, too, stands to its members in that same vital basic relation, that of the creditor to his debtors....The aim now is to preclude pessimistically, once and for all, the prospect of a final discharge...until at last the irredeemable debt gives rise to conception of irredeemable penance. (1989 [1887]: 70, 71, 91)

Where Beccaria attributes this indebtedness to a "contract," Nietzsche rejects such "sentimentalism," suggesting instead that "the welding of a hitherto unchecked and shapeless populace into a firm form was not only instituted by an act of violence but also carried to its conclusion by nothing but acts of violence" (1989 [1887]:86). That is, Nietzsche reminds us that the abstract liberal rule of law is the universalization of a particular, the particularity of the "master" (in Nietzsche's terms), and that the society sustained through abstract law is a divided hierarchical society. I've suggested above that we might read the so-called decline of communality associated with the elaboration of circuits and technologies of credit not as the replacement of interpersonal relations by systems but rather as the constitution of new social formations. Likewise, we might understand the so-called decline of communal social control (driven, per Colvin, by the very same economic development) and emergence of centralized and pervasive criminal justice practices—the Beccarian approach to law and the invention of the penitentiary—as the emergence of a new communality. On one hand, as Marx would argue, this new communality appears in the alienated and mystifying form of the liberal state, a form that, precisely through abstraction and the construction of equivalences ("the rule of law," the judge's syllogism), disavows the interested particular relations of civil society, those very social and economic interdependencies on which it is based. On the other, it is crucial to recognize that this new commu-

nality works not merely through abstraction but by a simultaneous particularization and abstraction that binds the particular subject to the
abstract, that enables the particular subject to function as the bearer of
abstract (liberal economic and political) subjectivity.

In this context, the invention of the penitentiary in the United
States, with its emphasis on labor and prayer, makes sense as an attempt
not only to extract payment but also to restore creditworthiness, to
enforce and instill the communal norms by which creditworthiness
is measured. Of course, such a project requires discerning, or rather
constituting, writing, the particularities by which creditworthiness is
established.

Foucault begins to trace the development of the technologies for
reading not merely the crime but the criminal—his "passions, instincts,
anomalies, infirmities, maladjustments, effects of environment and
heredity" (1977:17). And Leps (1990) follows up Foucault's work with
an account of the rise of positivist criminology. Their work suggests that
over the course of the nineteenth century, increasingly powerful epistemological tools were developed for writing and reading particularities such that particular people could be subjected to abstract justice.
The maturation of "the modern fact" enabled the identification of the
dangerous classes and their social contexts by visible, countable, and
statistically calculable traits. As a site of elaboration of social Darwinism
and eugenics, positivist criminology enabled not only the examination—quite literally the measurement—of the physical and moral fea-
tures of the individual criminal but also the reading of these particulars
as evidence of abstractions or generalities, as classed, raced, gendered
traits, as the product of unsanitary neighborhoods or hereditarily inferior families.

Foucault (1977:23) suggests that the new disciplinary apparatus,
which combined knowledge production with corrective punishment,
produced "individualization." But I would suggest that the process of
individualization is more dialectical than his account acknowledges:
criminology particularized the criminal, to a significant extent, not simply as an individual but as a member of a group, a race, a class, a neighborhood, a family. This attribution of communality did not, however,
displace the attribution, to abstract responsible individuals, of an
abstracted and calculated "debt to society," per Beccaria; rather, it

added to it, placing "criminals" in a double bind from which we have yet to extract them. The identification of social, racial, or gendered traits, for which presumably no individual can be held responsible, did not (and does not) prevent individuals from being sentenced—that is, still held individually responsible—to prison terms. Like the farmers Dudley describes, juridical subjects gain (or are denied) access to credit through a dynamic social accounting (an accounting that constitutes as much as it reflects social relations), even as, in the moment of foreclosure, we can see that they are also constituted as individual liberal subjects.[4]

Nietzsche points out that while punishment may have many purposes, it does not accomplish the purpose of interpellating subjects as social debtors: "[P]risons and penitentiaries are not the kind of hotbed in which this species of gnawing worm ["the feeling of guilt"] is likely to flourish" (1989 [1887]:81). By contrast, communality was and is deployed effectively to interpellate subjects as debtors to society. Family bonds or communal identities and commitments (communal debts) are appropriated to positively bind subjects to the circulation of state power (as they make willing subjects of capital [Joseph 2002:ch. 3]). The stigmatizing of familial and communal bonds and identities performed by criminology would seem to generate just the reverse— that is, communal membership as alienation from the state. Though the hegemonizing deployment of community is not apparent in criminology, as Zeman argues, criminology functions as a kind of mirror; so we can hypothesize that the criminalizing particularizations produced by criminology will be matched by positive particularizations such that visible performance of membership in the right race, the right family, the right class, brings social credit. Restorative justice, to which I will finally turn momentarily, by contrast with criminology, makes the hegemonizing process explicit; that is, it explicitly deploys communal obligation to induce willing subjection to the law. One might say it engages in a kind of credit-baiting.

ALTERNATIVE EPISTEMOLOGIES

Feminist and poststructuralist theorists have critiqued the social scientific methodology of induced abstraction, as well as the system of justice that operates through the calculation of debt. Various theorists have noted as a loss the loss of particularity in its reduction to abstraction, the ways that such reduction allows for calculation and the flow of capital, and the tendency of social scientists to deploy preexisting social categories as the categories into which particularities are abstracted, thus reaffirming existing social hierarchies.[5] At the same time, a great deal of political optimism has been placed on the deployment of antipositivist and anti-empirical epistemologies. Some have suggested that a focus on the singular or the narrative or the supplement might be (or reveal the ways those forms are) disruptive to the flows of capital and oppressive social classifications.[6] And certainly, it is crucial to seek out and attend to those moments in which abstraction must fail, where capital and power can't flow. However, as Derrida argues in *Given Time* (where he defines "the gift" as that which exceeds any economic circuit, precisely because it is annulled as a gift as soon as it is accounted or acknowledged),

> the overrunning of the circle by the gift, if there is any, does not lead to a simple, ineffable exteriority....It is this exteriority that sets the circle going, that puts the economy in motion....If one must *render an account* (to science, to reason, to philosophy, to the economy of meaning) of the circle effects in which a gift gets annulled, this account-rendering requires that one take into account that which while not simply belonging to the circle, engages in it and sets off its motion. (1992:30–31)

That is, if we hope to intervene, we need to attend to the ways the particular, the narrative, even the singular, enable abstraction and the circulation of power, knowledge, and capital, even as we recognize that something, something promising, escapes such accounts.

Recognizing the supplementarity of particularization and abstraction in the accounting of financial and criminal debt is useful because in each case both particularity and abstraction have been proposed as cures for the ills of the other. So with regard to the circulation of financial credit, redlining has been officially outlawed, even as the corner-store lender is nostalgically remembered as more humane than the contemporary credit card company (which exploits the poor not by denying them credit but by deliberately offering them credit).

Likewise, racial profiling is criticized, even as community policing and neighborhood watch programs, not to mention restorative justice, are promoted as re-creating long lost forms of local social control. If we understand that the circulation of abstract capital and the elaboration of the liberal state operate through a mode of accounting that simultaneously deploys abstraction and particularization, then we recognize that each is not likely to pose much of a barrier to the other, though we might hold out hope for an unaccountable excess of particularity.

Meanwhile, recognizing that accounting through processes of particularization and abstraction is a representational strategy, a performative act that constitutes creditworthiness by writing and reading, is also useful. The centrality of accounting suggests that epistemological interventions are possible, that alternative writings and readings might produce alternative particularizations and abstractions, might bind subjects differently or not at all. That is, without holding out for an unaccountable excess, we might take it upon ourselves to offer different accounts.

Restorative justice emerged in the 1970s but has gained substantial popularity in the last fifteen years or so. It is but one of an array of initiatives, such as community policing, community service sentences, and community justice, that explicitly invoke community as a key to (once again) reforming criminal justice. The restorative justice movement includes a dispersed and diverse array of initiatives taking place in New Zealand (where there is actually a national program) and in various locales in Australia, Britain, Canada, and the United States, including victim-offender mediation, family group conferencing, circle sentencing, and community reparative boards (Bazemore and Umbreit 2001). Contesting incarceration is not central to restorative justice rhetoric. Some of the sentences that emerge from restorative justice processes include time in prison; and John Braithwaite, author and editor of many books promoting restorative justice, proposes a "regulatory pyramid" (2002:31–32) that maintains incapacitating punishments as a final resort. However, restorative justice does claim to be a strategy for dramatically reducing the use of incarceration in that restorative justice processes more often result in financial restitution to the victim, community service orders, required participation in treatment programs, and apologies. For this reason, if for no other, it is worth giving restorative justice a serious and generous assessment.

And at least some advocates of restorative justice do claim to be making a profound critique of the whole framework of liberal criminal justice; in fact, the contrast between restorative justice and what they call retributive justice is often presented as a two-column list (Zehr 1990:184–185; Daly 2000:36).[7] They read liberal justice ("the justice paradigm," in Howard Zehr's terms) as focused on "retribution" and "revenge," in place of which they propose "healing" and ultimately the "reintegration" of the offender into the community. In place of the courtroom, where determinations of "what law was broken, who did it, and what do they deserve?" are made, they propose forums in which the determinations to be made are: "Who has been hurt?" "What are their needs?" and "Whose obligation are they?" In addition, "Instead of saying the state is the victim, restorative justice understands that communities and people are the victims, that real people are hurt" (NCCC 1996).[8] Where individual victims may or may not appear in court as witnesses, restorative justice gives individual victims (as well as offenders and community members) a central role and "voice" with the goal of offering "closure," which, restorative justice advocates claim, direct victims don't get through the existing criminal justice process. In place of assessing a debt to society, they propose a much more concrete form of debt paying that brings criminals and victims into direct interaction and accountability.

Advocates of restorative justice appear to have a Durkheimian perspective on criminal justice, which analyzes punishment as a ritual affirming social solidarity and social norms (Garland 1990). Whereas Foucault focuses on the emergence of the penitentiary as the most meaningful flashpoint in the history of punishment, advocates of restorative justice see the key moment as the establishment of the "king's peace," the "capture" of criminal justice from local communities by the state (Delgado 2000:755; Braithwaite 2002:5; Zehr 1990:115). They seem to see little difference between the strategies of sovereignty and discipline.[9] Where classical liberal criminology read (and reads) prior approaches to criminal justice as brutal and arbitrary, advocates of restorative justice idealize past modes, focusing on the centrality of shaming, fines, victim compensation, and social reintegration in a vast array of premodern and indigenous societies, rather than the centrality of corporal punishment and execution.[10] Crucially, while none of the contemporary sociological theories of criminal justice and punishment see crime control as the primary determinant of particular regimes of penality, advocates of restorative justice do see crime as the problem. They understand crime as a violation of social bonds that must be repaired (and sometimes as evidence of broken bonds).

Rejecting state control of criminal justice but reading crime as a violation of social bonds, advocates of restorative justice do not contest the assessment of debt but rather the abstraction of the creditor as society. In their accounting, the circuit of social obligation that crime violates is not the society bound by Beccaria's social contract, but rather family and community. Advocates suggest that the victim and offender, as well as a miscellany of others who might be present at a restorative justice process (social workers, teachers, police officers, the restorative justice facilitator), are members of a community. And family circle conferencing and circle sentencing require that victim and offender each be accompanied by family members and friends—their community (defined rather differently than it must be to include both victim, offender, and state functionaries). The offender and victim are required to tell their stories in the presence of these others, and it is through this storytelling that indebtedness is articulated: restorative justice advocates express the hope that in hearing the story of the victim, the offender will feel shame and remorse, offer an apology, and receive forgiveness. Kay Pranis, restorative justice planner for the Minnesota Department of Corrections, explicitly promotes the power of storytelling as a tool for building relationships and thus community (2001:6–8).[11]

Both the promise and limitations of restorative justice turn on what is enabled and foreclosed by this storytelling. The storytelling process is certainly an alternative to the Beccarian procedure of producing evidence and subjecting it to the judicial syllogism. And recognizing the faith placed in singularity and narrative by poststructuralist theorists, restorative justice's solicitation of singularity through a narrative form of accounting would seem to be a moment of promise. Barbara Hudson identifies just this promise, suggesting that

In terms of the critique of law posed by Derrida and other

deconstructionists, "justice" would be more closely approached [by restorative justice] than with a punitive system because the process would recognize the perpetrator and victim in their individuality rather than approximating the crime to a general legal category. (1998:241)[12]

But keeping in mind Derrida's articulation of justice, of the ethical relation, as "disadjustment," "asymmetry, "an-economic ex-position," the fulfillment of this promise would seem to depend on whether restorative justice processes aim at, or achieve, an open-ended relation of alterity, or whether they seek closure. The term "closure," in fact, figures prominently in restorative justice rhetoric (clearly borrowed from the victim's rights movement); and restorative justice does aim to achieve debt payment, restoration through restitution, a closing of accounts with regard to the immediate "crime" at hand. On the other hand, in aiming to restore community, it might in fact be understood to be seeking to open or reopen social relations, lines of credit as it were. Unfortunately, as I think will become clear, the credit relations aimed at here are more the permanent indebtedness, penance, and submission to norms of which Nietzsche writes than the responsibility to the (not fully knowable) "other" that Derrida invokes.

Some critics of and participants in restorative justice recognize that the intended closure might not be achieved because immediate communities (for example, families), as well as the larger community within which the offender and victim come together, are riven by power differences. Hudson's concern is that what will persist through and beyond the restorative justice ritual is not an open-ended ethical relation but rather a structural relation of domination. While advocates of restorative justice imagine that they can or should strive to create a Habermasian "ideal speech situation,"[13] she argues that in cases of racial or gendered violence (hate crimes, rape, and domestic violence), such an ideal cannot be achieved because the (white or male) offender has greater power than the victim (1998). Meanwhile, advocates do acknowledge that youthful offenders may not be comfortable speaking in the presence of adults; that differences of race, class, and gender might likewise impact the ability of participants to express their perspectives forcefully; that in bringing together families of young female offenders, it is crucial not to include adults at whose hands the young women may have suffered abuse; and that care should be taken not to simply "restore" existing gender hierarchies. In recognizing that the restoration of community might be a restoration of existing social hierarchies, the advocates would seem to reveal that the process itself is not informed by an adequate social analysis, a revelation confirmed by the fact that Braithwaite's answer to all such concerns is to place great faith in facilitators to deal with inequalities through careful selection and management of participants.

Others have expressed a concern (one that I share) not that the attempt to create (restore) community and achieve a Habermasian ideal speech situation might fail, but rather that it is a problematic goal. In "The Force of Community," George Pavlich reminds restorative justice advocates that "the quest for community has proved more than capable of unleashing an obsession with member purity, xenophobia, and an extreme focus on excluding traces of the 'other,' the 'strange,' and so on" (2001:59). Pavlich then recommends that restorative justice adopt a deconstructive conceptualization of community that focuses on "dissociation (rather than unity)" and that "requires all expressions of human solidarity to embrace the contingency of their limit formations" (59). That is, rather than taking either the internal unity of the community or its boundaries for granted, as somehow organic, Pavlich urges the active recognition of alterity within and a constant examination of the social processes that determine the identity of the community and its members. While Woolford and Ratner are concerned that Pavlich's proposal will produce only self-indulgent self-reflexivity (2003:187–188), it seems to me that we might take the imperative to examine constitutive social processes somewhat differently.

Restorative justice advocates might not seem to take community for granted insofar as their work assumes that communities are broken or violated. However, since they seem only to recognize the destructive role of modernity (capitalism and the liberal state) vis-à-vis community and not its constitutive role, there is a certain naturalization of community implicit (or sometimes explicit [see, for example, Pranis 1998: 1–2]) in their discourse. In proposing that power differences based on age, race, or gender can be addressed by ad hoc adjustments to participation, as well as in their pervasive use of the term community, restorative justice advocates would seem to specifically deny those constitutive social processes. As Ruth Morris (1996), advocate of transformative justice, argues, the restorative justice approach is easily co-optable by mainstream criminal justice because it accepts "the myth that problems in the world began with this offender" and ignores "structural injustice."[14] Not only are social formations such as race, gender, or class not addressed by ad hoc adjustments to the membership of a sentencing circle, but, as Delgado suggests, "such particularized mediation atomizes disputes, so that patterns, such as police abuse or the overcharging of black men, do not stand out readily" (2000:769). Delgado's apparent presumption that the mainstream criminal justice system will engage in what might be called "critical abstraction," the assembling of particulars to stand as evidence of systemic injustice, seems itself a bit optimistic; and, in fact, Angela Davis specifically contests the deployment of crime statistics, which she says renders "real human beings" "fetishistically exchangeable with their crimes in a seemingly race-neutral way" (1998:63).

However, it is crucial to note the potential for *critical* abstraction. As Hall elucidates in his reading of Marx's 1857 introduction to *Grundrisse*, Marx rejects abstraction in so far as it simply abstracts "'common' attributes" across historical particulars because that approach cannot enable us to "grasp, concretely, any single 'real historical stage of production'" (Hall 2003:120). Rather than rejecting abstraction altogether, Marx offers a different approach to abstraction. In this approach, any particular must be seen as a "complex concrete," defined as "a rich totality of many determinations and relations" (129). The apprehension of those "abstract determinations" and relations ("structural interconnections" [133]), the ability to "penetrat[e] behind the phenomenal forms of society to the hidden movements" (137), requires abstract thought, a deployment of abstractions that are themselves the products of history. For Hall, this last point, that the critical abstractions to be deployed are themselves the products of history, is crucial. For as Hall says, to read Marx "as if he is the theorist, solely, of the operation of 'a structure and its variations,' and not also and simultaneously, the theorist of its limit, interruption and transcendence [by history, in particular] is to transpose a dialectical analysis into a structural-functionalist one" (141).

It is just this kind of critical abstraction that is offered by the scholar-activists involved with Critical Resistance, a prison-abolition movement. For example, against the notion that there is a debt to be paid, Ruth Wilson Gilmore (1998–1999) argues that, viewed as a political economic phenomenon, the tenfold growth of the prison industrial complex over the last thirty years is not about extracting payment at all; rather, she proposes, prison is about excess. She maintains that the contemporary growth of the prison industrial complex is a "geographic solution to socio-economic problems," a response to a crisis of "surpluses of land, labor, finance capital and state capacity" (1998–1999:174). Her analysis has enabled the development of political alliances against the building of new prisons between those who are likely to be imprisoned and those who reside in the deindustrialized towns where prisons are meant to be built. Restorative justice seems unable and largely uninterested in generating this kind of knowledge. In fact, in particularizing too much, restorative justice might actually prevent the kinds of critical abstraction that Marx (and Hall) calls for.

In this vein, one might also wonder about the ability of restorative justice to address crimes that take place at a different scale, perpetrated by corporations or states against vast numbers of people (think of the Enron shareholders and employees). Braithwaite (2002), prepared to answer any complaint, proposes a form of restorative justice, which he calls responsive regulation, intended to address such situations. He suggests that even in the case of corporate criminals, it is more effective to hold them accountable in relation to moral standards articulated interpersonally than to hold them accountable to abstract laws and rules. While this may be true, Hudson's concern that the powerful carry their power into the restorative justice conference seems relevant here. And, in fact, given my account of bankruptcy law, it seems that we might not need to worry too much, in that restorative processes are already available to the creditworthy.

Meanwhile, despite its insistence on community, restorative justice does accept the abstract Beccarian social contract in that it accepts the validity of the laws that establish the initial positions of offender and victim; most restorative justice processes require that the offender has already been found guilty of or admitted to the crime. Braithwaite acknowledges this explicitly; and even as he urges that participation be managed to account for social inequality, he appears to be just as concerned that the facilitators manage the participants such that a "law abiding" consensus will outweigh any "law neutralizing" consensus that might be produced, if, say, too many of an offender's fellow gang members are present (2002:88–89). Pranis simply presumes that crime is there in proposing that community be mobilized against it (2001:4); and Daly, in arguing that restorative justice does (and should) actually include punishment, directly dismisses the notion that "the criminal justice system is unjust" (2000:40).[15]

The combination of accepting the legitimacy of the law and the crime while mobilizing family and community to repair the harm and reintegrate the offender lays bare the hegemonizing work of restorative justice. Although Braithwaite and, more persuasively, Woolford and Ratner (2003) do hold out the possibility that a circle conference might ultimately criticize the law that has been broken, it appears that in most cases the project is to mobilize communal commitments to parents and friends to provoke a commitment to obedience to abstract state law, despite the particularization of the state in the embodied victim (and the particularization of the punishment according to the consensus of the group). In fact, Braithwaite suggests that the presence of family members is crucial precisely because it might be one of them, rather than the offender, who feels shame in hearing the victim's story; and then it will be the relationship of the offender to his or her own family member that will motivate the desire to repair the harm through apology as well as more material forms of restitution (Daly 2000:43). Pranis argues that values and a sense of belonging are the most powerful forces in shaping behavior, that they function in the context of family and community, and that therefore family and community must be mobilized in response to crime (2001:4–5). In the approach proposed by Braithwaite, where incapacitating punishments such as incarceration are positioned as a last resort, the combination of a repressive state apparatus with an ideological state apparatus as described and criticized by Althusser is positively deployed (Walgrave 2000:170). Further, in deploying community to reaffirm the subject positions given by the law, the narrative possibilities—and thus the ethical possibilities—enabled by restorative justice are once again foreclosed.

A number of critics have, in effect, taken up Pavlich's suggestion and have examined the contingencies, the social processes, constituting this deployment of community. (Or one might say they have examined restorative justice as a "complex concrete" and have sought to grasp, critically, its abstract determinations.) Garland, for instance, has noted that the invocation of community in the context of criminal justice coincides precisely with the tenfold increase in incarceration in the United States and the emergence of law-and-order political regimes that have waged the "war on drugs," imposed mandatory sentencing, and eliminated rehabilitation programs over the last thirty years. He explains this coincidence by suggesting that both trends are aspects of an emerging "culture of control" that views crime as a problem of social control and seeks to mobilize public-private partnerships to "uphold restrictions and inculcate restraint" (2001:15). That is, families, communities, and nonprofit and for-profit nongovernmental organizations are mobilized to participate in social control (123). And as several critics point out, such a strategy clearly accords with the emphasis of neoliberalism on the privatization of state functions (Garland 2001:116–117; Lacey and Zedner 1995:310; Woolford and Ratner 2003:184–186). In other words, by situating restorative justice in the context of contemporary capitalism, and by using the Foucaultian analysis that advocates of restorative justice ignore, it becomes clear that, as in the case of financial credit and debt, in the context of juridical accounting the deployment of community does not effectively disrupt the circuits of power and capital.

In fact, it is precisely in the moments in which restorative justice deploys community—as a disavowal of structural inequalities, as a means of encouraging obedience to the law—that it is most likely to foreclose the very possibilities it opens. Its promise would seem to lie in the (im)possibilities offered by its inevitable failure to achieve its own goals of restitution and restoration, of community and closure. Counting on the (im)possibilities offered by inevitable failures as an intervention against the accounting that not only incarcerates too many people but also interpellates us all in domination and exploitation is a rather indirect approach. There is greater potential for political intervention in the deployment of critical abstraction than in the particularizing strategies deployed by restorative justice—but only if we recall that critical abstraction requires reading structures at their limit, as interrupted by the particularity of history and, maybe, community, understood not as the site of consensus or reparation but of credit, disadjustment, and alterity.

Notes

1. I do not take up the issue of time in this essay. The complexities of prison time, and the connection between prison time and the management of time through credit and debt, require a full-length essay of their own, one I hope to write in the near future.

2. In addition to the two million people incarcerated, approximately six million are under the noncustodial supervision of the criminal justice system. This fact has received far less attention from scholars and activists—and will not receive adequate attention here—although I think that any adequate critique of the contemporary criminal justice apparatus does need to account for its vast reach beyond prison walls.

3. As I discuss in chapter 5 of *Against the Romance of Community*, in *Trust*, Francis Fukuyama (1994) argues that trust is necessary to contemporary capitalism.

4. I do not have the space here to fully trace the history of criminology, but I should note that positivist criminology was supplanted in the twentieth century by a more sociological criminology that focused on criminal subcultures and social norming. While in this shift, the basis for identifying the communal particularity of the criminal shifted, the double bind appears to persist. In a late-1990s study of incarcerated female participants in a college-level educational program, Fine and others found that the women perceived proclaiming that they had become responsible individuals to be advantageous when attempting to gain the social credit they hoped would restore them as innocent rather than fraudulent bankrupts (Fine et al. 2001:13–18).

5. See, for example, Spivak (1994), J. W. Scott (1993), and A. Gordon (1997).

6. See, for example, Agamben (1993), A. Gordon (1997), and Bhabha (1994).

7. Daly presents the stark opposition between retributive and restorative justice offered by most proponents of restorative justice primarily to contest that opposition.

8. "Reintegration" is Braithwaite's term. Otherwise, all quotes in this passage are from the film *Restoring Justice* (NCCC 1996), in which Zehr is the principal narrator.

9. While the phrase "the king's peace" refers to the establishment of a criminal justice bureaucracy and centralization of power by William the Conqueror in eleventh-century Britain, preceding the emergence of the

penitentiary by centuries, in the United States the two flashpoints would appear to coincide; that is, the emergence of the centralized state necessary for the establishment of penitentiaries is narrated as corresponding to a breakdown of local social control and communal justice due to the expanding economy and greater geographic mobility of the late colonial and early postcolonial periods (Colvin 1997:32–46).

10. Their willingness to mobilize idealized examples from such a diverse array of cultures past and present should give one pause. See, for instance, the first few pages of Braithwaite (2002) and Zehr's (1990) chapter titled "Community Justice: The Historical Alternative."

11. Interestingly, storytelling is central not only to the process of restorative justice but also to the representation and promotion of restorative justice. Much of the restorative literature itself makes substantial use of stories to convey how restorative justice works: Braithwaite's book is full of boxes, each containing a narrative example; Zehr's book opens with a number of stories of restorative justice in action; even the U.S. Department of Justice bulletin prepared by Bazemore and Umbreit (2001) provides boxed sidebars as examples of each type of restorative justice.

12. Hudson makes an important mistake here, conflating "individuality" with "singularity." The category of the "individual" is inescapably tied to the dominant mode of accounting that Derrida rejects.

13. Braithwaite (2002:87–88) refers to Habermas in describing the goal and rewards of "undominated dialogue"; Pranis (2001:1–2) suggests that the consensus processes used are a new form of democracy.

14. Transformative justice, as proposed by Morris, is in many respects very similar to restorative justice in its shift from society and the state to community as the appropriate domain of justice and in that it "accepts the significance of the present act, validating the victim's wrong fully in the process." However, according to Morris (1996), "it goes on to examine and respond to the structural injustices in the life of the offender which contributed to the offense and need healing also if change is to occur."

15. The presumption of such a clear distinction between victim and offender is criticized by Alder (2000) in an essay on young female offenders that recognizes that many if not most young women who turn up as offenders have also been victimized.

9

Seeing Communities

Technologies of Visualization
in Conservation

Peter Brosius

At the beginning of the twenty-first century, as global environmental change proceeds at an unprecedented pace, conservation has become a central element in civic and political debates in the nations of both the North and the South. Responding to these debates, new forms of conservation practice are continually emerging. At the center of these debates is the concept of community. Indeed, tracking a parallel conversation in the field of development, one could summarize the last thirty years of conservation as an extended encounter between the community and its antinomies: the state, transnational conservation organizations, and other powerful agents. Topologies of conversation have continued to be discursively configured as efforts to mediate between these powerful agents and communities, expressed through any number of predicates (local, grassroots, "bottom-up," livelihood, culture, participation, "on the ground"). For the purposes at hand, I opt for an expansive notion of community that encompasses these predicates.

I want to frame my discussion of the idea of community within the context of these shifting discourses of conservation. A central premise of this volume is that the idea of community is never unproblematic. As several of the chapters illustrate, among the most persistent difficulties is arriving at a common understanding of how to even define this entity. My comments are premised on the idea that the difficulties we have faced in defining community are, first, a product of the fact that communities look very different from different locations or scales. As Donna Haraway (1991) and Neil Smith (1992) remind us, there is a politics of location and a politics of scale. Efforts to examine the nature of the idea of community, in specific contexts or in general, can thus only be productive when we acknowledge the multiscalar nature of our visions of this entity, and when we specify the scale, and the location, from which we see.

My purpose here, then, is to offer some comments about this association between representation and resolution by considering the relationship between *how* communities get constituted in conservation discourse and *who* does the constituting. I do so by examining a nascent set of strategies and practices being developed by major conservation organizations under the rubric ecoregional planning that increasingly place them in the position of viewing communities from "above."

My comments will proceed along a trajectory that tracks shifts in conservation practice in the past two decades. From the 1980s to the mid-1990s, we witnessed the proliferation of bottom-up models under the rubric community. In recent years, however, the "requiem for nature" argument has challenged the assumption that conservation and development are compatible, and we have witnessed a backlash that in some cases promotes coercive measures to achieve conservation goals (Oates 1999; Terborgh 1999; Wilshusen et al. 2002; Brechin and others 2002). Simultaneously, we have witnessed a broad-based reorientation of conservation organizations toward ecoregional approaches to conservation that obscure community.

I will consider each of these shifts in turn. I begin with a brief overview of my attempts, in collaboration with Anna Tsing and Charles Zerner, to address a series of key questions and concerns about community and conservation. Next, I briefly consider the backlash against such approaches that has appeared in recent years. I then examine some of the defining characteristics of one such response: the ecoregional approach to conservation. I trace the historical contours of its development both conceptually and institutionally, and I provide a series of examples. Finally, I show how ecoregional approaches are deeply imbricated with the emerging field of conservation finance.

What interests me about this shift toward ecoregional conservation is the potential it has to reconfigure our notions of the local. This cartographically enabled priority-setting approach, promulgated by large transnational conservation organizations, is based upon a series of visualization methods designed to make natural and cultural communities legible. In invoking the idea of legibility, I am drawing on the work of James Scott (1998), for whom legibility—achieved through a series of "state simplifications" designed to reduce the opacity of the local—is the "central problem of statecraft." It is also the central problem of conservation. What concerns me is how the forms of knowledge such approaches produce overwrite the specificities of location by all the visualizing techniques and structures of accountability that accompany ecoregional conservation.

COMMUNITY-BASED APPROACHES TO CONSERVATION

Various models of conservation incorporate, or claim to incorporate, the needs and priorities of local communities under the rubrics community-based conservation (CBC), community-based natural resource management (CBNRM), and other participatory, livelihood, or stakeholder-based approaches.[1] As Brosius, Tsing, and Zerner observe, such approaches

> are based on the premises that local populations have a greater interest in the sustainable use of resources than does the state or distant corporate managers; that local communities are more cognizant of the intricacies of local ecological processes and practices; and that they are more able to effectively manage those resources through local or "traditional" forms of access. In insisting on the link between environmental degradation and social inequity, and by providing a concrete scheme for action in the form of the CBNRM model, NGOs and their allies have sought to bring

about a fundamental rethinking of the issue of how the goals of conservation and effective resource management can be linked to the search for social justice for historically marginalized peoples. (1998:158)

These models have a history. In part they emerged in response to a steady series of critiques, primarily by southern (that is "Third World") intellectuals and activists, aimed originally at international agencies concerned with development and increasingly with the larger project of "sustainable development." They also resulted from the work of practitioners such as Robert Chambers (1983) and Michael Cernea (1985), reacting against the waste and inequity of traditional development project research, design, and implementation.

In the conservation realm, advocacy for community must be seen in the context of a series of other panaceas being proposed in the late 1980s and early 1990s: extractive reserves, debt-for-nature swaps, and the like. Through the advocacy of figures such as Janis Alcorn and Grazia Borrini-Feyerabend, a consensus began to emerge (in some quarters at least) that top-down approaches to conservation were likely to be successful only in limited cases, that conservation biology alone was inadequate as an exclusive framework for the development of conservation paradigms and initiatives, and that conservation organizations must make every effort to foster meaningful community participation in conservation and resource management. By the mid-1990s, in a variety of guises, community-based approaches to conservation had become established as the norm, and so-called ICDPs (integrated conservation and development projects) proliferated rapidly (Brown and Wyckoff-Baird 1993).

At a time when many donors, NGOs, conservation practitioners, and indigenous advocates were lauding the emancipatory potential for community-based approaches to conservation and resource management, Zerner, Tsing, and I felt there were "potentially problematic legal, political, and cultural complexities embedded in community-based programs" (Brosius, Tsing, and Zerner 1998:159) that were not being addressed. We were concerned that "both advocates and analysts must remain alert to the contested and changing variety of cultural and political agendas and contexts in which these programs are being imagined or implemented" (159). Several key questions have guided our efforts:

> Can CBNRM reconcile the goals of social justice and environmental sustainability? What opportunities for democratization and for effective environmental management does CBNRM offer? What are the possibilities that CBNRM may be appropriated or manipulated by actors whose interests are antithetical to the goals of social justice and environmental sustainability: multilateral financial institutions, national governments, or private sector interests? What potential problems exist for civil society and citizenship when CBNRM movements are linked to initiatives based on ethnicity and territory? What are the consequences when generalized models of CBNRM are inserted into specific contexts without attention to history, power relationships, or the politics of implementation? (Tsing, Brosius, and Zerner 1999:197)

We were especially concerned with three ways in which the emancipatory potential of CBC/CBNRM might be compromised. First, there was the broad question of how communities get constituted in conservation discourse. In this regard, we were concerned with the issue of "genericization": the model-building and "scaling-up" efforts of advocates and donors, we felt, "can too easily become embroiled in implementing management regimes in which concepts such as *community, territory, rights, resources, management, indigenous,* and *traditional* are used generically without regard to local contests and wide-ranging political stakes in these terms" (Brosius, Tsing, and Zerner 1998:159). Second, we were concerned with the potential for community-based initiatives to be coercive while being discursively configured as civil, consultative, participatory, and democratic: a form of political homeopathy (to paraphrase Wendy Kaminer) that prescribes or allows small, well-regulated doses of dissent as a way of circumscribing and constraining more substantive challenges to these projects. Seen from this perspective, "participation" represents a regime of civility intended to contain and domesticate dissent by creating a somewhat inauthentic "place at the table." Finally, we were concerned about what we perceived as a growing divergence in advocate and scholarly projects for understanding the situation of marginalized communities: advocates have found concepts of *indigenous, community, custom, tradition,* and *rights* useful in promoting possibilities for local empowerment in national and transnational policy discussions, while scholars have become increasingly aware of the fragility, mutability, hybridity, and political variability of these concepts. While some advocates are concerned about the political consequences of deconstructionist scholarly agendas, some scholars are concerned about the potential political and legal consequences of community-based advocacy programs in which rights to territory, resources and governance are linked to concepts of ethnicity, space, and indigenous identities. (Brosius, Tsing, and Zerner 1998:159)

What we did not anticipate in raising these issues was that a backlash was brewing among conservation biologists and practitioners against participatory or community-based approaches to conservation.

NARRATIVES OF URGENCY AND THE BACKLASH AGAINST COMMUNITY-BASED CONSERVATION

The biodiversity crisis narrative has a very long genealogy, exemplified in the work of figures such as Norman Myers (1979) and E. O. Wilson (1988),[2] and current expressions of urgency are an extension of this genealogy. John Terborgh notes that we are currently facing "the prospect of biological Armageddon" (1999:123). Soulé and Terborgh describe "a world in pieces" and warn that "each isolated remnant of nature is caught in a tightening tourniquet of civilization" (1999:12). They tell us that "humanity is alarmingly fecund: there are too many mouths to feed and too many dreams unrealized. And the ideological enemies of conservation will not rest until the last vestiges of creation are 'improved'" (x). The not-so-indirect implication is that the clock of biological extinction is ticking, and that even if our methods are imperfect, there is no time left to delay.

This sense of urgency about the state of global biodiversity must be viewed in relation to a series of conservation initiatives that are perceived as having failed. In the last two decades, we have witnessed a series of solutions—debt-for-nature swaps, extractive reserves, bio-prospecting, and others—proposed to supplement the protected area paradigm. Foremost among these proposed solutions have been the community-based approaches previously discussed. While all alternatives have come in for criticism by conservation biologists in recent years, by far the most ardent criticisms have been leveled at community-based conservation. Indeed, one could characterize the present mood as nothing short of a backlash (Brechin et al. 2002; Wilshusen et al. 2002).

Many conservation biologists feel that the emphasis on participation, development, and equity dilutes the main goal of conservation: saving species and habitats. What most concerns critics of CBC/CBNRM is that conservation organizations have allowed donors to shape their agendas. Terborgh (1999:164), for instance, criticizes the way the availability of funding from USAID led conservation organizations to embrace ICDPs. John Oates argues that the embrace of conservation with development by conservation organizations occurred "out of political and financial expediency, and particularly out of the desire to tap into the large sums of money becoming available from international development-aid organizations" (1999:xvii). Critics are unsparing in their condemnation of conservation organizations that have embraced community-based conservation. Terborgh argues:

> When conservation organizations begin to advocate sustainable use of tropical forests, it is a signal that conservation is on the run. Starting down the slippery road to sustainable use is stepping back from that crucial line in the sand that defines one's beliefs and principles. Sustainable use represents a gray zone where politics, economics, and social pressures, not science, decide what is good for humans, with scarcely a nod to nature. (1999:140)

Likewise, Soulé and Terborgh assert that "today it is evident that the effort to protect life on earth is failing—despite all the outpouring of feel-good news releases about sustainable development, integrated conservation and development, community-based conservation, ecosystem management, and sustainable forest management" (1999:4). Oates describes community-based approaches as an "alternative romantic myth" (1999:xi) and argues that "there are serious flaws in the theory that wildlife can best be conserved through promoting human economic development. It is a powerful myth that has made all those involved in its formulation feel good" (xv).

With this critique have come calls for a return to more authoritarian, top-down approaches: what Peluso (1993) has termed "coercive conservation." Oates, for example, calls for a return to the "reserve concept" and advocates "strong policing" to safeguard protected areas (1999:239–240). The most ardent proponent of authoritarian conservation is Terborgh, who advocates "building a bulwark of security around the last remnants of tropical nature" (1999:17) and believes that "a national parks agency with the best of intentions remains powerless without the backing of those who carry the guns" (163). According to Terborgh,

> The focus of conservation must therefore return to the make-it-or-break-it issue of actively protecting parks, a matter that hinges above all on the quality of enforcement. Active protection of parks requires a top-down approach because enforcement is invariably in the hands of police and other armed forces that respond only to orders from their commanders. (1999:170)

Terborgh further advocates the creation of "internationally financed elite forces within countries...legally authorized to carry arms and make arrests" (199).

DEFINING ECOREGIONAL CONSERVATION

In the last five years we have witnessed a decisive move away from community and participation as unifying principles of conservation and toward cartographically enabled priority-setting approaches. Foremost among these is ecoregional conservation planning. David Olson and his colleagues define ecoregions as "relatively large units of land containing a distinct assemblage of natural communities and species, with boundaries that approximate the original extent of natural communities prior to major land-use change" (Olson et al. 2001:933).

While the backlash against community-based conservation need not necessarily lead in the direction of ecoregional conservation, there is a degree of complementarity between them with respect to defining a successor project to community-based conservation, especially as a strategy to increase funding for conservation: ecoregional conservation is, after all, first and foremost concerned with identifying and prioritizing places for protection. This complementarity becomes evident in the agenda set out by Soulé and Terborgh. They describe the impetus for the founding of the Wildlands Project (cofounded by former Earth First! activist Mike Foreman) in the following terms:

> Tired of being on the losing side of this sad game of endless appeals, compromise, and attrition a group of conservation scientists and activists met in November 1991 to design a more effective way to protect nature, wilderness, and biodiversity. The principal rule of this approach is to honestly and boldly say what is required to save living nature in North America—how much land is required, where it is, and how the implementation should be phased over the coming decades. (Soulé and Terborgh 1999:xi)

The speed at which ecoregional conservation initiatives are proliferating today is nothing short of phenomenal, and making sense of this proliferation is a daunting task. Such initiatives are being undertaken by conservation organizations large and small, with the help of individual donors, large foundations, national governments, and multilateral banks. Different organizations have developed their own in-house strategic conservation planning initiatives: each employs its own methodological principles, and each is in the process of producing its own proprietary databases. One encounters a maze of idiosyncratic terminologies and acronyms and a dizzying array of emerging and shifting actors, organizations, and networks. In spite of efforts to achieve some sort of commensurability in the products of these initiatives, the issue of incommensurability looms large. In short, in the domain of ecoregional conservation, it is a time of Babel.

The task of succinctly defining ecoregional conservation is made difficult by the fact that so many actors and institutions have been involved. A considerable degree of diversity exists in what different organizations stress, and developments in this approach continue apace. Much of this paradigm is as yet unpublished or exists only in the gray literature. Nevertheless, one can discern several general characteristics of this emerging paradigm.

First, ecoregional conservation entails an effort to envision conservation at a larger scale than in the past: at the level of region, continent, or earth as a whole. In the past, conservation was largely focused on identifying and delineating discrete places for protection.[3] Ecoregional conservation seeks to move beyond the protected area paradigm because, conservation scientists increasingly believe, the focus on protected areas is too localized and does not provide a broad or representative enough perspective for the development of effective conservation strategies. More than simply enlarging scale, ecoregional conservation seeks to develop models that allow practitioners to "select conservation targets at multiple spatial scales and multiple levels of biological organization" (Nature Conservancy 2000:3–1). This approach allows planners to link conservation planning at the ecoregional scale with localized reserve design initiatives.

Second, ecoregional conservation approaches rely on powerful cartographic technologies, particularly the development of GIS databases from remote sensing imagery. This process allows for the development of multiple data layers that can incorporate information on the distribution of species and habitats, rates of disturbance, land tenure arrangements, political boundaries, and other types of data relevant to conservation planning. Such cartographic methods also have strategic value in allowing conservation organizations to produce compelling, visually exuberant images of regions and locations targeted for conservation. Associated with this advance, recent years have seen the development and application of a series of powerful algorithms that, linked with cartographic data, can be used for conservation forecasting, planning, and reserve selection. These technologies also provide the foundation for a kind of cartographic involution, in which finer and more detailed data "can be continually incorporated into a database that can be continually improved as new data are acquired" (Olson et al. 2001:936).

Third, ecoregional approaches expand not only the *spatial* scale for envisioning conservation but the *temporal* scale as well. That is, they provide practitioners with the means to approach conservation *strategi-*

cally. Ecoregional maps are *planning tools,* allowing conservation practitioners to establish *priorities* for future conservation investments. The emerging literature on ecoregional conservation presents the approach as an improvement over conventional "reactive" conservation, in which protected areas are established on an ad hoc basis leading to a "fragmented systems of parks and reserves in which some elements of the native biota are over-represented and others are not represented at all" (Soulé and Terborgh 1999:1). According to Terborgh, "Conservation emergencies…are the stuff of fund-raising campaigns, but they don't add up to a coherent plan for saving nature" (Terborgh 1999:8). Ecoregional conservation, then, provides a "proactive" approach to biodiversity planning (Environmental News Network 2001:1)

Fourth, ecoregional approaches are deeply imbricated with advances in the science of conservation biology. The scientific principles developed by conservation biologists have become part of the fabric of a proactive approach to conservation at extended spatial and temporal scales. Virtually all the conservation organizations that have adopted this approach stress that their efforts are firmly grounded in, and guided by, science. Conservation biology, which only began to emerge in the late 1970s (Terborgh 1999:17), is a relatively young discipline. The Nature Conservancy (TNC) did not hire its first scientist until the early 1970s, and then only to do biological inventory (Nature Conservancy 2000:1–1). Since its inception, conservation biology has been dedicated to using the conceptual tools of biology and ecology to further the instrumental goal of conservation. Its initial focus was to understand the biological significance of specific sites or species and to devise strategies to conserve them. However, a number of advances led to recognition of the need to think about conservation at a larger scale.

An important precursor was the work of MacArthur and Wilson (1967), which according to Noss "got many scientists and conservationists thinking seriously about the effects of habitat area and isolation on population persistence and species diversity" (2002:13). Another precursor was Richard Forman's work in landscape ecology, which focused on "factors that determine species distributions and abundances across large areas" (Noss 2002:13). Also notable were findings that demonstrated the role of top predators as a controlling influence "in the...maintenance of biodiversity" (Terborgh et al. 1999:40), which pointed to the need to consider the "habitat requirements of keystone species" (Soulé and Terborgh 1999:10) in the design of regional conservation networks. Conservation biologists increasingly recognized that habitat fragmentation was a major threat to the preservation of biodiversity. Additional insights into patterns of extinction compelled conservation biologists to expand the temporal scale of their assessments of threat, leading to calls for the preservation of larger areas and the establishment of corridors between protected areas.[4] Much work remains, and theoretical developments continue apace with attention to diversity indices, dynamic population models, and the long-term effects of global climate change, among other things.

Fifth, a salient characteristic of ecoregional conservation is the degree to which the production of maps is guided by biological rather than political criteria. In part, this process is simply a function of scale: as the scale of vision is enlarged, boundaries are increasingly likely to get crossed. It is also a product of the recognition that "the distribution of species and communities rarely coincides with political units" (Olson et al. 2001:937). As Terborgh argues, "Biodiversity transcends national boundaries and belongs to no one" (1999:198). This is not to say that conservation biologists consider political boundaries to be irrelevant—merely secondary. It is worth asking what the consequences are when, to quote Olson and Dinerstein, "The analysis of social, political, economic or cultural data is best brought into the analysis *after* the biological priorities have been determined" (1997).

Two recent conservation initiatives exemplify the shift to ecoregional conservation: the World Wildlife Fund's Global 200 and the Nature Conservancy's Conservation by Design. The Global 200 is an initiative undertaken by the WWF Conservation Science Program to identify "the Earth's most biologically outstanding terrestrial, freshwater and marine habitats" (Olson et al. 2000). Primarily the brainchild of David Olson and Eric Dinerstein, the Global 200 follows earlier efforts by WWF to undertake regional analyses, most notably the 1995 conservation assessment of Latin America and the Caribbean (Dinerstein et al. 1995). The Global 200 is based on a "representation approach." This approach recognizes a hierarchy of scales at which to encompass global biodiversity: three realms (terrestrial, freshwater, marine), fourteen major habitat types or MHTs (for instance, boreal forests and taiga, flooded grasslands and savannas), unique biogeographic realms (for instance, Afrotropical, Nearctic), and 238 ecoregions (hence the Global 200).

As Olson and others note, "Most conservation biologists recognize that although we cannot save everything, we should at least ensure that all ecosystem and habitat types are represented within regional conservation strategies" (2000:2). As significant as what is considered in identifying the 238 ecoregions of the Global 200 is what is not considered. According to Olson and others, "We did not use ecological function, conservation feasibility (that is, political, social, economic, cultural factors), or human utility as discriminators to identify the Global 200.... We reiterate that *The Global 200* is focused on biological values as the critical first step in setting global conservation priorities" (5–6). Olson and others characterize the initiative as "a map guiding conservation investments so that a comprehensive plan eventually can be achieved by the global conservation community and the world's nations" (21). They recognize that this is a very tall order but argue that "the widespread destruction of the Earth's biodiversity occurring today must be matched by a response on an order of magnitude greater than currently exists. *The Global 200* provides a necessarily ambitious template for a global conservation strategy" (21).

The Nature Conservancy's strategic vision for ecoregional conservation is termed Conservation by Design. A recent TNC publication described the genealogy of this vision as follows:

> Historically, ecological systems were seen as static and predictable, with biodiversity viewed largely in terms of species richness and rarity. The Nature Conservancy's early conservation approach reflected this view, evolving from one of opportunism during its formative years in the 1950s and '60s to the strategic acquisition of preserves for rare species and communities during the 1970s and '80s. However, because of the complex and dynamic nature of natural systems, current scientific thinking emphasizes the need to conserve biodiversity at multiple scales within an ecosystem or landscape context, along with the ecological processes that sustain it. (Poiani and Richter n.d.)

According to TNC president Steven McCormick, Conservation by Design

> directs us to systematically identify the array of places around the globe that embrace the full spectrum of the Earth's natural diversity; to develop the most effective strategies to achieve tangible, lasting results; and to work collaboratively to catalyze action at a scale great enough to ensure the survival of entire ecosystems. (Nature Conservancy 2001:1)

Conservation by Design is defined as a "portfolio approach" dedicated to conserving "portfolios of functional conservation areas within and across ecoregions" (Nature Conservancy 2001:4). It is premised on four core concepts: (1) ecoregions; (2) ecological systems; (3) functional conservation areas; and (4) functional landscapes. In identifying ecoregions as a core concept, TNC is asserting that "ecoregions, not political boundaries, provide a framework for capturing ecological and genetic variation in biodiversity across a full range of environmental gradients." Ecological systems are groups

> of interconnected natural communities...that are linked together by ecological processes. Primary emphasis in portfolio design will be placed on conserving the highest quality examples of ecological systems and second, on viable populations of native species not captured within these ecological systems. (Nature Conservancy 2001:4)

Functional conservation areas range in scale from specific sites to landscapes and can encompass a range of levels of biological complexity, from single species to entire ecological systems. Functional landscapes "represent particularly effective and efficient geographical units for conserving biodiversity [that are]...Large, complex, multi-scale, and relatively intact" (Nature Conservancy 2001:4).

As with other major conservation organizations engaged in developing and promoting ecoregional conservation initiatives, TNC places considerable emphasis on measuring the success of its efforts. This work includes providing quantitative measures of success both in the maintenance of "biodiversity health" and in threat abatement. Further, TNC seeks to provide more general measures of organizational performance overall (Nature Conservancy 2001:8–9).

INSTITUTIONAL OPPORTUNITIES AND ENTANGLEMENTS: ECOREGIONAL CONSERVATION AND FINANCE

It would be a mistake to assume that the history of ecoregional conservation could be told only with reference to its technical and scientific foundations, or even with reference to the conceptual and ideological shifts within conservation circles. The history of ecoregional conservation is also the history of institutions, which became aware of the possibilities it presented for attracting donor support. In the pursuit of sustained funding, expressions of urgency are no longer enough. Conservation organizations need to give *shape* to that urgency and demonstrate that they are guided by a strategic vision that will allow them to direct their efforts effectively and efficiently in the task of saving nature. Donors demand not only strategic visions but also structures of accountability and ways of measuring the success of initiatives they fund. Ecoregional conservation provides all these and more: a complete package. As an enterprise dedicated to visualizing and prioritizing places for protection, and in providing both a coherent vision and a set of powerful tools, it moves conservation away from the domain of crisis-response and toward that of strategic management. This approach has enormous appeal to donors, and it has shaped the way conservation organizations now go about their work.

The point here is that only when the paradigm of protection and preservation, informed by conservation biology, became linked with the impetus to articulate strategic organizational goals did ecoregional planning emerge as a successor project to community-based conservation and become central to the vision of major conservation organizations. Thus in the last few years conservation organizations have become increasingly concerned with the development of vision statements and strategic plans as a way of attracting donor funding. In developing comprehensive packages such as the Global 200 and Conservation by Design, they have employed methods equivalent in many respects to what in the world of marketing is known as branding.

Understanding the reorientation of major conservation organizations toward ecoregional approaches to conservation requires that we recognize the ways in which these organizations have reshaped both their broad strategic visions and the practices that characterize their work so as to attract donor support. One manifestation of this process is the recent emergence of the field of conservation finance. I am not prepared here to offer a comprehensive history of conservation finance: it is a history that is yet to be told and a history still very much in the making.[5]

Recognition of the need for innovative ways to finance conservation is not in itself a new thing. In the late 1980s, Tom Lovejoy proposed the idea of "debt-for-nature swaps," a considerable number of which were subsequently negotiated by WWF and other conservation organizations. In the early 1990s, we witnessed the introduction of conservation trust funds, some forty of which have been established to date. Around the same time, we saw a series of proposed market-based approaches: certification schemes and the like. In short, several elements of a conservation finance approach have been around for more than a decade, but it is only in the last couple of years that we have seen this process coalesce into a coherent new subfield intended both to bring all these approaches into a single frame of reference and to develop new approaches. Several factors have played a role in the development of conservation finance as a field.

One such development was the founding of the Global Environment Facility (GEF) following the 1992 Rio Summit. A partnership between United Nations Development Program (UNDP), United Nations Economic Program (UNEP), and the World Bank, the GEF over the last ten years has made large amounts of funding available for biodiversity conservation. Along with funding, the GEF has demanded rigorous standards of accountability, and it promotes a series of so-called monitoring and evaluation tools to assist in the task. The use of such tools has now become virtually obligatory in contemporary conservation programs, even those with no links to GEF funding. To a much greater degree than before, major conservation organizations have been compelled to apply such tools to measure the success of their efforts.

Another factor in the development of conservation finance has been the growth of the "new philanthropy." The greater the percentage of revenues that conservation organizations devote to fund-raising, the lower their rating by organizations that track and evaluate philanthropy. As a result, major conservation organizations have tended to redirect their fund-raising efforts from expensive mass mailings toward a smaller number of wealthy corporate and individual donors or family foundations. Like the GEF, corporate donors are not satisfied with lofty conservation goals and good intentions: they demand measurable results of success for projects they fund. And increasingly, individual donors and family foundations are just as demanding. Many donors targeted by conservation organizations represent a new generation of entrepreneurs who made their fortunes in the 1990s high-tech economy. As one TNC development officer explained to me, many of these individuals want to be directly involved with the projects they fund, and as self-made entrepreneurs, they are much more "hardheaded and businesslike in their expectations" of conservation outcomes. They want to see measurable results.

The emergence of ecoregional conservation models has simultaneously raised estimates of the cost of preserving biodiversity, provided a compelling justification for the need to invest so much, and provided the institutional structures to "capture" and administer the funds necessary to do the job. Given these three developments, conservation organizations, along with many donors who support them, increasingly have come to recognize the need to think about funding for conservation in fundamentally new ways. This process has taken a number of different forms, but the end result has been the emergence of conservation finance as a distinct enterprise. In the last few years we have seen the publication of a number of in-house reports and how-to manuals on conservation finance (Bayon, Lovink, and Veening 2000; Cohen, Maguire, and Kloss 2001; Phillips 2000; WWF 2001), along with the creation of organizational initiatives, alliances, and special funds. Allow me to briefly provide three examples.

As one of the largest conservation organizations, WWF has long been a major conservation fund-raiser. For instance, over a period of three years, from 1999 to 2001, its Living Planet Campaign raised some $177 million. A significant portion of this money came from some 2,800 individual "Partners in Conservation." While such capital campaigns will continue to be a centerpiece of conservation fund-raising, they are only part of the story. In June 2000, WWF founded its Center for Conservation Finance (CCF), dedicated to building "the next generation of conservation-finance models—models that can be replicated in every corner of the world" (WWF 2002b). In defining its mission, the CCF web site notes:

> One of the greatest challenges facing global conservation is

the overwhelming lack of resources for funding long-term comprehensive programs. This challenge becomes all the more daunting as WWF and its partners pioneer large-scale, ecoregion-based conservation efforts that demand correspondingly large investments. (WWF 2002a)

WWF cites as an example its involvement in a project to protect 10 percent of the Brazilian Amazon, requiring an investment of some $280 million.

In pursuit of its vision, WWF hired a number of financial experts from multilateral banks and top Wall Street investment firms: Goldman Sachs, J. P. Morgan, and others. These individuals are working to develop a series of innovative financial instruments—environmental taxes, conservation easements, trading systems, environmental investment funds, and others—to "generate conservation capital" and "leverage money for the environment."

Yet another example of this shift is the Conservation Finance Alliance (CFA), a partnership between TNC, the Wildlife Conservation Society, Conservation International, the World Conservation Union, Ramsar, and the World Bank. Established in early 2002, the CFA is still very much in the formative stage. It was created "to catalyze increased and sustainable public and private financing for biodiversity conservation to support the effective implementation of Multilateral Environment Agreements...and other commitments to conservation" (CFA 2002). As part of its preliminary program of action, CFA is presently engaged in an effort to "map conservation funding supply and demand" and to establish a "Conservation Finance Communication Strategy" stressing the importance of "sustainable conservation financing to key audiences" (Maguire 2002:1).

Finally, yet another manifestation of the emergence of conservation finance is the Critical Ecosystem Partnership Fund (CEPF), an initiative of Conservation International, GEF, and the World Bank. The aim of the CEPF is "to invest at least $150 million over the next five years to advance biodiversity conservation projects in critical ecosystems that harbor the richest variety of life" (CEPF 2001b). What distinguishes this fund from other sources of support for conservation is that each expenditure is guided by an "ecosystem profile" that combines conventional threat assessments with "assessments of investment that is already taking place. The analysis identifies investment gaps, leveraging opportunities, and broad strategic funding directions for the CEPF" (CEPF 2001a).

One of the most significant entailments of conservation finance is its impact on how conservation is both conceptualized and administered. That is, it represents an attempt to shift conservation discourse away from romantic, scientific, or crisis narratives and toward a discourse of investment. To some extent, this process is a function of the fact that conservation finance has adopted some of the valorizing strategies of ecological economics; forests and other ecosystems are "natural capital" that provide "ecological services." But the approach goes well beyond that. The thoroughgoing adoption of investment discourse represents an effort to fundamentally reframe the conservation enterprise in neoliberal terms.

This shift is especially evident in WWF's Center for Conservation Finance initiative. The key document produced by the CCF is framed through its very title as a "business plan," though we are warned in the front that "This document is not a prospectus or offering document. Words or expressions such as 'investment,' 'broker,' and other financial terminology are used metaphorically...they do not imply that your contribution to protecting the environment's future will generate profit or financial gain" (WWF 2001:ii). With this proviso, we are introduced to the CCF as an "entrepreneurial program" of WWF. CCF employers are "critical human capital," individual donors are "clients" or "venture philanthropists," and a review of the center's activities is labeled "Product Descriptions." The overall purpose of this document is to construct conservation finance as an investment (indeed, the word "investment" is italicized in every instance of usage in this document) and WWF as a broker: "WWF has earned an international reputation as an honest, trusted, and forward-thinking conservation broker" (5). In describing its marketing strategy, the business plan notes that "the Center's parent, WWF, allows it to capitalize on the organization's worldwide reputation and globally recognized panda logo and trademarks" (14). In a 2000 article on conservation philanthropy in *Barron's*, WWF's new approach was described in the context of the aforementioned effort to protect 10 percent of the Amazon: "The WWF set out to make the Amazon project look like an investment, one that provided financial assurances and measurable outcomes" (Alderman 2000:P23). WWF's Private Sector Advisory Task Force subsequently began establishing "procedures that will ensure the Amazon project meets blue chip investment standards," identifying "five key areas that need to be addressed: business planning, financial controls, disclosure and reporting to donors, management structure and asset management" (Alderman 2000:P23).

WWF is not alone in promulgating this discursive shift. Recall that TNC's Conservation by Design is described as a "portfolio approach" to conservation. In the Critical Ecosystem Partnership Fund, Conser-vation International (CI) "serves as Fund manager, ensuring quality and accountability. In addition, CI develops ecosystem profiles to guide investments and supervises regional Hotspot alliances created through the fund" (CEPF 2001b). In reference to its "biodiversity conservation investments" in the context of the CEPF, CI "seeks investors who would like to contribute to this innovative funding mechanism" (CEPF 2001b). The Conservation Finance Alliance promotes "the application of a *business approach* toward financing protected areas." This approach "uses— quite deliberately—the language of business, employing such terms as 'products,' 'goods and services,' 'customers' and 'marketing.' The idea is to encourage PA managers to see their job, in part, as running a business" (Cohen, Maguire, and Kloss 2001). This statement is followed by a proviso that the use of a business approach is merely a means to an end and should not displace the core value of conservation. Likewise, a World Conservation Union document published by the World Commission on Protected Areas promotes a business approach in the pursuit of "sustainable finance." Among other things, this approach entails "defining relevant customers and identifying ways of capturing a fair return from them" (Phillips 2000:5). Key to this approach is the identification and cultivation of protected area "customer groups." In a section entitled "Managing Customer Groups," the reader is informed of four categories of customer: neighbors and residents; commercial customers, including visitors; bioregional customers; and global customers (13). "Protected area managers need to 'service' both their public customers and their private customers, and receive a fair return from both through appropriate financial mechanisms" (12). Further, "A financial plan requires the protected area manager to know who the customers of his or her protected area are, and how their interests might be captured so as to provide financial support to the area" (21).

One critical tangible effect of this discursive shift is that measuring the success of conservation investments has become absolutely obligatory. This process has been going on in conservation for some time, but the increasing centrality of conservation finance invests it with additional momentum. Thus we observe "monitoring and evaluation" (M&E) becoming a central component of nearly every major conservation initiative, along with the emergence of a cadre of specialists to coordinate and administer these measures and enforce standards of accountability. This process has important implications for how conservation is conceptualized, planned, and administered.

One of my purposes in juxtaposing ecoregional conservation and conservation finance is to show that they are not unrelated. Beyond the simple fact that conservation finance is often framed as a necessary entailment of ecoregional conservation, it is possible to discern several forms of complementarity between them. There is first a strong discursive complementarity: the narratives of long-term planning, priority setting, the management of "portfolios" of both protected areas and funds, and M&E situate both these developments within the same discursive frame. Second, there is a kind of strategic complementarity in the sense that ecoregional initiatives, viewed as exercises in branding, provide a locus around which to both justify and structure large conservation investment packages. Finally, there is a broader complementarity that aligns ecoregional conservation and conservation finance with national and transnational neoliberal development agendas. To the extent that ecoregional conservation initiatives become an extension of the spatializing practices of the state, achieved in conjunction with financial instruments developed in partnership with multilateral development banks, it becomes difficult to distinguish where conservation ends and neoliberalism begins.[6]

DISCUSSION: COMMUNITIES AND ECOREGIONS

Conservation initiatives take shape because certain places, or the species that inhabit them, are perceived to be at risk. What lies behind this deceptively simple observation is a series of questions concerning how and by whom such perceptions of risk are formed. Posing such questions is all the more critical today because of the shifts in the theory and practice of conservation I have described here. My purpose has been to provide a genealogy of ecoregional conservation, as well as an account of the assumptions that underlie it and the practices that have come to define it. As I have shown, ecoregional conservation and allied projects such as conservation finance must be located within the context of a long series of shifts that have moved through conservation discourse over time; that have at times invoked, and at other times effaced, histories of human presence in the landscape. What ecoregional conservation represents is nothing less than a new regime of enclosure, and the consequences of this development are anything but trivial. The comprehensive vision it promotes, the tools it deploys in pursuit of that vision, the proprietary databases it produces, and the emerging complementarities of spatial planning and investment have the potential to reshape the contours of the relationship between humanity and nature for generations to come. It therefore behooves us to carefully consider what is at stake, and for whom, in this proliferation of efforts to classify and map the ecoregions of the world, to establish a set of comprehensive blueprints for the future of the planet, and to forge a new discursive order linking conservation and finance. What I would like to do now is lay out some elements for thinking about ecoregional conservation, and consider a series of questions regarding its prospects and its potential.

If we have learned one thing over the last several years, it is that maps and other technologies of visualization have the potential to be both emancipatory and reactionary. As Sousa Santos argues, "Ours is not a simple moment of oppression and victims; it is a moment of a double crisis of regulation and emancipation" (1998:531). And Sachs asks, is ecology "about to transform itself from a knowledge of opposition to a knowledge of domination...reshaped as expert neutral knowledge, until it can be wedded to the dominating world view?" (1993:xv). Put another way, are we witnessing the emergence of a parallel to what Scott termed "state simplifications" that "enable much of the reality they depict to be remade" (J. C. Scott 1998:3)? Are we then, in our critiques, developing "a case against the imperialism of high-modernist, planned social order" (6) that is "calculated to make the terrain, its products, and its workforce more legible—and hence manipulable—from above and from the center" (2)? As Scott argues, "The clarity of the high-modernist optic is due to its resolute singularity. Its simplifying fiction is that, for any activity or process that comes under its scrutiny, there is only one thing going on" (347). At what point do organizations engaged in ecoregional conservation become agents of "homogenization, uniformity, grids, and heroic simplification" (8)? Taking another tack, David Harvey has drawn on Hajer's ideas about "ecological modernization" to argue that

> the authoritarian solution [to environmental problems] rests upon the application of techniques of scientific-technical rationality within an administrative state armed with strong regulatory and bureaucratic powers in liaison with "big" science and big corporate capital. The centerpiece of the argument here is that our definition of many ecological problems...is necessarily science led and that solutions equally depend upon the mobilization of scientific expertise and corporate technological skills embedded within a rational...process of political-economic decision-making. (1996: 177–178)

One could cite any number of similar such statements of concern about regimes of environmental governmentality, and such concerns are quite valid. However, there is another side to this argument that cannot easily be dismissed. In opposition to the preceding, one could argue that ecoregional conservation initiatives can be viewed as a kind of counter-mapping exercise against extractive forms of resource use.[7] Given the low value conventionally afforded biodiversity (Bayon, Lovink, and Veening 2000), is it not a good idea to use the "master's tools" to preserve it? Is it not better that maps, financial instruments, and other such embodiments of power be directed toward the protection of biodiversity rather than enriching the shareholders and CEOs of extractive industries? In a world characterized increasingly by corporate hegemony, don't we want organizations like WWF and TNC to be more powerful? Conservation is expensive, and becoming more so all the time. We should not expect conservation organizations to be effective if they cannot compete in domains where power and influence are unapologetically exercised as a matter of course. As Soulé and Terborgh argue,

> Maps stimulate desires—for territory, for natural resources, for real estate development, even for conservation. Therefore the ideology of those who produce land-use maps is important. If developers are the only people mapping the land's future use, then they control the land-use agenda....If maps are the agenda, then conservationists must enter the mapping arena....Such maps must be honest, scientifically rigorous, and inspiring so that the hegemony of the growth myth can be offset by the notion that the long-term interests of society are well served by a sufficient system of protected areas. (1999:13–14)

Are we, then, merely stuck with a conundrum here, or can we somehow analyze our way out of this? I'm not sure. But I do think that we can at least try to move beyond generalized statements of concern about the politics of legibility and high-modernist ecology, and perhaps try to specify a bit more precisely what is at stake in the recent turn toward the place-making (and place-effacing) practices of ecoregional conservation planning. I see five issues that might be productively addressed.

The first concerns what might be termed the assertion of cartographic naturalism. By this I suggest that those who produce ecoregional maps take them to be unmediated representations of biophysical reality. For example, the description of one ecoregional initiative on the Nature Conservancy web site is labeled "When Nature Draws the Maps."[8] Likewise, the Wildlife Conservation Society describes its Living Landscapes initiative as setting "priorities for conservation by looking through the eyes of wildlife."[9] The many strategic mediations involved in the making of ecoregional maps, each subject to extensive commentary by their designers—decisions about scale, biogeographical boundaries, and "potential natural vegetation"—are made to disappear in the final product, which is then taken to represent the actual or potential natural state of the world.

This situation in turn leads us to consider a second issue: the problem of the effacement of history when ecoregional maps overwrite human presence in the landscape. This process is achieved several ways. One is through the aforementioned cartographic privileging of natural boundaries over political boundaries. Another is the overwriting of human use of the environment in the production of both maps and the strategic plans they generate, whether in the guise of land classification categories, assumptions about "potential natural vegetation," "rewilding," or the establishment of corridors. Reflect, for example, on the implications for local populations of the "Congo Basin Wilderness Area," as depicted in a Conservation International "hotspots" map, an area currently inhabited by many millions of people (Diane Russell, pers. comm., November 28, 2001). Another form of effacement is the coding of people as threats. What happens when all the cartographic and algorithmic visualizing power I have described is turned on the assessment of threat, and "disturbed" establishes itself as a stand-in for "inhabited"? Each of these issues raises the question of how assumptions about human communities become coded or elided cartographically in ecoregional maps, and how this in turn produces capillary processes of power by which visualizations are transferred from map to ground. Of particular interest to me is how such methods produce topologies for environmental intervention while distancing "bioplanners" from the human effects of their interventions.

The third issue I see arising from the turn to ecoregional conservation relates to what Neil Smith (1992) has called the "politics of scale." As Smith notes, "The theory of geographical scale—more correctly the theory of the production of geographical scale—is grossly underdeveloped." In spite of substantial progress in the ten years since Smith's article appeared, we have some way to go in understanding the intersections of environmental discourses and the politics of scale. Of course, as I have shown, ecoregional conservation is fundamentally about scale, both enlarging the scale of environmental interventions and linking information created at different scales into a single strategic blueprint for the future at an extended temporal scale. Scale, then, is more than "a purely technical matter" (Harvey 1996:203). All the talk we hear about ecoregions, mega-reserves, mega-transects, conservation priorities, and the strategic management of conservation portfolios should lead us to question how spatial and temporal scales are constructed and legitimized in the domain of ecoregional conservation. What, for instance, is the relationship between findings in conservation biology regarding the significance of keystone predators in top-down ecological processes and assertions of the importance of top-down models of environmental management suggested by the ecoregional conservation paradigm?

Fourth, regarding the relation between ecoregional conservation and conservation finance, we must continue to ask: What becomes of nature when biodiversity is coded as "natural capital" or as "comparative advantage" (Bayon, Lovink, and Veening 2000)? What are the implications when those who claim to speak for nature refer to themselves as "conservation brokers"? And what are the implications for local communities when conservation organizations must provide tangible measures of the success of their investments over three-year funding cycles? When conservation organizations must be more accountable to "investors," do they not become less accountable to local communities? The concerns of those of us who take discourse seriously are not put to rest by assurances that all this language of capital and finance is mere metaphor. All the codings and elisions I have described have instrumental effects that cannot be easily dismissed.

Finally, it is worthwhile to consider how the proliferation of ecoregional conservation initiatives and databases have led, following Bruno Latour, to the creation of a series of closely linked "centers of calculation" (Latour 1988). As noted, we are living in a time of environmental enclosure, and the enclosures being produced are emerging from a series of proprietary maps and databases designed and constructed by a relatively small number of practitioners in the North, mostly in the United States. As one proponent of ecoregional conservation remarked to me, somewhat tongue in cheek, "The future of the planet is being mapped out by about seven guys in Washington D.C." We have much to learn about how ecoregional conservation initiatives move out—already made—from this center of calculation, through the circuits and networks of national and transnational conservation organizations, national governments, donors, and beyond. What is at stake here is echoed in Hardt and Negri's *Empire*:

> What we are witnessing is a new planetary order, the consolidation of its administrative machine, and the production of new hierarchies of command over global space. Who will decide on the definitions of justice and order across the expanse of this totality in the course of its process of consti-

tution?...Who will be able to unify the process of suspending history and call this suspension just? (2000:19)

I began this essay by suggesting that communities may look very different depending on the location and scale from which they are seen, and by arguing that efforts to examine the nature of the idea of community can be productive only when we acknowledge the multiscalar nature of our visions of this entity. My broader goal in the foregoing discussion has been to pose a series of questions about this relation between representation and resolution. I have, in a sense, been trying to understand the consequences for the analysis of community when we look at them not, as we are accustomed to, from "the ground," but through a universalizing, pixilated global optic from on high. Certainly this process has important implications for the ability of conservation practitioners to hear local voices, perceive local realities, and take account of local particularity in the design and implementation of conservation initiatives. Equally consequential, however, such technologies of visualization entail broader structures of intervention, structures of accountability, and structures of deference. They thus have the potential to transfigure the contours of power in novel ways—ways we cannot yet imagine. If these developments were provoked, even in small measure, by the failures of community-based conservation efforts, which in turn can be attributed partially to idealistic assumptions about "community," then we have a powerful illustration of the need to pay more analytical attention to the concept.

Notes

1. See Brosius, Tsing, and Zerner 1998; Kemf 1993; Lynch and Talbot 1995; McNeely 1995; Pye-Smith, Borrini-Feyerabend, and Sandbrook 1994; Stevens 1997; Western and Wright 1994.

2. One could, of course, trace the narrative of environmental crisis back much further. Here I refer to those instances in which environmental threat is coded specifically as a biodiversity crisis.

3. The genealogy of ecoregional conservation must be written against a backdrop of advances in cartographic technologies and methodologies for visualizing space at different scales of resolution. The conceptual basis for an ecoregional approach lay in a series of maps and methods developed between the

1960s and 1980s, most notably by Robert Bailey of the U.S. Forest Service (Bailey 1998) and James Omernik, who produced a 1987 ecoregional map of the United States for the EPA (Omernik 1987). Subsequently, Reed Noss developed a "regional landscape approach" (Noss 1983), and Michael Scott developed the "gap analysis" approach, "a process by which species and natural communities not adequately represented in conservation lands are identified" (Scott and Jennings 1998:37). These maps and methods became the basis for further developments in ecoregional conservation.

4. Conservation International's effort to designate biodiversity "hotspots"—a term originally coined by Norman Myers and subsequently promoted by Russ Mittermeier—was one such response, and was accompanied by a proliferation of approaches that stressed the need to integrate core areas, corridors, and buffer zones in the design of protected areas; the MAB Biosphere Reserve concept is the most prominent such approach.

5. It is worth noting that many conservationists consider increased levels of funding by large donors to be deeply problematic. Oates, for instance, complains that "much of international conservation has come to operate as a business" (1999:236), and he worries that this infusion of money has corrupted conservation organizations' vision (237). Likewise, Terborgh argues that large conservation organizations have become "prisoners of the bottom line" (1999:8).

6. Ecoregional conservation lends itself to a neoliberal agenda in other ways as well. William Wolmer of the University of Sussex has examined linked transboundary protected area and regional economic integration initiatives in southern Africa (Wolmer 2002). Wolmer describes the South African government's Spatial Development Initiative, intended to establish development corridors for private sector investment, in conjunction with a broader regional planning initiative. In the years ahead, observers of contemporary conservation should keep track of this development of integration of biodiversity conservation with regional economic integration.

7. One might cite here the case of former USGS employee Ian Thomas, who was fired by the Bush administration in 2001 for posting USGS-produced maps of caribou calving grounds in the vicinity of the Arctic National Wildlife Refuge on the USGS Web site.

8. http://nature.org/wherewework/northamerica/states/idaho/science/art423.html

9. http://wcs.org/8190

10

The Politics of Community

Some Notes from India

Gyanendra Pandey

It will be clear by now just how unstable the conceptual terrain of community is. The contributors to this volume decided to approach this conceptual instability, or ambiguity, not so much by mapping the diverse meanings of the term as by exploring the different circumstances in which the idea of community has been deployed and by critiquing the history of its production and use in different contexts.

Earlier chapters have shown that with all its slipperiness, community acts as a powerful code word in the organization of contemporary society. Almost always, the expression evokes a place, a group of people, and a feeling (see chapter 1, this volume). Obviously, the notion of place has been modified considerably by such constellations as diasporic communities (Khan and Lees, this volume), the community of cricket lovers, or indeed the international working class. In its Indian usage, as is well known, the term most commonly refers to religious community. It is frequently applied to regional or linguistic communities, sometimes to castes or caste conglomerations, but rarely to the nation. It may also be used to refer to women (but not men), to the poor (although the category seems to have disappeared from much of the reigning discourse), to rich teenagers (to cite a recent example), to beggars, lepers, and unemployed youth, and of course to other groups identified by local residence, occupation, or interest.

Some of these examples would seem to trouble Raymond Williams's famous characterization of community as a "warmly persuasive word" that "[u]nlike all other terms of social organization (*state, nation, society,* and so on)...seems never to be used unfavourably" (1976:76). Nevertheless, something of that claim—or feeling—remains, and it is perhaps this texture, or feel, that gives the idea of community its unusual place in the history of modern times.

Yet the notion of community has clearly performed other functions as well. In much colonial and some postcolonial writing, for instance, it served as a marker of the primitive, or at least the premodern, as I shall try to show later in this essay. Again, one may take a rather different example from a body of work with which I have been closely associated. In critiques of the narrative of capital and of authorized histories of the nation-state, such as those presented in *Subaltern Studies,* community has been used to focus an alternative domain—or locus—of power. Within *Subaltern Studies* itself, notions of community, and the work that the word does, have changed over time. It may help to spell out these changes very briefly to underline my point about the very different uses of the concept of community in different contexts.

In the examination of the general problem of politics and the state in a large agrarian society, earlier writings in *Subaltern Studies* began with a proposition about the availability—or persistence—of a "communal" mode of power, distinguished by the priority of a collective bond, in which individual and sectional interests derive from this prior collectivity. It was suggested that this communal mode existed alongside the rather better known "feudal" and "bourgeois" modes of power, the one characterized by a frequent use of physical force to ensure domination, the other by consultative procedures including (at its peak) the establishment of authority through institutions of representative government (see Chatterjee 1983). It was the imbrication of these different kinds of politics, these writers claimed, that made for the specificity of politics in the subaltern domain—and by extension of the politics of the anticolonial struggle as a whole.

Several major changes have occurred since the days of the early *Subaltern Studies*—in South Asia as well as in the analytical priorities of students of South Asia. For one thing, there is now a much more significant (and powerful) urban section in the society than there was even two decades ago. At the same time, and in part because of the efficacy of those earlier critiques, we have seen a disappearance (or at least a considerable weakening) of the "transition" narrative—and with that, for reasons that have to do with the whole history of our times, the disappearance (or weakening) of the belief in a self-evident revolutionary class. Finally, this same period has seen the emergence of the "problem" of secularism, at any rate as a theoretical issue—the problem, in other words, of the recognition and representation of "difference."

Recently, a great deal of critical scholarship on South Asia has engaged the question of secularism—with the description of the fragile, unstable, shifting character of people's multiple community affiliations (that is, of the diverse, overlapping, converging, or polarizing assemblages, networks, solidarities, and aspirations they inhabit), and with the projection of this multiplicity and changeability as the ground for conversation or negotiation between and among different communities, as well as between communities and the state.

What should be apparent, even from these brief remarks, is the underlying question of the politics that always, necessarily, goes with the deployment of community—not only in the "real" world "out there" but also in our academic deliberations. With that as background, let me move to a closer examination of the concept as it appears in a variety of intellectual/political discourses in colonial and postcolonial India.

Probably the first point to be made is that in South Asia, the notion of community is crucially implicated in, if not constituted by, the project of modernity, and more specifically nationhood. Through the nineteenth and twentieth centuries on the subcontinent, community—and the idea of community—is constructed in the course of the assembling of the "modern": the state, nation, history. It is produced in the very same operation, at the same time, as a necessary condition of the birth and advance of modernity, even as it is produced as a singular and substantive entity that is seen as being both primordial and antiquated—a relic of history.

In a sense, of course, this is what happens not only in India/South Asia but also in Europe, the so-called cradle of modernity (see Creed, chapter 2, this volume). In the distribution of assets (or attributes) in the mirror of modernity, nationhood has been the mark of the modern, what all great countries and peoples have achieved. Community is what existed before. There is a slight complication. The nation, too, is after all a community. It is *the* modern political community. So thoroughly was this community naturalized, however, with the nation coming to be seen as the natural condition for the modern political existence of all peoples, that it quickly came not to be referred to as community at all.

While the nation was assumed to be the modern political community, representative democracy (government of the people, by the people) came to be seen as the (ideal) modern political condition—in India as in Europe. A central issue that then arose related to the arrangements required for the realization of this ideal. This issue led on to the matter of majorities and minorities, and of how the people of a territory (or the communities to which they belonged) were to find political representation in the almost natural unit called the nation-state. It was on this question that the experience of colonialism became especially significant.

A key mark of colonial and postcolonial polities is that they have been seen, and continue to be seen, as social/political orders constituted by community or group ties as much as (if not more than) by individual interests. It has been suggested that in these societies, which have been deprived of the secularizing and individualizing histories of the absolutist states in Europe, there is an unusual tension between the community and the individual as the bearer of rights. While it is not clear to me that this is a problem of colonial and postcolonial societies alone, the consequences this "difference" has had in the deployment of community in political life have surely been decisive.

John Kelly and Martha Kaplan put forward an important argument about the primacy of state and nation in the postcolonial world. Emphasizing decolonization and the birth of the United Nations as moments that established the nation-state as the global norm, they urge us to consider a wider range of forces than is usually admitted in the imagining of community "in hopes of rediscovering the...nation as an extraordinary, special case, a case not only of Enlightenment but also of imperial imagination, the single 'community' imagining itself to monopolize a social space." "Exactly when, and why," they ask, "did who decide to share homogenous, empty space-time, and the nation-state as a political form, with a globe full of others? Who turned Others into 'communities' of 'locals,' and why?" (Kelly and Kaplan 2001:25–26, 55, 95).

Community, in perhaps the most widely prevalent modernist reading, lies outside the nation-state (or more broadly the state) and outside history. Let me illustrate the proposition by quick reference to one of the great philosophers of modernity, Hegel. History for Hegel is the progress of freedom; and freedom is possible only in the state. "The story of individuals alone, and even of individuals in the still emotional, irrational community of the family, is not yet history." "Peoples may have continued a long life before they reach their destination of becoming a state": but this is "*pre-history*." "A community which acquires a stable existence and elevates itself into a state requires more than merely subjective mandates of government, sufficient only for the needs of the moment. It requires rules, laws, universal and universally valid norms." (Hegel 1953 [1837]:xxxi, 74, 76). Hegel's comments on India elaborate the argument:

> India not only has old books of religion and brilliant works of poetry but also old codes of law—which above were mentioned as a condition of the formation of history—and yet it has no history. In that country the impulse of organization, which begins to differentiate society, was immediately petrified into the natural distinctions of castes....Because of that bondage of the caste system, in all historical relation there is wild arbitrariness, ephemeral bustling, indeed, raging without a final purpose of progress or development. (1953 [1837]:76–77)

There are two different invocations of community in these quotations: (1) the natural, irrational community of the family, and (2) an incipient organization, in India frozen into castes. What marks both is the absence of satisfactory differentiation, of historical purpose, of universality, and of adequate organization, otherwise known as the state.

In line with Hegel's thinking, history was long written up as an account of the career of the "organized" (the state, the nation, the revolutionary party, capitalism, science), although the "unorganized" frequently showed up in the narrative—as an interruption, an outbreak of violence, the presence of discontent, or, to put it in more general terms, the resistance of the nonmodern (or the insufficiently modern). It is only in the last few decades that elements of the latter kind have come to be acknowledged as a part of history, as benign or even necessary supplements to modernity. This shift has been accompanied by the official recognition of indigenous people's rights, multiculturalism, alternative medicine, and so on, in some parts of the world. Before this change, the "unorganized" appeared in history only as a disturbance.

How did these "local others," these nonstate elements, excluded from history, respond to their exclusion? To ask this question is to restore the agency and politics of the marginalized and the disprivileged. For the answer is that they did so by *organizing* and demanding a place among the "organized"; by becoming communities that were politicized, that hovered on the boundaries of the "modern," contending for entry into its most advanced sectors: communities that frequently presented themselves in the image of the nation.

At times, the production of such community has followed directly from the initiatives of the modern (especially the colonial) state. Mahmood Mamdani suggests that this was the case with the Hutu/Tutsi division in Rwanda. "The idea that the Tutsi were superior because they came from elsewhere," he notes, "and that the difference between them and the local population was a *racial* difference, was an idea of colonial origin." The rival European powers were all persuaded that wherever there was evidence of organized state life in Africa, the ruling groups must have come from outside. In another move, the Tutsi were "racialized" in Rwanda and Burundi, "not just through an ideology but through a set of institutional reforms that the ideology inspired" (Mamdani 2001:80).

Key institutions, such as schools, local administration, taxation, and even the church, were organized around an "active acknowledgment of these identities." The regime issued official identity cards confirming every individual as Hutu or Tutsi, barring the small number of Twa, thereby converting a constructed political difference between Hutu and Tutsi into a legislated racial difference. After the 1933 census, the rise of a Hutu individual to Tutsi status, or the fall of a Tutsi to Hutu status, was no longer possible. The identities "Hutu" and "Tutsi" became permanent and frozen (Mamdani 2001:80, 87, 88, 101), with the tragic and ironic consequence that victims of Hutu or Tutsi violence have in the recent years of genocide sometimes been identified by their identity cards alone (Mamdani 2003:230).

The procedures and points of initiative have not always been the same, but the process of constructing such "racialized," "primordial" identities has gone on apace in all parts of the colonized world, not to mention the colonizing world. In all "direct-rule colonies," Mamdani notes, the colonial power "constructed the colonized along a majority/minority axis, an indigenous majority and a so-called nonindigenous minority...Hindu and Muslim in India, Sinhalese and Tamil in Sri Lanka." The presumed difference was in every case "a construction more political than historical" (Mamdani 2001:100).

We need to highlight another route to these constructions, however, one that is likely to have affected the indirectly ruled as much as the colonies of direct rule. This process is the appropriation and deployment of new opportunities by members of the colonized groups themselves. I turn to an examination of this trend in the following pages.

In the nineteenth century, propagandists and publicists among the Hindu, Muslim, Sikh, and other religious groupings on the Indian subcontinent moved to appropriate marginal populations (for the first time, Hindu leaders classified the "untouchables" as unambiguously Hindu), to purify their communities (Muslims must not be contaminated by Hindu practices and vice versa), and to establish distinct and separate identities (among religious groupings, most notably in the case of the Sikhs). In this way, notions of an "all-India Hindu community," an "all-India Muslim community," and a "Sikh community" distinct from the Hindus gradually took hold in the later nineteenth and early twentieth centuries. And on this basis, new kinds of struggles for Muslim and Sikh homelands arose later in the twentieth century (to be matched at a later stage, from the 1980s on, by the most ironic of them all—the movement for a "Hindu homeland" in the Hindu-majority country of India).

The articulation of these new, subcontinent-wide communities of religion, and their political demands, have provided some of the most dramatic departures in South Asian political history in the colonial and postcolonial periods. The emergence of castes as political actors—with a relatively reduced social significance but much increased political consequence—has been almost as important. Once "caste" had come to replace the unchanging "village community" as the defining feature of Indian society in colonial discourse (Cohn 1987; Dirks 2001; R. S. Smith 1985), and census operations from the 1870s on began the process of identifying, enumerating, and ranking all castes and subcastes throughout the country, a number of results quickly followed.

"Caste" tended to replace "subcaste" as the effective unit of endogamy and commensality (although such distinction was, and remains, difficult to maintain on the ground). Subcaste names became markedly less salient as caste names came to be more widely adopted; and whereas caste appellations had earlier been ways of designating identities, privileges, and disprivileges that were more locally specific, being confined in many cases to a small area or group of villages, castes or "caste clusters" now emerged as significant interregional categories.

These newly refashioned castes and subcastes sometimes demanded recognition as having a more respectable, higher status than their neighbors, or census officials or other observers, assigned to them. Innovative Sanskritization (upward mobility) movements arose, with attendant caste histories, caste associations, and caste conflicts (compare Srinivas 1972). In one province, Bihar, the census commissioner observed in 1911 that the flood of petitions he had received asking for a change of caste name and a higher place in the order of precedence was so great that the weight of the paper alone amounted to 1.5 maunds (Government of India 1912:part 1, 440). In Madras an agricultural caste group loosely described as Palli, or Vanniyar, had organized at the time of the 1872 census to petition for Kshatriya ("aristocratic") status. In 1901 the census commissioner commented on their "widespread organization." By 1931 the title Palli had disappeared from the census: only Vanniyakula Kshatriya remained. Yet the caste organization persisted and developed fresh political ambitions. In 1935 the Vanniyakula Kshatriyas (recently given official recognition as some sort of "upper caste") asked for proportional representation in the appointments reserved for "backward castes" in the presidency! (Dirks 2001:223, 238–239).

In this way, some widespread and even interregional constellations of castes emerged as new kinds of community—with greatly extended social and political links, meeting points, and even marriage networks. One of the most notable examples of such new articulations is that of the all-India collectivity called the untouchables. These were scattered and not always consistently identifiable local groups, traditionally denied access to various kinds of common resources and facilities owing to the menial and "dirty" work they performed (or with which they were once associated) and considered to be extremely polluting. They were now allocated more distinctly to a fifth ("fallen" or "aberrant") category of Hindu society, below the four classical caste clusters. As the pace of state intervention and modern politics increased, untouchable groups came to be enumerated and classified. In 1935 they were listed in a schedule of "depressed castes" drawn up as part of a revised Government of India Act, a schedule that was carried over almost unchanged into the Indian constitution of 1950.

Since the 1920s, if not a little earlier, the "community" of untouchables has been a major factor in Indian politics. (At least one political leader in the 1920s thought the best "solution" to the "problem" of untouchables was to divide them equally between Hindus and Muslims!) The names they have been given, or claimed, since then speak of the changing temper of politics ranging around untouchable, or ex-untouchable, groups. Gandhi renamed them Harijans, or "children of God." The constitutional provisions mentioned above christened them the scheduled castes. Militant leaders of the community now call themselves Dalit, or the downtrodden and oppressed.

More recently, the "other backward castes"—socially and economically depressed groups situated just on the border of the "clean" lower and middle castes but not falling into the category of the Dalits or ex-untouchables[1]—have emerged as another constitutional category, and a more visible and organized political force. At various times in the late nineteenth and the twentieth century, and very forcefully in recent decades, the politics of such "depressed" groups has expanded further to encompass all the lower castes and classes in a new "community," sometimes calling itself the Dalitbahujan samaj (the "oppressed majority," roughly speaking). On the one hand, then, as one commentator puts it, "We have the supremely paradoxical phenomenon of low-caste groups asserting their very backwardness in the caste hierarchy to claim discriminatory privileges from the state" (Chatterjee 1993:198). On the other hand, the current politics of militant assertion—like the politics of Sanskritization, Islamization, and the more general upward mobility that they have supplanted—produce new "communities" making unaccustomed demands for an alteration of existing social and political arrangements.

As already noted, except for the nation, or communities that establish themselves as potential nations (politically deprived of their rights or tactically surrendering them for the time being), all such groups have been projected as being, to a greater or lesser extent, "premodern." What marks them in common, however, is the very fact of their articulation in relation to the modern state or to incipient statehood. These are at bottom *political communities*: constituted in relation to modern political arrangements and mobilized largely for purposes of participation in public affairs.

One could push the argument further. In all the examples cited above, the relationship between communities and political movements seems to be peculiarly inverted. It is almost as if the political category gives rise to the social unit from which it supposedly draws its life rather than the other way around, although of course there is a cyclical process at work here. I have made this argument before in relation to the history of "communalism," that curious colonial label for the allegedly historical condition of suspicion, fear, and hostility between members of different religious and racial communities—Hindu/Muslim or Hindu/Sikh in northern India; Brahman/non-Brahman in southern and western India; Sinhala/Tamil in Sri Lanka; Malays, Chinese, and Indians in Malaysia; and people of European, African, and Indian background in the West Indies (Pandey 2005).

In this instance, the adjective "communal" derives from "communalism," not from "commune," "the Paris Commune," or "community," as it does in most of the rest of the world. And the religious or racial "community" in question springs from the fact (as it is asserted) of being "communalist" and the practice of what is called communalism. In the same way, I suggest, it is "casteism" that has given rise to the existence of castes as we know them, much as "nationalism" has given rise to the new political communities we call nations. It is no accident—on the contrary it is a necessary part of the politics that produces them—that these communities should come to be reified in the course of their formation and their mobilization.

Thus we arrive at a number of paradoxes found at the heart of the concept of community as it is used in many parts of the world today: contradictions that are to some extent irresolvable. I suspect there would be wide agreement among contemporary social scientists and historians that the modern community is a *politicized* community. For until that is its condition, the so-called community—of religion, caste, language, race, whatever—would appear to be rather too differentiated and unorganized to enter into the kind of dialogue or conversation in the legal-constitutional domain of the state in which all such social groups are now implicated. Indeed, I am tempted to paraphrase Benedict Anderson and say that "all communities larger than primordial villages of face-to-face contact (and perhaps even these) are *political*" (see B. Anderson 1991:6), although I would put "primordial" under the qualifying sign of inverted commas.

To be effective, however, and sometimes even to gain recognition as a community, it seems necessary at the same time for this sort of social group to claim to be a natural unit, long in existence—one that acquires its authority on grounds of being an affective, moral collectivity that is less a matter of choice than of birth. This is one contradiction that modern communities and political thinkers alike have to live with.

Different kinds of community come up for discussion in this paper. An aspect of these, however self-consciously political they may be—and I obviously include the nation in this list—is that they are usually conjured up as moral collectivities, with clear notions of the members' moral/ethical norms and responsibilities. They are projected not only as historically constituted collectivities, bound by common practices, experiences, and memories, but often also as "natural" entities, in the image of the family—Hegel's first elementary moment of social life, based not on contract but in love—and precisely for that reason immune against externality and secession. Family, caste, religious community, and (curiously) nation become homologous.

It is no surprise to find members of caste, religious community, or nation being described as members of an extended family, and the nation being worshipped as the motherland or fatherland. A particularly striking example of this situation was provided by the actions of large numbers of middle-class housewives in Calcutta when Gandhi began a "fast unto death" to try and stop violence between Hindus and Muslims in the city in 1946: in home after home, women refused to eat on the argument that it would be a sin for them to do so while Bapu—that is "Father" (the father of these families as well as of the nation)—went without food (Chakrabarty 2000:39).

It is this moral, affective quality that consciously or unconsciously gives to many modern communities their particular emotional appeal and their authority, enabling them to provide the kind of comfort, the sense of belonging and home, that they are said to provide. Yet there is a second question that they must confront at some point. This question has to do with acceptance in the regime of modernity: for not every kind of affective, moral, or for that matter political community is equally acceptable here.

India's first prime minister, Jawaharlal Nehru, the "scientific," "socialist" leader of the country's struggle for democracy and liberation, provides a very good example of modernist thinking on this issue. In the final years of British colonial rule, leading up to partition and independence, Nehru repeatedly disparaged the idea of Pakistan and a separate Muslim nation on the subcontinent as a sham, an artificial creation and a manipulation of vague fears by well-defined vested interests. "To think in terms of Pakistan when the modern trend is towards the establishment of a world federation is like thinking in terms of bows and arrows as weapons of war in the age of the atom bomb," he wrote. "The whole mentality behind this conception of bows and arrows and Pakistan is most dangerous" (Nehru 1984:187). To think in terms of "India" and a modern national army for India was far from anachronistic. The idea was, on the contrary, one with "the trend of world history." This argument was but one way of naturalizing and elevating the nation, the community, called India.

To this day, Indian scholars and students are unfailingly amused by any talk of two or three thousand years of "Pakistani history," yet they think nothing of studying and assimilating an "Indian history" said to originate in an equally if not more ancient past. Nehru himself provided the substance of this argument about the natural, eternal nation, in spite of his constant references to scientific advance and modern political arrangements and choices. "Some kind of a dream of unity has occupied *the mind of India* since the dawn of civilization." And again: "Some powerful impulse, some tremendous urge, or ideas of the significance of life…was impressed upon *the subconscious mind of India* when *she was fresh and young* at the very dawn of her history" (Nehru 1961:63, 147).

Communities, too, are divided into the "good" and the "bad," depending to a large extent, I suggest, on how well or how poorly they are thought to correspond to the requirements of modernity. "Good" and "bad" communities are sometimes equated with the natural and the unnatural, and (incongruously, given that last set) with the progressive modern on the one hand and a comatose premodern on the other. The issue at stake is the recognition or nonrecognition of particular communities as legitimate political actors. A brief discussion of the Muslim minority and its place in the public life of independent India may help illustrate the point.

What marked out all the politicized communities of the era of anticolonial struggle on the Indian subcontinent, whether they were based on region, religion, caste, class, language, or race, was an aspiration to citizenship and democratic rights. What marked some of them more than others—those that were numerically small, educationally or economically backward, or politically threatened by the advance of industrial organization and modern capitalist society—was an anxiety about the conditions of this future citizenship, leading them to organize and agitate to turn those conditions into the most favorable ones possible. It was this process that gave force to what was called communalism and communalist demands.

We may recall that the term "communalism" was commonly applied in colonial times to describe the conflict between Brahmans and non-Brahmans and the emergence of a powerful non-Brahman movement in southern India. Likewise, the debate on the communal question at the Round Table Conferences of 1930–1932, and the Communal Award that followed, was concerned with the political weightage to be granted not only to religious minorities and the Anglo-Indians but also to the so-called untouchables (the scheduled castes and tribes of the Government of India Act of 1935 and the Indian constitution of 1950). What was at issue in this politics of communalism was the place that would be found for diverse social-political communities in the affairs of the larger political community, itself claiming the status of nation-statehood.

The situation has since changed. While the ideals and images, policies and practices of the nation and its state continue to be contested, the nation-state now exists as a powerful and tangible material, intellectual, and spiritual force. It lays down the terms of debate in a way that is definitive, setting out what is acceptable and unacceptable, moral and immoral, legal and illegal. The notion of "good" and "bad" community is invoked in this context. The nation obviously becomes the supreme example of the good (compare Chatterjee 1986, 1993). People may still belong to sundry communities, apart from the nation, but permission to belong and to proclaim such belonging depends to a large extent on the "lesser" community's conformity or lack of conformity to the current state of the national project, or to put it more bluntly, on whether it is seen as threatening to the nation(al) community or not.

Members of marginal, subordinated, or politically disadvantaged communities, who were and often continue to be the proponents of communalist standpoints and the makers of communalist demands, are now formally citizens. At the same time, they are seen as belonging to preconstituted and sometimes constitutionally recognized "minority communities." These communities may continue to participate in political affairs, but in conditions that are very different from those that obtained before. Their culture and interests, inclinations and "passions" are known from the start. They appear as frozen entities, denied the possibility of internal difference, political agency, and change, even as they become objects of political manipulation and governmentality in a new way.

In moments of heightened political tension or agitation, the citizenship of men and women belonging to these communities may easily become suspect. The case of the Indian Muslims is in this sense paradigmatic. For given the partition of the subcontinent, they have lived almost continuously since 1947 under the shadow of the suspicion of harboring loyalties to Pakistan. In these times of tension, the members of such a minority community are always in danger of emerging as an easily targeted "fifth column" to be watched and controlled by the government: citizens yet aliens. Curfews, imposed neutrally over particular territories, towns, and villages, often affect only these suspect citizens; surveillance procedures apply primarily to them (see Rai 1987, 2002:211–212).

These are sections of the population that once claimed their say in debates about political futures. The state now returns to them with a different project. It seeks to "discipline" them in the midst of much rhetorical talk of richness and variety, the coexistence of cultures, and (though the term has not really caught on in India) multiculturalism. In certain circumstances, of which we have seen far too many examples in recent times, in India as in other parts of the world, the wielders of state power adopt more extreme measures. Because these "minorities" are collectivities with different (or in extremist accounts "abnormal") values, customs, and practices, people with a peculiar (and obviously "unwarranted") sense of independence and pride, those in power sometimes join hands with local hoodlums and sectarian militias to attack and if possible destroy them as moral/ethical communities and networks of sustenance.

The members of such collectivities thus come to be portrayed, and (unfortunately) widely viewed, as people who are unlike "us" modern individuals: populations that are not used to the practice of reason and that cannot control their passions or their primitive beliefs. Minorities are targeted for alleged deviation from "national" and "modernist" norms. Muslims in India, and increasingly the very small community of Christians, too, come under suspicion because of their link to "foreign" (antinational) religions, hence to "foreign" (antinational) forces and more recently in the case of the Muslims to what is widely proclaimed as a worldwide network of terrorism. In the instance of the Christians, let it be noted, the "national" trumps even the (Christian European) "modern"!

There are of course other kinds of "communities" that have gained constitutional and political recognition in independent India, among them the Dalits (scheduled castes and tribes) and the "other backward castes" (OBCs) mentioned earlier, and the community of "women" that has been at the center of political debate more recently. This particular debate, on the question of adequate political representation for women, bears consideration for a moment, not only because it once again sets out the difficulties involved in the adjustment of the claims of certain communities against others but also because it reintroduces the notion of natural, essential communities in a different (biological) way—and thereby underlines the political contests and choices that go into any such production.

The question of seats especially reserved for women had come up at the time of the framing of the Indian constitution but was rejected by female representatives on the ground that women were not so weak as to require special representation and that full and equal adult franchise—rather than the representation of sectional interests—was the way forward for a rich, equal, and indivisible nation. The Dalits were given special weightage for an initial period of ten years, but it was understood that this was a purely temporary measure until free and compulsory education and economic development enabled oppressed groups to get over the disabilities they had long suffered. In the event, the reservations for Dalits, in legislative bodies, public services, and educational institutions, have continued to this day. In terms of reservations in public services and educational institutions, though not in the legislatures, the OBCs have been added to the list of "protected" groups, nationally since 1989 and rather earlier in the legislative enactments of various provinces. It was against this background (and in the context of the rise of powerful women's campaigns against sati, rape, dowry deaths, and other acts of violence against women, as well as against drinking, the sharp rise in prices of essential commodities, and widespread corruption in public life) that the question of special quotas for women in legislative bodies at the national, provincial, and local levels was raised again—this time by several women's groups.

In 1993 the constitution was amended to provide for a 33 percent reservation for women in local self-government institutions of all kinds. In 1996 another amendment proposed a 33 percent reservation for women in Parliament. Reintroduced in slightly modified forms in 1998 and 1999, this amendment is still awaiting passage—for the question of the empowerment of women, upon which the supporters of this bill staked their position, came up immediately against the question of the empowerment of lower-caste women—the question of "quotas within quotas," as the issue has been termed in the Indian debate.

The arguments put forward by those in favor of the amendment were straightforward enough. First, women were underrepresented in the political institutions of the country: this imbalance, which has persisted far too long, now needs to be corrected. Secondly, women in Parliament would act as a strong lobby and change the tone and temper, as well as the content, of debates. These arguments proceeded on the basis of a belief in the existence of a homogenous category of women and made large assumptions about the "softening" effects of women's "gentle" nature, as well as about the effects of their socialization and their social commitments and obligations. All this is open to challenge—but that has not been the ground of opposition to this measure.

Significantly, the most passionate opposition to the bill did not come from those who argued that the nation should be recognized as one, homogenous and undifferentiated. Some prominent female activists and spokespersons, who had earlier opposed special representation for women on the premise that this would be an admission of women's inferiority and a further sectionalization (and distortion) of the notion of abstract citizens and "one-person, one-vote" democracy, now adopted a quite different stand. "Our position represented an ideological and conceptual shift," one wrote, "which was to develop into a search for a new identity for ourselves in the maelstrom of the politics of nation building" (Mazumdar 1997:15).

The most forceful opposition in this phase of "nation building" came instead from those who said that such a marking of inherited privilege and disprivilege in the nation, and therefore among women, too, should be extended further. A Dalit quota had been included within the terms of the Women's Reservation Bill. However, there was no quota for the OBCs, in part because they had no reserved quota of seats in the legislatures in the first place. Parties and leaders representing these castes, which now have considerable clout in the provinces and are important parts of the ruling coalitions at the center, argued that the introduction of the bill in this form was simply a means of strengthening upper-caste/middle-class control over the legislature. Certainly, the move had the backing of all the "mainstream" parties supported by the upper castes and middle classes.

Sharad Yadav and Mulayam Singh Yadav, two top OBC leaders, were among the most vocal opponents of the measure, arguing that it was "anti-backward [caste]," "anti-minority," and "anti-dalit." The

Bahujan Samaj Party leader, Mayawati, who is also the first female Dalit chief minister of any Indian province, supported the OBC leaders, demanding the reservation of 50 percent of the legislative seats for women, with separate quotas within this number for the OBCs and the "minorities" as well as for Dalits. Uma Bharati, a female backward-caste member of Parliament from the party then in power at the center (the Bharatiya Janata Party), and later chief minister of the large central Indian province of Madhya Pradesh, opposed her own party's leadership on this issue. She supported the move to establish reserved seats for women but demanded special allocations for backward-caste and Dalit women, since women from these communities were, as she put it, doubly oppressed. Not surprisingly, speaking as she did not only from her backward-caste position but also from that of the Hindu right wing, Uma Bharati rejected the idea of a quota for Muslim women even as she conceded that they were among the most oppressed. "In a secular constitution," she declared, "there can be no place for reservations based on religion" (see Menon 2000:3838).

Once again, the larger question is how the wider political community called the nation is to be seen and represented. Gandhi had opposed any talk of constitutional reservations for women on the grounds that women should be homemakers and the right arms of men, not seekers of political power for themselves. He had also seen demands for weightage or special electorates as signs of "antinational betrayal." Perhaps along similar lines, but even more crassly, a leading Indian newspaper asked, in the course of the debate on the Women's Reservation Bill, whether Parliament was to be "parcelled into lots of the historically oppressed, leaving the rest of mainstream India to its own devices?" (John 2000:3824; Menon 2000:3838).

One other question asked by commentators on the women's bill needs to be foregrounded. Why, they asked, is the category of "women" so widely and readily acceptable to the dominant political elite, which is much more qualified in its acceptance of backward castes or religious minorities as politically legitimate communities? The answer is to be found, I suggest, not only in the fact that "women" are still seen as an irreducible, biological category, in a way in which religious or caste groupings are not, but also because as a collectivity, women are seen as less threatening to existing social and political arrangements. The point to be made about all this, as numerous analysts since Simone de Beauvoir (1997 [1949]) have noted, is that the construction of "women" as the subjects or agents of history must also be seen as a political project: "women" as a category can be brought into being only through politics.

It is the politics of the recognition or nonrecognition of different kinds of community that we need to attend to more carefully, and I return to this in the last part of this chapter through a consideration of the issue as it appears in the complex and still unfamiliar thought of M. K. Gandhi.

Much has been written about Gandhi's philosophy and his unusual techniques of political mobilization and agitation. One aspect of his thinking that may yet repay more extended scrutiny is his understanding of community. In Gandhi's view, individuals everywhere were born into well-established territorial and cultural communities. The individual, the (social, political, or religious) community, and humankind were "ontologically and morally inseparable." Every individual was "an integral part" of a specific community, with whose members he or she was in intimate contact, of whose values and needs he or she had an instinctive understanding, and whose welfare demanded his or her primary attention. It was only through service to one's own community, Gandhi contended, that one could serve other communities and humanity at large. By the same token, there was generally no reason to change one's native (religious or social) attachments, for the true principles of morality or religion were universal and unchanging (Parekh 1989; Chatterjee 1986:ch. 4).

When a society was made up of different cultural and religious communities, Gandhi saw little merit in seeking to homogenize them or even subject them to one uniform set of laws. He insisted that such a society should cherish its diverse communities and respect their languages, cultural practices, personal laws, and educational institutions. Indian society consisted of a range of such communities—Hindus, Muslims, Christians, and so on, as well as the castes and regions to which they belonged. The ideal polity for this country (and for all others, Gandhi would have said) was a federation of communities.

The challenge, of course, was to find a language of communication, and negotiation, between what could sometimes appear as very different kinds of communities with very different sets of values, arguments, and practices. Gandhi was willing to accept these different values and internal reasons as entirely different versions of truth ("One person's truth may appear as another's untruth"), and he urged everyone to follow the dictates of his or her own truth. He did this in the name of a higher Truth, that of nonviolence and love, which for him formed the basis of all religions and hence the basis of the religious politics he advocated. Ahimsa—nonviolence and love—was to serve as the protocol for relationships and conversations among all such political "antagonists" (see Skaria 2002).

One difficulty that remained was that some truths (including perhaps those of Enlightenment Rationality and modern secular politics) do not conceive of, or allow, the coexistence of multiple truths in this way, and some (including those of Enlightenment Rationality) believe in the need to obliterate other "truths" in order to establish the Truth. What of those who will not, and perhaps cannot, define God in the nebulous, always open way preferred by Gandhi, or accept his proposition about the fundamental identity of all truths? How are conversations to be developed between such groups? I shall leave this question for another discussion, since it is not central to the argument I am making here.

Let me simply reiterate that Gandhi stressed the importance of *conversation* as the means to the resolution of "difference" in society, national or international. Ideally, this conversation would take place between parties on the basis of an "absolute difference" and an "equality" that were the conditions of neighborliness and friendship. At the same time he proposed different kinds of dialogue as being necessary to political negotiation between people placed at different levels in the social-political hierarchies of the actual world. He advocated the attitude of *mitrata* (friendship) toward equals, for example between Hindus and Muslims; of *seva* (service) toward subordinates (in Gandhian terms "unfortunates"), as in the relations between upper castes and "untouchables"—the Mahatma's Harijans; and of *satyagraha* (the appeal for justice through noncooperation) toward the dominant, as in the case of the Indian population in relation to its British rulers (Skaria 2002).

"Gandhi assumed that loyalty to religion and community was the dominant loyalty in India," writes an astute student of the Mahatma's early political campaigns. And further: "Because Gandhi had a realistic picture of India as a loose constellation of classes, communities and religious groups, he was able to activate the peoples of the subcontinent in a way no one had done before, or has since" (Kumar 1983:51, 53). The problem with the Gandhian approach, as described here, is a tendency to rather too easily "fix" groups of people in a specified place in the social hierarchy (that of equal, dominant, or subordinate, to be met with "friendship," "noncooperation," or "service") and to homogenize whole groups of people so that they can be so fixed.

Were the Muslims of the subcontinent in fact quite so undifferentiated as Gandhi proclaimed? What were the grounds for his postulation of Muslims as one seamless bloc, allowing "absolute difference" and "full equality" between them and the (similarly undifferentiated and seamless) "Hindu" community? And why was it that the Muslims were to be treated as equals, while the Dalits were fit only to be classed as unfortunates, children—even if Gandhi anointed them *daridranarayan* (God in the form of the poor). For we should remember that while Gandhi pronounced "untouchability" a sin and an "accretion" on Hinduism, he refused to accept the demands of the untouchables for representation as a separate community.

It is not surprising that in this negotiation of the problem of unity and difference, even Gandhi, the great champion of communities of birth and inheritance, was not in a position to admit all claims to community. However, it is worth pausing a moment to think of his criteria for admission or nonadmission. In India, as Partha Chatterjee has observed,

> the problem of unifying the opposed requirements of sepa-
> rateness and dependence has been concretely addressed
> [and even here with partial success] only at the level of the
> structure of federalism, a level where the problem is seen as
> permitting a territorial resolution....In other domains, of
> which caste is a prime example, politics has drifted from one
> contentious principle to another (bourgeois equality, caste-
> class correlation, discriminatory privileges for low castes
> through state intervention, and so on) without finding ade-
> quate ground on which it can be superceded by a new uni-
> versal form of community. (1993:198–199)

275

Gandhi refused to grant the Dalits the separate status they demanded—because this would have amounted to a fracturing of his cherished notion of the "Hindu" community. He was in anguish over the demand for Pakistan as a separate state for the Indian Muslims. All such judgments followed from vigorous political contestation between different conceptions of the political community, past, present, and future—a fact that the Mahatma never fully accepted.

In Gandhi, then, we have a thinker who, unlike Nehru and a whole range of other liberal modernists, saw existence in communities (including the religious community) as natural and ethical. For there was simply no other place for individuals to be. He also conceded in many ways that the life of communities was a political matter in that it involved choices as well as privileges and responsibilities. Yet the acknowledgement of such choice never went far enough, precisely because of the return to an argument about the "natural" boundaries of community and place of belonging.

We are well aware of how Dalit and Muslim political leaders, Ambedkar and Jinnah among them, responded to Gandhi's scheme of politics and political negotiation. Who is it, they might have asked, who so arrogantly claims the right to assign to all the people of the subcontinent such a clear, unambiguous, and (one might say) permanent place in the amazing hierarchy of "equals," "subordinates," and "superordinates" that Gandhi drew up? Who is it who can deny us our politics?

That said, I want to conclude with the thought that we still have the need for an idea, concept, dream such as community—with the proviso that this notion be rigorously historicized. A distinguished colleague, anthropologist, and historian of Central Africa points out that on that continent, community—with all its accompanying claims of autochthony and allochthony—has now become a dirty word (Peter Geschiere, pers. comm., March 2003; compare Watts, this volume).[2] My first response is to note that "state," too, has become a dirty word—and not only in Africa. And with "community" and "state," perhaps "politics" and "politicians," and "nation," too. Which leaves the question: What words are we left with?

Notes

1. Again, it is important to stress that these boundaries are extremely hazy, and established to a large extent only by constitutional fiat or political prescription. What complicates the situation even more is that there are depressed castes of the same kind and status as the scheduled castes or the other backward castes that are not given the same constitutional protection because they were not identified in lists drawn up by particular constitutional or inquiry commissions, or because they are not Hindu but are Muslim or Christian in terms of religious denomination.

2. Kelly makes a point of a similar kind in response to Chatterjee's *The Nation and Its Fragments*, expressing his "initial feeling of sheer shock, and continuing disquiet, when reading Partha Chatterjee's praise...for the concept of community and for *jatis* [castes] as communities of struggle, his praise for minorities empowering themselves with claims to historically organic, particularistic rights and interests" (Kelly and Kaplan 2001:98). Apparently, community has become an already-known dirty word in the discussion of India's political future, too.

References

Abercrombie, Thomas
1998   Pathways of Memory and Power: Ethnography and History among an Andean People. Madison: University of Wisconsin Press.

Adebayo, A.
1993   Embattled Federalism. New York: Peter Lang.

Agamben, Giorgio
1993   The Coming Community. Michael Hardt, trans. Minneapolis: University of Minnesota Press.

Agrawal, Arun, and Clark C. Gibson
1999   Enchantment and Disenchantment: The Role of Community in Natural Resource Conservation. World Development 27(4):629–649.

Agrawal, Arun, and Clark C. Gibson, eds.
2001   Communities and the Environment: Ethnicity, Gender, and the State in Community-Based Conservation. New Brunswick, NJ: Rutgers University Press.

Alagoa, M.
2001   The Report of the Nembe Peace and Reconciliation Committee. Port Harcourt, Nigeria: Rivers State Government.

Alder, Christine
2000   Young Women Offenders and the Challenge for Restorative Justice. *In* Restorative Justice: Philosophy to Practice. Heather Strang and John Braithwaite, eds. Pp. 105–119. Burlington, VT: Ashgate Publishing Company.

Alderman, L.
2000   Saving the Forest. Barron's, December 18: P22–P23.

Allen, Catherine J.
1988   The Hold Life Has: Coca and Cultural Identity in an Andean Community. Washington, DC: Smithsonian Institution Press.
1997   When Pebbles Move Mountains: Iconicity and Symbolism in Quechua Ritual. *In* Creating Context in Andean Cultures. Rosaleen Howard-Malverde, ed. Pp. 73–84. Oxford Studies in Anthropological Linguistics. Oxford: Oxford University Press.

Alonso, Ana Maria
1988   The Effects of Truth: Re-Presentations of the Past and the Imagining of Community. Journal of Historical Sociology 1(1):33–57.

REFERENCES

Althusser, Louis
1971   Ideology and Ideological State Apparatuses. *In* Lenin and Philosophy and Other Essays. Ben Brewster, trans. New York: Monthly Review Press.

Altink, Henrice
2004   "To Wed or Not to Wed?": The Struggle to Define Afro-Jamaican Relationships, 1834–1838. Journal of Social History 38(1):81–111.

Amit, Vered
2002   Reconceptualizing Community. *In* Realizing Community: Concepts, Social Relationships and Sentiments. Vered Amit, ed. Pp. 1–20. London: Routledge.

Amit, Vered, ed.
2002   Realizing Community: Concepts, Social Relationships and Sentiments. London: Routledge.

Anderson, Benedict
1983   Imagined Communities: Reflections on the Origin and Spread of Nationalism. London: Verso.
1991   Imagined Communities: Reflections on the Origin and Spread of Nationalism. Rev. edition. New York: Verso.

Anderson, Perry
2001   Scurrying toward Bethlehem. New Left Review 10:5–30.

Andolina, Robert J.
2001   Between Local Authenticity and Global Accountability: The Ayllu Movement in Contemporary Bolivia. Paper prepared for the workshop "Beyond the Lost Decade: Indigenous Movements and the Transformation of Development and Democracy in Latin America," Princeton University, March 2–3.

Apffel-Marglin, F., and PRATEC, eds.
1988   The Spirit of Regeneration: Andean Culture Confronting Western Notions of Development. London: Zed Books.

Appadurai, Arjun
1993   Patriotism and Its Futures. Public Culture 5(3):411–429.
1996   Modernity at Large: Cultural Dimensions of Globalization. Minneapolis: University of Minnesota Press.

Apter, D.
2005   The Pan African Nation. Chicago: University of Chicago Press.

Arensberg, Conrad M.
1961   The Community as Object and as Sample. American Anthropologist 63:241–264.

Arensberg, Conrad M., and Solon T. Kimball
1940   Family and Community in Ireland. Cambridge, MA: Harvard University Press.

Arnold, Denise
1988   Matrilineal Practice in a Patrilineal Setting: Ritual and Metaphors of Kinship in an Andean Ayllu. Ph.D. dissertation, University of London.
1997   Introducción. *In* Parentesco y género en los Andes, vol. 1: Mas allá del silencio: Las fronteras del género en los Andes. Denise Arnold, ed. Pp. 13–52. La Paz: Biblioteca de Estudios Andinos.
1998   De "castas" a "kastas" enfoques hacia el parentesco andino. *In* Parentesco y género en los Andes, vol. 2: Gente de carne y hueso: Las tramas del parentesco en los Andes. Denise Arnold, ed. Pp. 15–66. La Paz: Biblioteca de Estudios Andinos.

Ash, Robert C.
2000   Mountains Suspended by a Hair: Eruv, a Symbolic Act by Which the Legal Fiction of Community Is Established. Ph.D. dissertation, Leicester University.

al-Azmeh, A.
2002   Postmodern Obscurantism and the "Muslim Question." *In* Socialist Register. L. Panitch and C. Leys, eds. Pp. 28–50. New York: Monthly Review Press.

Bailey, Robert
1998   Ecoregions: The Ecosystem Geography of the Oceans and Continents. New York: Springer-Verlag.

Balibar, Etienne, and Emmanuel Wallerstein
1992   Race, Nation, Class: Ambiguous Identities. London: Verso.

Banfield, Edward
1958   The Moral Basis of a Backward Society. Glencoe, IL: Free Press.

Barrow, Christine
1988   Anthropology, the Family, and Women in the Caribbean. *In* Gender in Caribbean Development. Patricia Mohammed and Catherine Shepherd, eds. Pp. 156–169. Cave Hill, Barbados: University of the West Indies.
1996   Family in the Caribbean: Themes and Perspectives. Kingston, Jamaica: Ian Randle.

Barry, A., T. Osborne, and N. Rose
1993   Liberalism, Neoliberalism, and Governmentality: An Introduction. Economy and Society 22:265–266.

Bastien, Joseph W.
1978   Mountain of the Condor: Metaphor and Ritual in an Andean Ayllu. Saint Paul: West Publishing Co.

Bates, Crispin
2001   Introduction: Community and Identity among South Asians in Diaspora. *In* Community, Empire and Migration: South Asians in Diaspora. Crispin Bates, ed. Pp. 1–45. London: Palgrave.

REFERENCES

Bauman, Zygmunt
2001   Community: Seeking Safety in an Insecure World. Cambridge: Polity Press.

Baumann, Gerd
1996   Contesting Culture: Discourses of Identity in Multi-Ethnic London. Cambridge: Cambridge University Press.

Bayon, R., J. S. Lovink, and W. J. Veening
2000   Financing Biodiversity Conservation. Washington, DC: Sustainable Development Department, Inter-American Development Bank.

Bazemore, Gordon, and Mark Umbreit
2001   Comparison of Four Restorative Conferencing Models. Juvenile Justice Bulletin, NCJ 184738. Washington, DC: Office of Juvenile Justice and Delinquency Prevention, U.S. Department of Justice.

Beaumont, Gustave de, and Alexis de Tocqueville
1964   On the Penitentiary System in the United States and Its Application in
[1833]   France. Carbondale, IL: Southern Illinois University Press.

Beccaria, Cesare
1963   On Crimes and Punishments. Henry Paolucci, trans. Indianapolis:
[1764]   Bobbs-Merrill Company.

Bechofer, Yosef Gavriel
1998   The Contemporary Eruv: Eruvin in Modern Metropolitan Areas. Jerusalem: Feldheim Publishers.

Beirne, Piers
1994   Origins and Growth of Criminology. Aldershot, NH: Dartmouth Publishing Company.

Berger, Peter L., and Thomas Luckmann
1966   The Social Construction of Reality: A Treatise in the Sociology of Knowledge. New York: Doubleday.

Berlant, Lauren
1991   The Anatomy of National Fantasy. Chicago: University of Chicago Press.

Bhabha, Homi K.
1990   DissemiNation: Time, Narrative, and the Margins of the Modern Nation. *In* Nation and Narration. Homi Bhabha, ed. Pp. 291–322. New York: Routledge.
1994   The Location of Culture. London: Routledge.

Bilby, Kenneth
1999   Neither Here Nor There: The Place of "Community" in the Jamaican Religious Imagination. *In* Religion, Diaspora, and Cultural Identity. John Pulis, ed. Pp. 311–335. Amsterdam: Gordon and Breach.

Blair, Tony
2001   Opportunity for All, Responsibility from All: A New Commitment to Neighbourhood Renewal. Electronic document, http://www.socialexclu

sionunit.gov.uk/media/speeches/PM_speech.doc, accessed January 10, 2003.

Blok, Anton

1974   The Mafia in a Sicilian Village. Prospect Heights, IL: Waveland Press.

Bloom, Stephen

2000   Postville: A Clash of Cultures in Heartland America. San Diego: Harcourt.

Boyarin, Jonathan

1997   Circumscribing Constitutional Identities in Kiryas Joel. Yale Law Journal 106(5):1537–1570.

Boyarin, Jonathan, and Daniel Boyarin

1993   Diaspora: Generation and the Ground of Jewish Identity. Critical Inquiry 19:693–725.

Brah, Avtar

1996   Cartographies of Desire. New York: Routledge.

Braithwaite, John

2002   Restorative Justice and Responsive Regulation. Oxford: Oxford University Press.

Brana-Schute, Gary

1979   On the Corner: Male Social Life in a Paramaribo Creole Neighborhood. Assen, Netherlands: Van Gorcum.

Brechin, S. R., P. R. Wilshusen, C. L. Fortwangler, and P. C. West

2002   Beyond the Square Wheel: Toward a More Comprehensive Understanding of Biodiversity Conservation as Social and Political Process. Society and Natural Resources 15(1):41–64.

Brereton, Bridget

1979   Race Relations in Colonial Trinidad, 1870–1900. New York: Cambridge University Press.

Brettschneider, Marla

1996   Multiculturalism, Jews, and Democracy: Situating the Discussion. *In* The Narrow Bridge: Jewish Views on Multiculturalism. Marla Brettschneider, ed. Pp. 1–24. New Brunswick, NJ: Rutgers University Press.

Brodkin, Karen

1998   How Jews Became White Folks and What That Says about Race in America. New Brunswick, NJ: Rutgers University Press.

Brosius, J. Peter, Anna Lowenhaupt Tsing, and Charles Zerner

1998   Representing Communities: Histories and Politics of Community-Based Natural Resource Management. Society and Natural Resources 11(2):157–168.

Brown, Jacqueline Nassy

1998   Black Liverpool, Black America, and the Gendering of Diasporic Space. Cultural Anthropology 13(3):291–325.

REFERENCES

Brown, Susan Love
2002   Intentional Community: An Anthropological Perspective. Albany: State University of New York Press.

Brown, Michael, and Barbara Wyckoff-Baird
1993   Designing Integrated Conservation and Development Projects. Washington, DC: Biodiversity Support Program.

Brubaker, Rogers, and Frederick Cooper
2000   Beyond "Identity." Theory and Society 29:1–47.

Brush, Stephen B.
1977   Mountain, Field and Family: The Economy and Human Ecology of an Andean Village. Philadelphia: University of Pennsylvania Press.

Buck-Morse, S.
2003   Thinking Past Terror. London: Verso.

Burawoy, Michael
2003   For a Sociological Marxism: The Complementary Convergence of Antonio Gramsci and Karl Polanyi. Politics and Society 31(2):193–261.

Byres, Terence J., and Henry Bernstein
2001   From Peasant Studies to Agrarian Change. Journal of Agrarian Change 1:1–56.

Calhoun, C. J.
1980   Community: Toward a Variable Conceptualization for Comparative Research. Social History 5:105–129.

Cancian, Frank
1992   The Decline of Community in Zinacantan. Stanford, CA: Stanford University Press.

Castells, Manuel
1997   The Power of Identity. Malden, MA: Blackwell.

Castro Pozo, Hildebrando
1924   Nuestra comunidad indígena. Lima: Editorial "El Lucero."

CEPF. *See* **Critical Ecosystem Partnership Fund**

Cernea, Michael, ed.
1985   Putting People First: Sociological Variables in Rural Development. New York: Oxford University Press.

CFA. *See* **Conservation Finance Alliance**

Chakrabarty, Dipesh
2000   Provincializing Europe: Postcolonial Thought and Historical Difference. Princeton, NJ: Princeton University Press.

Chambers, Robert
1983   Rural Development: Putting the Last First. London: Longman.

Chatterjee, Partha
1983   More on Modes of Power and the Peasantry. *In* Subaltern Studies: Writings

on South Asian History and Society, vol. 2. Ranajit Guha, ed. Pp. 311–349. Delhi: Oxford University Press.

1986   Nationalist Thought and the Colonial World: A Derivative Discourse. London: Zed Books.

1993   The Nation and Its Fragments: Colonial and Postcolonial Histories. Princeton, NJ: Princeton University Press.

Chevannes, Barry

2003   The Role of the Street in the Socialization of Caribbean Males. *In* Gender and the Culture of Sexuality in the Caribbean. Linden Lewis, ed. Pp. 215–233. Gainesville: University Press of Florida.

Choque, María Eugenia, and Carlos Mamani

2001   Reconstitución del ayllu y derechos de los pueblos indígenas: El movimiento indio en los Andes de Bolivia. Journal of Latin American Anthropology 6(1):202–224.

Clark, David B.

1973   The Concept of Community: A Re-Examination. Sociological Review 21(3):397–416.

Clarke, Edith

1957   My Mother Who Fathered Me. London: George Allen and Unwin.

Clarke, James W.

1998   The Lineaments of Wrath: Race, Violent Crime and American Culture. New Brunswick, NJ: Transaction Publishers.

ClearWater

2003   Back from the Brink. London: ClearWater.

Clifford, James

1994   Diasporas. Cultural Anthropology 9(3):302–338.

Clifford, M.

2001   Political Genealogy after Foucault. London: Routledge.

Cohen, Anthony P.

1985   The Symbolic Construction of Community. Chichester, UK: Ellis Horwood; London: Tavistock.

2002   Epilogue. *In* Realizing Community: Concepts, Social Relationships and Sentiments. Vered Amit, ed. Pp. 165–170. London: Routledge.

Cohen, Jeffrey H.

2000   Cooperation and Community: Economy and Society in Oaxaca. Austin: University of Texas Press.

Cohen, S., P. Maguire, and D. Kloss

2001   Mobilizing Funding for Biodiversity Conservation: A User-Friendly Training Guide for Understanding, Selecting, and Implementing Conservation Finance Mechanisms. Electronic document, www.conservationfinance.org/Documents/Training_Manual/htm_files/Home.htm, accessed August 19, 2005.

REFERENCES

Cohen, Yehudi

1956   Structure and Function: Family Organization and Socialization in a Jamaican Community. American Anthropologist 58:664–686.

Cohn, Bernard S.

1987   An Anthropologist among the Historians and Other Essays. New Delhi: Oxford University Press.

Coleman, Peter J.

1974   Debtors and Creditors in America: Insolvency, Imprisonment for Debt, and Bankruptcy, 1607–1900. Madison: State Historical Society of Wisconsin.

Collier, Paul

2000   The Economic Causes of Civil Conflict and Their Implications for Policy. Washington, DC: World Bank.

2003   Breaking the Conflict Trap. London: Oxford University Press.

Collins, Jane L.

1986   The Household and Relations of Production in Southern Peru. Comparative Studies in Society and History 28(4):651–671.

Colvin, Mark

1997   Penitentiaries, Reformatories and Chain Gangs: Social Theory and the History of Punishment in Nineteenth-Century America. New York: St. Martin's Press.

Comaroff, J., and J. L. Comaroff

1989   The Colonization of Consciousness in South-Africa. Economy and Society 18(3):267–296.

Conservation Finance Alliance (CFA)

2002   Conservation Finance Alliance. Electronic document, www.conservationfinance.org, accessed October 31, 2002.

Cooper, Davina

2002   Out of Place: Symbolic Domains, Religious Rights and the Cultural Contract. *In* Land and Territoriality. Michael Saltman, ed. Pp. 93–111. Oxford: Berg.

Coronil, Fernando

1997   The Magical State: Nature, Money and Modernity in Venezuela. Chicago: University of Chicago Press.

Creed, Gerald W.

2004   Constituted Through Conflict: Images of Community (and Nation) in Bulgarian Rural Ritual. American Anthropologist 106(1):56–70.

Creed, Gerald W., and Barbara Ching

1997   Recognizing Rusticity: Identity and the Power of Place. *In* Knowing Your Place: Rural Identity and Cultural Hierarchy. Barbara Ching and Gerald W. Creed, eds. Pp. 1–38. New York: Routledge.

Crehan, Kate
1997   The Fractured Community: Landscapes of Power and Gender in Rural
         Zambia. Berkeley: University of California Press.
2002a   Silencing Power: Mapping the Social Terrain in Post-apartheid South
         Africa. *In* Contested Terrains, Constructed Categories: Contemporary
         Africa in Focus. George C. Bond and Nigel C. Gibson, eds. Pp. 173–193.
         Boulder, CO: Westview Press.
2002b   Gramsci, Culture and Anthropology. Berkeley: University of California
         Press; London: Pluto Press.

Critical Ecosystem Partnership Fund (CEPF)
2001a   Ecosystem Profiles. Electronic document, www.cepf.net/he/ecosystem_
         profiles.htm, accessed November 9, 2001.
2001b   Investors. Electronic document, www.cepf.net/he/investors.htm, accessed
         November 9, 2001.

Daly, Kathleen
2000   Revisiting the Relationship between Retributive and Restorative Justice. *In*
         Restorative Justice: Philosophy to Practice. Heather Strang and John
         Braithwaite, eds. Pp. 33–54. Burlington, VT: Ashgate Publishing Company.

Daniels, Christine
1995   "Without Any Limitacon of Time": Debt Servitude in Colonial America.
         Labor History 36(2):232–250.

Danzger, Herbert
1989   Returning to Tradition: The Contemporary Revival of Orthodox Judaism.
         New Haven, CT: Yale University Press.

Davila, Arlene M.
2001   Latinos, Inc.: The Marketing and Making of a People. Berkeley: University
         of California Press.

Davis, Angela
1998   Race and Criminalization: Black Americans and the Punishment Industry.
         In The Angela Davis Reader. Joy James, ed. Pp. 61–73. London: Blackwell.

Dean, Mitchell
1999   Governmentality. London: Sage.

de Beauvoir, Simone
1997   The Second Sex. London: Vintage.
[1949]

de la Cadena, Marisol
2000   Indigenous Mestizos: The Politics of Race and Culture in Cuzco, Peru,
         1919–1991. Durham, NC: Duke University Press.

Delgado, Richard
2000   Goodbye to Hammurabi: Analyzing the Atavistic Appeal of Restorative
         Justice. Stanford Law Review 52:751–775.

References

Derrida, Jacques
1992   Given Time: I, Counterfeit Money. Peggy Kamuf, trans. Chicago: University of Chicago Press.
1994   Specters of Marx. Peggy Kamuf, trans. New York: Routledge.

Di Chiro, Giovanna
1996   Nature as Community: The Convergence of Environment and Social Justice. *In* Uncommon Ground: Rethinking the Human Place in Nature. William Cronon, ed. Pp. 298–320. New York: W. W. Norton.

Dinerstein, Eric, David M. Olson, Douglas J. Graham, Avis L. Webster, Steven A. Primm, Marnie P. Bookbinder, and George Ledec
1995   A Conservation Assessment of the Terrestrial Ecosystems of Latin America and the Caribbean. Washington, DC: World Bank.

Dirks, Nicholas B.
2001   Castes of Mind: Colonialism and the Making of Modern India. Princeton, NJ: Princeton University Press.

Doheny-Farina, Stephen
1996   The Wired Neighborhood. New Haven, CT: Yale University Press.

Donham, Donald L.
2002   On Being Modern in a Capitalist World: Some Conceptual and Comparative Issues. *In* Critically Modern: Alternatives, Alterities, Anthropologies. Bruce M. Knauft, ed. Pp. 241–257. Bloomington: Indiana University Press.

Douglass, Lisa
1992   The Power of Sentiment: Love, Hierarchy, and the Jamaican Family Elite. Boulder, CO: Westview Press.

Dudley, Kathryn
2000   Debt and Dispossession: Farm Loss in America's Heartland. Chicago: University of Chicago Press.

Dundes, Alan
2002   The Shabbat Elevator and Other Sabbath Subterfuges. Lanham, MD: Rowman and Littlefield.

Earls, John, and Irene Silverblatt
1978   La realidad física y social en la cosmología andina. Actes du XLIIe Congres International des Americanistes 4:299–325.

Ebeku, K.
2003   Nigerian Supreme Court and Ownership of Offshore Oil. Natural Resources Forum 27:291–299.

Edelman, Marc
1999   Peasants Against Globalization: Rural Social Movements in Costa Rica. Stanford, CA: Stanford University Press.

Environmental News Network
2001   Scientists Develop Mathematical Model for Conservation Forecasting.

Electronic document, http://enn.com/news.enn-stories/2001/10/
10232001/model_45329.asp, accessed October 23, 2001.

Environmental Rights Actions (ERA)

2000   The Emperor Has No Clothes. Benin City, Nigeria: Environmental Rights
         Action.

ERA. *See* **Environmental Rights Action**

Erikson, Erik

1964   Inner and Outer Space: Reflections on Womanhood. Daedalus
         93(2):582–606.

Etzioni, Amitai

1998   The New Golden Rule: Community and Morality in a Democratic Society.
         New York: Basic Books.

Ferguson, James

1992   The Country and the City on the Copperbelt. Cultural Anthropology
         7(1):80–92.

1994   The Anti-Politics Machine: Development, Depoliticization, and
         Bureaucratic Power in Lesotho. Minneapolis: University of Minnesota
         Press.

Fernandez, James W.

1965   Symbolic Consensus in a Fang Reformative Cult. American Anthropologist
         67:902–929.

**Fine, M., M. E. Torre, K. Boudin, I. Bowen, J. Clark, D. Hylton, M. Martinez,
R. A. "Missy" Roberts, P. Smart, and D. Upegui**

2001   Participatory Action Research: Within and Beyond Bars. *In* Qualitative
         Research in Psychology: Expanding Perspectives in Methodology and
         Design. P. Camic, J. E. Rhodes, and L. Yardley, eds. Pp. 173–198.
         Washington, DC: American Psychological Association.

Firth, Raymond

1957   Factions in Indian and Overseas Indian Societies I: Introduction. British
         Journal of Sociology 8:291–342.

Fondahl, Gail

1998   Gaining Ground? Evenkis, Land, and Reform in Southeastern Siberia.
         London: Allyn and Bacon.

Fonrobert, Charlotte

2003   The Political Symbolism of the Eruv in Rabbinic Judaism. Paper presented
         at the conference Jewish Conceptions and Practices of Space, Stanford
         University, May 18–19.

Forero, Juan

2003   Native Latins Are Astir and Thirsty for Power. With Larry Rohter. New
         York Times, March 22: A3.

Forrest, T.

1995   Politics and Economic Development in Nigeria. Boulder, CO: Westview.

REFERENCES

Foucault, Michel
1977   Discipline and Punish. New York: Vintage.
1982   The Subject and Power. *In* Beyond Structuralism and Hermeneutics. H.
         Dreyfus, ed. Pp. 208–226. Chicago: University of Chicago Press.
2000   Power, vol. 3. James Faubion, ed. New York: New Press.

Fowler, Robert Booth
1991   The Dance with Community: The Contemporary Debate in American
         Political Thought. Lawrence: University Press of Kansas.

Fraser, N., and A. Honneth
2003   Redistribution or Recognition? London: Verso.

Frazier, E. Franklin
1966   The Negro Family in the United States. Chicago: University of
[1939] Chicago Press.

Freedman, Samuel
2000   Jew vs. Jew: The Struggle for the Soul of American Jewry. New York: Simon
         and Schuster.

Freeman, Carla
2000   High Tech and High Heels in the Global Economy. Durham, NC: Duke
         University Press.

Frynas, G.
2000   Oil in Nigeria. Hamburg: LIT.

Fukuyama, Francis
1994   Trust: The Social Virtues and the Creation of Prosperity. New York: Free
         Press.

Furnivall, J. S.
1956   Colonial Policy and Practice. New York: New York University Press.
[1939]

Furro, T.
1992   Federalism and the Politics of Revenue Allocation in Nigeria. Ph.D.
         dissertation, Clark Atlanta University.

Gans, Herbert
1962   The Urban Villagers: Group and Class in the Life of Italian-Americans.
         New York: Free Press.

Ganzfried, Rabbi Solomon
1927   Code of Jewish Law (Kitzur Schulchan Aruch). Hyman Goldin, trans. New
         York: Hebrew Publishing Company.

Garland, David
1990   Punishment and Modern Society. Chicago: University of Chicago Press.
2001   The Culture of Control. Oxford: Oxford University Press.

Gilmore, Ruth Wilson

1998– Globalization and U.S. Prison Growth: From Military Keynesianism to

1999 Post-Keynesian Militarism. Race and Class 40(2/3):171–188.

Gilroy, Paul

1987 "There Ain't No Black in the Union Jack": The Cultural Politics of Race and Nation. Chicago: University of Chicago Press.

1991 "There Ain't No Black in the Union Jack": The Cultural Politics of Race and Nation. With a new foreword by Houston A. Baker Jr. Chicago: University of Chicago Press.

1993 The Black Atlantic. Chicago: University of Chicago Press.

Glick Schiller, Nina, and Georges Fouron

2001 Georges Woke Up Laughing: Long-Distance Nationalism and the Search for Home. Durham, NC: Duke University Press.

Gmelch, George, and Sharon Gmelch

1997 The Parish behind God's Back. Ann Arbor: University of Michigan Press.

Gopinath, Gayatri

1995 "Bombay, U.K., Yuba City": Bhangra Music and the Engendering of Diaspora. Diaspora 4(3):303–321.

2005 Impossible Desires: Queer Diasporas and South Asian Public Cultures. Durham, NC: Duke University Press.

Gordon, Avery F.

1997 Ghostly Matters: Haunting and the Sociological Imagination. Minneapolis: University of Minnesota Press.

Gordon, C., ed.

1980 Knowledge/Power. London: Harvester.

Gould, Jeffrey

1998 To Die in This Way: Nicaraguan Indians and the Myth of Mestizaje, 1880–1960. Durham, NC: Duke University Press.

Government of India

1912 Census of India, 1911, vol. 5: Bihar and Orissa. Calcutta: Government Press.

Gramsci, Antonio

1971 Selections from the Prison Notebooks. Quintin Hoare and Geoffrey Nowell Smith, eds. London: Lawrence and Wishart.

1977 Selections from Political Writings 1910–1920. Quintin Hoare, ed. London: Lawrence and Wishart.

1985 Selections from Cultural Writings. David Forgacs and Geoffrey Nowell Smith, eds. London: Lawrence and Wishart.

Gray, Patty A.

n.d. The Obshchina in Chukotka: Local Self-Government and Urge to Centralize. Unpublished manuscript.

REFERENCES

Greenberg, James B.

1995   Capital, Ritual, and Boundaries of the Closed Corporate Community. *In* Articulating Hidden Histories: Exploring the Influence of Eric R. Wolf. Jane Schneider and Rayna Rapp, eds. Pp. 67–81. Berkeley: University of California Press.

Gregg, Veronica

2001   Caribbean Women and the Question of Knowledge. Paper presented at the conference Atlantic Crossings: Women's Voices, Women's Stories from the Caribbean and the Nigerian Hinterland, Dartmouth College, May 18–20.

Halberstam, Judith

2004   In a Queer Place and Time: Transgender Bodies, Subcultural Lives. New York: New York University Press.

Hall, Stuart

1990   Cultural Identity and Diaspora. *In* Identity: Community, Culture, Difference. J. Rutherford, ed. Pp. 222–237. London: Lawrence and Wishart.

1999   Thinking the Diaspora: Home-Thoughts from Abroad. Small Axe 6:1–18.

2003   Marx's Notes on Method: A "Reading" of the "1857 Introduction." Cultural Studies 17(2):113–149.

Halter, Marilyn

2000   Shopping for Identity: The Marketing of Ethnicity. New York: Schocken Books.

Hamilton, Richard F.

1996   The Social Misconstruction of Reality: Validity and Verification in the Scholarly Community. New Haven, CT: Yale University Press.

Hammer, J.

1996   Nigerian Crude. Harper's Magazine, June: 58–68.

Hansen, Karen V.

1994   A Very Social Time: Crafting Community in Antebellum New England. Berkeley: University of California Press.

Haraway, Donna

1991   Simians, Cyborgs, and Women: The Reinvention of Nature. New York: Routledge.

Hardt, Michael, and Antonio Negri

2000   Empire. Cambridge, MA: Harvard University Press.

Hart, Gillian

2003   Disabling Globalization. Berkeley: University of California Press.

Harvey, David

1987   The Urban Experience. Baltimore: Johns Hopkins University Press.

1996   Justice, Nature and the Geography of Difference. Oxford: Blackwell.

2003   The New Imperialism. London: Clarendon.

Hegel, G. W. F.

1953   Reason in History: A General Introduction to the Philosophy of History.

[1837]   Robert S. Hartman, trans. Indianapolis: Bobbs-Merrill.

Heilman, Samuel

1976   Synagogue Life: A Study in Symbolic Interaction. New Brunswick, NJ:
          Transaction.

Heilman, Samuel, and Steven Cohen

1989   Cosmopolitans and Parochials: Modern Orthodox Jews in America.
          Chicago: University of Chicago Press.

Henriques, Fernando

1949   West Indian Family Organization. American Journal of Sociology
          55(1):30–37.

Herskovits, Melville

1958   The Myth of the Negro Past. Boston: Beacon Press.

[1941]

Hillery, George A., Jr.

1955   Definitions of Community: Areas of Agreement. Rural Sociology
          20:111–123.

Hintzen, Percy

1989   The Costs of Regime Survival: Racial Mobilization, Elite Domination and
          Control of the State in Guyana and Trinidad. Cambridge: Cambridge
          University Press.

Hoffert, Paul

2000   All Together Now: Connected Communities: How They Will Revolutionize
          the Way You Live, Work, and Play. Toronto: Stoddart.

Hoggart, Richard

2002   No Sell-Out: Adult Education and the Uses of Literacy. First of the Month
          4(2):13–15.

HRW. *See* **Human Rights Watch**

Hudson, Barbara

1998   Restorative Justice: The Challenge of Sexual and Racial Violence. Journal
          of Law and Society 25(2):237–256.

Human Rights Watch (HRW)

1995   The Ogoni Crisis Report no. 7/5. New York: Human Rights Watch.

2002   The Niger Delta: No Democratic Dividend. New York: Human Rights
          Watch.

2003   Testing Democracy Report no.15/9. New York: Human Rights Watch.

2005   Violence in Oil Rich Rivers State in 2004. New York: Human Rights Watch.

Hummon, David M.

1990   Commonplaces: Community Ideology and Identity in American Culture.
          Albany: State University of New York Press.

Huntington, Samuel P.
1998　The Clash of Civilizations and the Remaking of World Order. New York: Touchstone.

Ikein, A.
1990　The Impact of Oil on a Developing Country. New York: Praeger.

Ikelegbe, A.
2001　Civil Society, Oil and Conflict in the Niger Delta Region of Nigeria. Journal of Modern African Studies 399(3):437–469.

Ikporukpo, C.
1996　Federalism, Political Power and the Economic Power Game: Control over Access to Petroleum Resources in Nigeria. Environment and Planning Series C 14:159–177.

Isbell, Billie Jean
1978　To Defend Ourselves: Ecology and Ritual in an Andean Village. Austin: University of Texas Press.

Isbell, William H.
1997　Mummies and Mortuary Monuments: A Postprocessual Prehistory of Central Andean Social Organization. Austin: University of Texas Press.
2000　What We Should Be Studying: The "Imagined Community" and the "Natural Community." In The Archaeology of Communities: A New World Perspective. Marcello A. Canuto and Jason Yaeger, eds. Pp. 243–266. London: Routledge.

Janowitz, Morris
1967　The Community Press in an Urban Setting: The Social Elements of Urbanism. 2nd edition. Chicago: University of Chicago Press.

Jensen, S.
2004　Claiming Community. Critique of Anthropology 24(2):179–207.

John, Mary E.
2000　Alternate Modernities? Reservations and Women's Movement in 20th Century India. Economic and Political Weekly (Bombay), October 28: 3824.

Jones, Steve, ed.
1999　Doing Internet Research: Critical Issues and Methods for Examining the Net. Thousand Oaks, CA: Sage.

Joseph, Miranda
2002　Against the Romance of Community. Minneapolis: University of Minnesota Press.

Joyce, Patrick
2003　The Rule of Freedom. London: Verso.

Julien, Catherine
2000　Reading Inca History. Iowa City: University of Iowa Press.

Kanter, Rosabeth Moss
1972   Commitment and Community: Communes and Utopias in Sociological Perspective. Cambridge, MA: Harvard University Press.

Kapucinski, R.
1982   The Shah of Shahs. New York: Vintage.

Karl, T.
1997   The Paradox of Plenty. Berkeley: University of California Press.

Katznelson, Ira
1991   Between Separation and Disappearance: Jews on the Margins of American Liberalism. *In* Paths of Emancipation: Jews, States, and Citizenship. Pierre Birnbaum and Ira Katznelson, eds. Pp. 157–205. Princeton, NJ: Princeton University Press.

Keane, J.
1998   Civil Society. Cambridge: Polity Press.

Kelly, John
1991   A Politics of Virtue. Chicago: University of Chicago Press.
2001   "They Cannot Represent Themselves": Threats to Difference and So-Called Community Politics in Fiji from 1936 to 1947. *In* Community, Empire and Migration: South Asians in Diaspora. Crispin Bates, ed. Pp. 46–86. London: Palgrave.

Kelly, John D., and Martha Kaplan
2001   Represented Communities: Fiji and World Decolonization. Chicago: University of Chicago Press.

Kemedi, V.
2002   Oil on Troubled Waters. Environmental Politics Working Papers no. 15. Berkeley: University of California.

Kemf, E.
1993   Indigenous Peoples and Protected Areas: The Law of Mother Earth. London: Earthscan.

Khan, Aisha
1994   Juthaa in Trinidad: Food, Pollution, and Hierarchy in a Caribbean Diaspora Community. American Ethnologist 21(2):245–269.
2004   Callaloo Nation: Metaphors of Racial and Religious Identity among South Asians in Trinidad. Durham, NC: Duke University Press.

Khan, S.
1994   Nigeria: The Political Economy of Oil. London: Oxford University Press.

Kirp, David L.
2000   Almost Home: America's Love-Hate Relationship with Community. Princeton, NJ: Princeton University Press.

Kitching, Gavin
1980   Development and Underdevelopment in Historical Perspective. London: Methuen.

REFERENCES

Klare, M.
2001   Resource Wars. Boston: Beacon Press.

Kloss, D.
2001   Sustainable Financing of Biodiversity and Protected Areas. Eschborn, Germany: GTZ.

Kumar, Ravinder
1983   Essays in the Social History of Modern India. Calcutta: Oxford University Press.

Lacey, Nicola, and Lucia Zedner
1995   Discourses of Community in Criminal Justice. Journal of Law and Society 22(3):301–325.

Laclau, Ernesto
1996   Emancipation(s). London: Verso.

Latour, Bruno
1988   The Pasteurization of France. Cambridge, MA: Harvard University Press.

Leeds, Anthony
1973   Locality Power in Relation to Supralocal Power Institutions. *In* Urban Anthropology: Cross-Cultural Studies of Urbanization. Aidan Southall, ed. Pp. 15–41. New York: Oxford University Press.

Leps, Marie-Christine
1990   Apprehending the Criminal. Durham, NC: Duke University Press.

Le Roy Ladurie, Emmanuel
1974   The Peasants of Languedoc. John Day, trans. Urbana: University of Illinois Press.

Lewis, Gordon K.
1968   The Growth of the Modern West Indies. New York: Monthly Review Press.

Lewis, Linden, ed.
2003   The Culture of Gender and Sexuality in the Caribbean. Gainesville: University Press of Florida.

Lewis, Oscar
1960   Tepoztlan: Village in Mexico. New York: Holt, Rinehart and Winston.

Li, Tania Murray
1996   Images of Community: Discourse and Strategy in Property Relations. Development and Change 27(3):501–527.

2001   Boundary Work: Community, Market and State Reconsidered. *In* Communities and the Environment: Ethnicity, Gender, and the State in Community-Based Conservation. Arun Agrawal and Clark C. Gibson, eds. Pp. 157–179. New Brunswick, NJ: Rutgers University Press.

Lieber, Michael
1981   Street Life: Afro-American Culture in Urban Trinidad. Cambridge, MA: Schenkman.

Locke, Adrian

1999   From Ice to Icon: El Señor de Qoyllur Rit'i as Symbol of Native Andean Catholic Worship. Paper presented in the Department of Art History and Theory at the University of Essex, January 28. Electronic document, http://www2.essex.ac.uk/arthistory/arara/papers/p2.1.html, accessed December 2002.

Low, Setha

2003   Behind the Gates: Life, Security, and the Pursuit of Happiness in Fortress America. New York: Routledge.

Lowenthal, David

1985   The Past Is a Foreign Country. Cambridge: Cambridge University Press.

Luhmann, Niklas

1979   Trust and Power: Two Works. Chichester, UK: Wiley.

Lutz, Catherine, and Lila Abu-Lughod

1990   Language and the Politics of Emotion. Cambridge: Cambridge University Press.

Lynch, O., and K. Talbot

1995   Balancing Acts: Community-Based Forest Management and National Law in Asia and the Pacific. Washington, DC: World Resources Institute.

MacArthur, R. H., and E. O. Wilson

1967   The Theory of Island Biogeography. Princeton, NJ: Princeton University Press.

Macas, Luis

2000   Indigenous Institutions: The Llacta-Ayllu. Rimay: Bulletin of the Indigenous Sciences and Cultures (IISC) 2(17). Electronic document, http://icci.nativeweb.org/boletin/17, accessed December 2002.

MacDonald, Scott B., and Albert L. Gastman

2001   A History of Credit and Power in the Western World. New Brunswick, NJ: Transaction Publishers.

Macfarlane, Alan

1977   History, Anthropology and the Study of Communities. Social History 2:631–652.

Maguire, P.

2002   Unpublished summary of Sustainable Conservation Finance Retreat, Saint Michaels, Maryland, February 12–13.

Mallon, Florencia E.

1983   The Defense of Community in Peru's Central Highlands: Peasant Struggle and Capitalist Transition, 1860–1940. Princeton, NJ: Princeton University Press.

1995   Peasant and Nation: The Making of Postcolonial Mexico and Peru. Berkeley: University of California Press.

Mamdani, Mahmood
1996   Citizen and Subject. Princeton, NJ: Princeton University Press.
2001   Beyond Native and Settler as Political Identities: Overcoming the Political Legacy of Colonialism. Comparative Studies in Society and History 43(4):651-664.
2001   When Victims Become Killers: Colonialism, Nativism, and the Genocide in Rwanda. Princeton, NJ: Princeton University Press.
2003   From Conquest to Consent as the Basis of State Formation: Reflections on Rwanda. *In* The Forging of Nationhood. G. Pandey and P. Geschiere, eds. Pp. 227–270. New Delhi: Manohar.

Mann, Bruce H.
2002   A Republic of Debtors: Bankruptcy in the Age of American Independence. Cambridge, MA: Harvard University Press.

Mariátegui, José Carlos
1971   Seven Interpretative Essays on Peruvian Reality. Marjory Urquidi, trans. Austin: University of Texas Press.
1991   Mariátegui: Textos básicos. Selección prólogo y notas introductorias de Aníbal Quijano. Lima: Fondo de cultura económica.

Markowitz, Fran
1993   A Community in Spite of Itself: Soviet Jewish Émigrés in New York. Washington, DC: Smithsonian Institution Press.

Martin, S., and A. Subramanian
2003   Addressing the Resource Curse: An Illustration from Nigeria. IMF Working Paper, July 2003. Washington, DC: IMF.

Marx, Karl
1977   Capital, vol. 1. Ben Fowkes, trans. New York: Random House.
[1867]

Masuda, S., Izumi Shimda, and Craig Morris, eds.
1985   Andean Ecology and Civilization: An Interdisciplinary Perspective on Andean Ecological Complementarity. Tokyo: University of Tokyo Press.

Matthews, Dom Basil
1971   Crisis of the West Indian Family: A Sample Study. Westport, CT:
[1953]   Greenwood Press.

Mayer, Enrique
1992   Peru in Deep Trouble: Mario Vargas Llosa's "Inquest in the Andes" Re-examined. *In* Rereading Cultural Anthtropology. George E. Marcus, ed. Pp. 181–229. Durham, NC: Duke University Press.
2002   The Articulated Peasant: Household Economies in the Andes. Boulder, CO: Westview Press.

Mayer, Enrique, and Ralph Bolton, eds.
1977   Andean Kinship and Marriage. Washington, DC: American Anthropological Association.

Mazumdar, Vina

1997   Historical Soundings. Special issue "Empowering Women," Seminar no. 457 (September 1997). New Delhi, India.

Mbembe, Achille

2000   At the Edge of the World. Public Culture 12(1):259–284.

McNeely, J., ed.

1995   Expanding Partnerships in Conservation. Washington, DC: Island Press.

Menon, Nivedita

2000   Elusive "Woman": Feminism and Women's Reservation Bill. Economic and Political Weekly (Bombay), October 28: 3838.

Meranze, Michael

1996   Laboratories of Virtue: Punishment, Revolution, and Authority, 1760–1835. Chapel Hill: University of North Carolina Press.

Mercer, Kobena

1994   Welcome to the Jungle: New Positions in Black Cultural Studies. London: Routledge.

Mikhailov, Nikolai V.

2002   The Collective Psychology of Russian Workers and Workplace: Self-Organization in the Early Twentieth Century. Gerald D. Surh, trans. *In* New Labor History: Worker Identity and Experience in Russia, 1840–1918. Michael Melancon and Alice K. Pate, eds. Pp. 77–94. Bloomington, IN: Slavica Publishers.

Miller, Daniel, and Anthony Carter

2001   The Dialectics of Shopping. Chicago: University of Chicago Press.

Miller, Jonathan

2003   Ruling on Religious Markers, but No End to Fight. New York Times, June: 2324.

Mintz, Sidney

1966   The Caribbean as a Socio-Cultural Area. Journal of World History 9(4):912–937.

Mitchell, Timothy

2002   Rule of Experts: Egypt, Techno-Politics, Modernity. Berkeley: University of California Press.

Mohammed, Patricia

1988   The Caribbean Family Revisited. *In* Gender in Caribbean Development. Patricia Mohammed and Catherine Shepherd, eds. Pp. 156–169. Cave Hill, Barbados: University of the West Indies.

Mohapatra, Prabhu

1996   Longing and Belonging: The Dilemma of Return among Indian Emigrants to the West Indies, 1880–1940. South Asian Studies Seminar, Centre for South Asian Studies, Cambridge University.

Moore, Donald

1998   Clear Waters and Muddied Histories: Environmental History and the Politics of Community in Zimbabwe's Eastern Highlands. Journal of Southern African Studies 24(2):377–403.

Morris, Ruth

1996   Restored to What? Electronic document, http://www.md-justice-policy-inst.org/Rmorris1.html, accessed December 2002.

Muldrew, Craig

1998   The Economy of Obligation: The Culture of Credit and Social Relations in Early Modern England. New York: St. Martin's Press.

Murdoch, Jonathan, and Neil Ward

1997   Governmentality and Territoriality: The Statistical Manufacture of Britain's "National Farm." Political Geography 16:307–324.

Murra, John V.

1975   Formaciones económicas y políticas del mundo andino. Lima: Instituto de Estudios Peruanos.

1978   La organización económica y política del estado Inca. Mexico, DF: Siglo XXI.

Myers, Norman

1979   The Sinking Ark: A New Look at the Problem of Disappearing Species. Oxford: Pergamon Press.

Naanen, B.

1995   Oil Producing Minorities and the Restructuring of Nigerian Federalism. Journal of Commonwealth and Comparative Politics 33(1):46–58.

Nakamura, Lisa

2002   Cybertypes: Race, Ethnicity, and Identity on the Internet. New York: Routledge.

Nandy, Ashis

1990   Dialogue and the Diaspora. Third Text 11:99–108.

Nash, June

1967   Death as a Way of Life: The Increasing Incidence of Homicide in a Maya Community. American Anthropologist 69:451–470.

National Council of Churches of Christ in the USA (NCCC)

1996   Restoring Justice. 51 min. Presbyterian Church, USA. Louisville, KY.

Nature Conservancy

2000   Designing a Geography of Hope: A Practitioner's Handbook to Ecoregional Conservation Planning, vols. 1 and 2. Washington, DC: Nature Conservancy.

2001   Conservation by Design: A Framework for Mission Success. Washington, DC: Nature Conservancy.

NCCC. *See* **National Council of Churches of Christ in the USA**

Nehru, Jawaharlal
1961   The Discovery of India. Bombay: Allied Publishers.
1984   Selected Works of Jawaharlal Nehru, vol. 14. New Delhi: Nehru Memorial
        Fund.

Neusner, Jacob
1984   A History of the Jews in Babylonia. Chico, CA: Scholars Press.
1998–   Judaism and Its Social Metaphors: Israel in the History of Jewish Thought.
1989   Cambridge: Cambridge University Press.

Niethammer, L.
2003   The Infancy of Tarzan. New Left Review 19:79–92.

Nietzsche, Friedrich
1989   On the Genealogy of Morals. Walter Kaufman and R. J. Hollingdale, trans.
[1887] New York: Vintage Books.

Nigerian Federal Government
1987   Report of the Political Bureau. Lagos: Federal Government Printers.
1996   Ogoni Crisis. Lagos: Ministry of Information, Nigerian Federal
        Government.

Nisbet, Robert A.
1953   The Quest for Community. New York: Oxford University Press.

NNPC
2004   Niger Delta: A Report on the Niger Delta Youths Stakeholders Workshop.
        Port Harcourt, Nigeria: NNPC/AAPW.

Noss, Reed F.
1983   A Regional Landscape Approach to Maintain Diversity. BioScience
        33(11):700–706.
2002   Context Matters: Considerations for Large-Scale Conservation.
        Conservation in Practice 3(3):10–19.

Oates, John F.
1999   Myth and Reality in the Rain Forest: How Conservation Strategies Are
        Failing in West Africa. Berkeley: University of California Press.

Obi, C.
2001   The Changing Forms of Identity Politics in Nigeria. Uppsala, Sweden:
        Africa Institute.
2004   The Oil Paradox. Working Paper no. 73, University of Leipzig Papers on
        Africa. Leipzig: University of Leipzig.

Ojo, O.
2002   The Niger Delta. Research Report no. 49. Ibadan, Nigeria: Development
        Policy Center.

Okilo, M.
1980   Derivation: A Criterion of Revenue Allocation. Port Harcourt, Nigeria:
        Rivers State Newspaper Corporation.

REFERENCES

Okonta, I.

2001   The Struggle of the Ogoni for Self-Determination. Ph.D. dissertation. Oxford University.

2004   Resource Control and the Political Economy of Nigeria. Unpublished manuscript, University of California, Berkeley.

Okonta I., and O. Douglas

2001   Where Vultures Feast. San Francisco: Sierra Club.

Okpu, U.

1977   Ethnic Minority Problems in Nigerian Politics. Stockholm: Wiksell.

Olson, David, and Eric Dinerstein

1997   Ecoregional-Based Conservation Planning: Identifying Priority Sites and Activities within Ecoregions. Unpublished paper. Washington, DC: World Wildlife Fund.

Olson, D. M., E. Dinerstein, R. Abell, T. Allnutt, C. Carpenter, L. McClenachan, J. D'Amico, et al.

2000   The Global 200: A Representation Approach to Preserving the Earth's Distinctive Ecosystems. Washington, DC: World Wildlife Fund.

Olson, D. M., E. Dinerstein, E. D. Wikramanayake, N. D. Burgess, G. V. N. Powell, E. C. Underwood, J. A. D'Amico, et al.

2001   Terrestrial Ecoregions of the World: A New Map of Life on Earth. BioScience 51(11):933–938.

Omernik, James

1987   Ecoregions of the Coterminous United States. Annals of the Association of American Geographers 7(1):118–125.

Orlove, Benjamin

1977   Alpacas, Sheep, and Men: The Wool Export Economy and Regional Society in Southern Peru. New York: Academic Press.

Orta, Andrew

2001   Remembering the Ayllu, Remaking the Nation: Indigenous Scholarship and Activism in the Bolivian Andes. Journal of Latin American Anthropology 6(1):198–201.

Osaghae, E.

1995   The Ogoni Uprising. African Affairs 94:325–344.

Pandey, Gyanendra

2001   Remembering Partition: Violence, Nationalism and History in India. New York: Cambridge University Press.

2005   The Construction of Communalism in Colonial North India, 2nd ed. New Delhi: Oxford University Press.

Parekh, Bhiku

1989   Gandhi's Political Philosophy: A Critical Examination. Notre Dame, IN: University of Notre Dame Press.

Pavlich, George

2001   The Force of Community. *In* Restorative Justice and Civil Society. Heather Strang and John Braithwaite, eds. Pp. 56–68. Cambridge: Cambridge University Press.

Peck, Jamie, and Neil Brenner

2002   Political Economies of Scale: Fast Policy, Interscalar Relations, and Neoliberal Workfare. Economic Geography 78:331–359.

Peluso, N.

1993   Coercing Conservation: The Politics of State Resource Control. *In* The State and Social Power in Global Environmental Politics. R. Lipschutz and K. Conca, eds. Pp. 46–70. New York: Columbia University Press.

Phillips, A.

2000   Financing Protected Areas: Guidelines for Protected Area Managers. Gland, Switzerland: IUCN.

Plant, Raymond

1978   Community: Concept, Conception and Ideology. Politics and Society 8(1):79–107.

Poiani, K., and B. Richter

n.d.   Functional Landscapes and the Conservation of Biodiversity. Working Papers in Conservation Science no. 1. Washington, DC: Nature Conservancy.

Polanyi, Karl

1945   The Origins of Our Time. Boston: Beacon.

Poll, Solomon

1962   The Hasidic Community of Williamsburg. New York: Free Press.

Poovey, Mary

1998   A History of the Modern Fact: Problems of Knowledge in the Sciences of Wealth and Society. Chicago: University of Chicago Press.

Popkin, Samuel L.

1979   The Rational Peasant: The Political Economy of Rural Society in Vietnam. Berkeley: University of California Press.

Poulantzas, Nicos

1978   State, Power, Socialism. London: New Left Books.

Pranis, Kay

1998   Engaging the Community in Restorative Justice. Balanced and Restorative Justice Project (Grant 95-JN-FX-0024). Washington, DC: Office of Juvenile Justice and Delinquency Prevention, U.S. Department of Justice.

2001   Building Justice on a Foundation of Democracy, Caring and Mutual Responsibility. Saint Paul: Minnesota Department of Corrections, Community and Juvenile Services Division.

REFERENCES

Prell, Riv-Ellen
1999   Fighting to Become Americans: Jews, Gender and the Anxiety of Assimilation. Boston: Beacon Press.

Price, Richard
1971   Studies of Caribbean Family Organization: Problems and Prospects. Daedalo 7(14):23–58.

Purdy, Matthew
2001   A Wire-Thin Line Sharply Divides a Suburb's Jews. New York Times, March 25: 35.

Putnam, Laura
2002   The Company They Kept: Migrants and the Politics of Gender in Caribbean Costa Rica, 1870–1960. Chapel Hill: University of North Carolina Press.

Putnam, Robert
2000   Bowling Alone: The Collapse and Revival of American Community. New York: Simon and Schuster.

Pye-Smith, C., G. Borrini-Feyerabend, and R. Sandbrook, eds.
1994   The Wealth of Communities: Stories of Success in Local Environmental Management. Hartford, CT: Kumarian Press.

Rai, Vibhuti Narain
1987   Shahar mein curfew. New Delhi: Rajkamal Prakashan.
2002   An Open Letter to My Fellow Police Officers. In Gujarat. S. Varadarajan, ed. Pp. 211–213. New Delhi: Penguin Books.

Raj, Dhooleka
2003   Where Are You From? Middle-Class Migrants in the Modern World. Berkeley: University of California Press.

Reddock, Rhoda
1998   The Indentureship Experience: Indian Women in Trinidad and Tobago, 1845–1917. In Women Plantation Workers: International Experiences. Shobhita Jain and Rhoda Reddock, eds. Pp. 29–48. New York: Oxford.
2004   Interrogating Caribbean Masculinities: An Introduction. In Interrogating Caribbean Masculinities: Theoretical and Empirical Analyses. Rhoda Reddock, ed. Pp. xiii–xxxiv. Mona, Jamaica: University of the West Indies Press.

Reddock, Rhoda, ed.
2004   Interrogating Caribbean Masculinities: Theoretical and Empirical Analyses. Mona, Jamaica: University of the West Indies Press.

Redfield, Robert
1941   The Folk Culture of Yucatan. Chicago: University of Chicago Press.
1955   The Little Community: Viewpoints for the Study of a Human Whole. Chicago: University of Chicago Press.

Rilke, Rainer Maria

1946   Sonnets to Orpheus. 2nd edition. J. B. Leishman, trans. London: Hogarth Press.

Rix, Vikki

1996   Social and Demographic Change in East London. *In* Rising in the East: The Regeneration of East London. Tim Butler and Michael Rustin, eds. Pp. 20–60. London: Lawrence and Wishart.

Robotham, Donald

2000   Blackening the Jamaican Nation: The Travails of a Black Bourgeoisie in a Globalized World. Identities 7(1):1–37.

Rodman, Hyman

1971   Lower Class Families: The Culture of Poverty in Negro Trinidad. New York: Oxford University Press.

Roitman, Janet

2003   Unsanctioned Wealth; or the Productivity of Debt in Northern Cameroon. Public Culture 15(2):211–237.

Rosaldo, Renato

1989   Culture and Truth: The Remaking of Social Analysis. Boston: Beacon Press.

Rose, Nikolas

1999   Powers of Freedom: Reframing Political Thought. Cambridge: Cambridge University Press.

Rose, Richard

1999   Living in an Antimodern Society. East European Constitutional Review 8(1/2):68–75.

Roseberry, William

1991   Potatoes, Sacks, and Enclosures in Early Modern England. *In* Golden Ages, Dark Ages: Imagining the Past in Anthropology and History. William Roseberry and Jay O'Brian, eds. Pp. 19–47. Berkeley: University of California Press.

Ross, Michael

2001   Does Oil Hinder Democracy? World Politics 53:325–361.

Rostworowski de Diez Canseco, María

1977   Etnía y sociedad: Costa peruana prehispánica. Lima: Instituto de Estudios Peruanos.

Rubenstein, Hymie

1987   Coping with Poverty: Adaptive Strategies in a Caribbean Village. Boulder, CO: Westview Press.

Rutherford, Jonathan

1990   The Third Space: Interview with Homi Bhabha. *In* Identity: Community, Culture, Difference. Jonathan Rutherford, ed. Pp. 207–221. London: Lawrence and Wishart.

Sachs, Wolfgang, ed.

1993   Global Ecology: A New Arena of Political Conflict. London: Zed Books.

Saro-Wiwa, K.

1989   On a Darkling Plain. Port Harcourt, Nigeria: Saros International
        Publishers.

1992   Genocide in Nigeria. Port Harcourt, Nigeria: Saros International
        Publishers.

1995   A Month and a Day. London: Penguin.

Scheele, Raymond

1956   The Prominent Families of Puerto Rico. *In* The People of Puerto Rico.
        Julian Steward, Robert A. Manners, Eric R. Wolf, Elena Padilla Seda,
        Sidney W. Mintz, and Raymond Scheele, eds. Pp. 418–462. Urbana:
        University of Illinois Press.

Scherer, Jacqueline

1972   Contemporary Community: Sociological Illusion or Reality? London:
        Tavistock.

Schofield, Barry

2002   Partners in Power: Governing the Self-Sustaining Community. Sociology:
        The Journal of the British Sociological Association 36:663.

Schwartz, Moshe, Susan Lees, and Gideon M. Kressel, eds.

1995   Rural Cooperatives in Socialist Utopia: Thirty Years of Moshav
        Development in Israel. Westport, CT: Praeger.

Scott, J. M., and M. D. Jennings

1998   Large-Area Mapping of Biodiversity. Annals of the Missouri Botanical
        Gardens 85(1):34–47.

Scott, James C.

1998   Seeing Like a State: How Certain Schemes to Improve the Human
        Condition Have Failed. New Haven, CT: Yale University Press.

Scott, Joan W.

1993   The Evidence of Experience. *In* The Lesbian and Gay Studies Reader.
        Henry Abelove, Michele Barale, and David Halperin, eds. Pp. 397–415.
        New York: Routledge.

Seltzer, Robert

1980   Jewish People, Jewish Thought. Upper Saddle River, NJ: Prentice Hall.

Sheffer, Gabriel

2003   Diaspora Politics: At Home Abroad. Cambridge: Cambridge University
        Press.

Shepherd, Verene

1998   Indian Migrant Women and Plantation Labour in Nineteenth- and
        Twentieth-Century Jamaica: Gender Perspectives. *In* Women Plantation
        Workers: International Experiences. Shobhita Jain and Rhoda Reddock,
        eds. Pp. 89–106. New York: Oxford.

Sherman, Lawrence W.

2003   Reason for Emotion: Reinventing Justice with Theories, Innovations and Research—the American Society of Criminology 2002 Presidential Address. Criminology 41(1):1–37.

Shohat, Ella, and Robert Stam

1996   From the Imperial Family to the Transnational Imaginary: Media Spectatorship in the Age of Globalization. *In* Global Local: Cultural Production and the Transnational Imaginary. Rob Wilson and Wimal Dissanayake, eds. Pp. 145–169. Durham, NC: Duke University Press.

Silverman, Sydel

1979   The Peasant Concept in Anthropology. Journal of Peasant Studies 7(1):49–69.

Simey, Thomas

1946   Welfare and Planning in the West Indies. Oxford: Clarendon.

Sivan, Emmanuel

1995   The Enclave Culture. *In* Fundamentalisms Comprehended, vol. 5. Martin Marty and Scott Appleby, eds. Pp. 11–68. Chicago: University of Chicago Press.

Skaria, Ajay

2002   Gandhi's Politics: Liberalism and the Question of the Ashram. South Atlantic Quarterly 101:4.

Skinner, G. William

1971   Chinese Peasants and the Closed Community. Comparative Studies in Society and History 13:270–281.

Smart, Alan

2001   Unruly Places: Urban Governance and the Persistence of Illegality in Hong Kong's Urban Squatter Areas. American Anthropologist 103:30–44.

Smith, M. G.

1965   The Plural Society in the British West Indies. Berkeley: University of California Press.

1973   A Survey of West Indian Family Studies. *In* Work and Family Life: West Indian Perspectives. Lambros Comitas and David Lowenthal, eds. Pp. 365–408. Garden City, NY: Anchor Press.

Smith, Neil

1992   Geography, Difference and the Politics of Scale. *In* Postmodernism and the Social Sciences. J. Doherty, E. Graham, and M. Malek, eds. Pp. 67–91. London: Routledge.

Smith, R. T.

1956   The Negro Family in British Guiana. London: Routledge and Kegan Paul.

1967   Social Stratification, Cultural Pluralism and Integration in West Indian Societies. *In* Caribbean Integration: Papers on Social, Political, and Economic Integration. Sybil Lewis and Thomas G. Mathews, eds. Pp. 226–258. Rio Piedras: Institute of Caribbean Studies, University of Puerto Rico.

REFERENCES

Smith, Richard Suarez

1985 Rule-by-Records and Rule-by-Reports: Complementary Aspects of the British Imperial Rule of Law. Contributions to Indian Sociology, n.s., 19:1.

Soulé, M., and J. Terborgh, eds.

1999 Continental Conservation: Scientific Foundations of Regional Reserve Networks. Washington, DC: Island Press.

Sousa Santos, B. de.

1998 Why We Can't Afford to be Innocent: Comments on Papers by Price, Hancock, and Reyna. Identities 4(3–4):529–533.

Spivak, Gayatri

1994 A Critique of Postcolonial Reason. Cambridge, MA: Harvard University Press.

1996 The Spivak Reader: Selected Works of Gayatri Chakravorty Spivak. Donna Landry and Gerald MacLean, eds. New York: Routledge.

Srinivas, M. N.

1972 Social Change in Modern India. Bombay: Asia Publishing House.

Stallybrass, Peter, and Allon White

1986 The Politics and Poetics of Transgression. Ithaca, NY: Cornell University Press.

Starn, Orin

1992 Missing the Revolution: Anthropologists and the War in Peru. In Rereading Cultural Anthropology. George E Marcus, ed. Durham, NC: Duke University Press.

1994 Rethinking the Politics of Anthropology: The Case of the Andes. Current Anthropology 35(1):13–28.

1999 Nightwatch: The Politics of Protest in the Andes. Durham, NC: Duke University Press.

Stein, Maurice Robert

1960 The Eclipse of Community: An Interpretation of American Studies. Princeton, NJ: Princeton University Press.

Stevens, S.

1997 Conservation through Cultural Survival: Indigenous Peoples and Protected Areas. Washington, DC: Island Press.

Stolcke, Verena

1995 Talking Culture: New Boundaries, New Rhetorics of Exclusion in Europe. Current Anthropology 36(1):1–24.

Suberu, R.

2004 Pseudo-Federalism and the Crisis of Revenue Allocation. In Nigeria's Struggle for Good Governance. A. Agbaje, L. Diamond, and E. Onwudiwe, eds. Pp. 29–47. Ibadan, Nigeria: University of Ibadan Press.

Suttles, Gerald D.
1972   The Social Construction of Communities. Chicago: University of Chicago Press.

Taussig, M.
1993   Mimesis and Alterity. London: Routledge.

Taylor, Avram
2002   Working Class Credit and Community Since 1918. New York: Palgrave MacMillan.

Terborgh, J.
1999   Requiem for Nature. Washington, DC: Island Press.

Terborgh, J., J. A. Estes, P. Paquet, K. Ralls, D. Boyd-Herger, B. J. Miller, and R. F. Noss
1999   The Role of Top Carnivores in Regulating Terrestrial Ecosystems. *In* Continental Conservation: Scientific Foundations of Regional Reserve Networks. M. Soulé and J. Terborgh, eds., Pp. 39–64. Washington, DC: Island Press.

Thomas, Alan
1992   Non-governmental Organisations and the Limits to Empowerment. *In* Development Policy and Public Action. Marc Wuyts, Maureen Mackintosh, and Tom Hewitt, eds. Pp. 117–146. New York: Oxford University Press.

Thorns, David C.
1976   The Quest for Community: Social Aspects of Residential Growth. New York: John Wiley and Sons.

Toyo, E.
2002   Revenue Allocation and the National Question. *In* The National Question in Nigeria. A. Momoh and S. Adejumboi, eds. Pp. 69–96. Aldershot, UK: Ashgate.

Trillin, Calvin
1994   Drawing the Line. New Yorker, December 12: 50.

Trouillot, Michel-Rolph
2002   Otherwise Modern: Caribbean Lessons from the Savage Slot. *In* Critically Modern: Alternatives, Alterities, Anthropologies. Bruce M. Knauft, ed. Pp. 220–237. Bloomington: Indiana University Press.

Tsing, A. L., J. P. Brosius, and C. Zerner
1999   Assessing Community-Based Natural-Resource Management. Ambio 28(2):197–198.

Ukeje, C.
2001   Oil Communities and Political Violence. Terrorism and Political Violence 14(4):15–36.

Unger, Roberto Mangabeira
1975   Knowledge and Politics. New York: Free Press.

REFERENCES

Valcárcel, Luis E.
1927   Tempestad en los Andes. Biblioteca "Amauta." Lima: Editorial Minerva.

Vertovec, Steven
1996   "Official" and "Popular" Hinduism in the Caribbean: Historical and
            Contemporary Trends in Surinam, Trinidad, and Guyana. *In* Across the
            Dark Waters: Ethnicity and Indian Identity in the Caribbean. David
            Dabydeen and Brinsley Samaroo, eds. Pp. 108–130. London: Macmillan.

WAC/SPDC
2004   Peace and Security in the Niger Delta. Port Harcourt, Nigeria: Shell.

Walgrave, Lode
2000   Restorative Justice and the Republican Theory of Justice. *In* Restorative
            Justice: Philosophy to Practice. Heather Strang and John Braithwaite, eds.
            Pp. 165–183. Burlington, VT: Ashgate Publishing Company.

Wall, Helena M.
1990   Fierce Communion: Family and Community in Early America. Cambridge,
            MA: Harvard University Press.

Waters, Mary C.
2001   Growing Up West Indian and African American: Gender and Class
            Differences in the Second Generation. *In* Islands in the City: West Indian
            Migration to New York. Nancy Foner, ed. Pp. 193–215. Berkeley: University
            of California Press.

Watts, Michael
1998   Islamic Modernities? *In* Cities and Citizenship. J. Holston, ed. Pp. 67–102.
            Durham, NC: Duke University Press.
2000   Struggles over Geography. The 1999 Hettner Lectures. Heidelberg:
            University of Heidelberg.
2004   Resource Curse? Geopolitics 9(1):50–80.

Weinreich, Max
1967   The Reality of Jewishness versus the Ghetto Myth: The Socio-linguistic
            Roots of Yiddish. *In* To Honor Roman Jakobson. Pp. 2199–2211. The
            Hague: Mouton.

Weismantel, Mary
1989a   Food, Gender and Poverty in the Ecuadorian Andes. Philadelphia:
            University of Pennsylvania Press.
1989b   Cooking Houses and Sleeping Houses: The Zumbagua Household as
            Constituted Process. *In* The Household Economy: Reconsidering the
            Domestic Mode of Production. Richard R. Wilk, ed. Pp. 55–72. Boulder,
            CO: Westview Press.
1995   Making Kin: Kinship Theory and Zumbagua Adoptions. American
            Ethnologist 22(4):685–709.
2001   Cholas and Pishtacos: Stories of Race and Sex in the Andes. Chicago:
            University of Chicago Press.

West India Royal Commission

1945   West India Royal Commission Report. Presented by the Secretary of State for the Colonies to Parliament by Command of His Majesty. London: His Majesty's Stationary Office.

Western, D., and M. Wright, eds.

1994   Natural Connections: Perspectives in Community-Based Conservation. Washington, DC: Island Press.

Weston, Kath

1991   Families We Choose: Lesbians, Gays, Kinship. New York: Columbia University Press.

Whitt, Laurie Anne, and Jennifer Daryl Slack

1994   Communities, Environments and Cultural Studies. Cultural Studies 8(1): 5–31.

Williams, Raymond

1973   The Country and the City. New York: Oxford University Press.

1976   Keywords. New York: Oxford University Press.

Wilshusen, P. R., S. R. Brechin, C. L. Fortwangler, and P. C. West

2002   Reinventing a Square Wheel: Critique of a Resurgent "Protection Paradigm" in International Biodiversity Conservation. Society and Natural Resources 15(1):17–40.

Wilson, E. O.

1988   BioDiversity. Washington, DC: National Academy Press.

Wilson, Peter

1973   Crab Antics. New Haven, CT: Yale University Press.

Wilson, Samuel M., and Leighton C. Peterson

2002   The Anthropology of Online Communities. Annual Review of Anthropology 31:449–467.

Wolf, Eric R.

1957   Closed Corporate Communities in Mesoamerica and Java. Southwestern Journal of Anthropology 13:1–18.

1986   The Vicissitudes of the Closed Corporate Peasant Community. American Ethnologist 13:325–329.

Wolmer, W.

2002   Transboundary Conservation: The Politics of Ecological Integrity in the Great Limpopo Transfrontier Park. Unpublished manuscript.

Woolford, Andrew, and R. S. Ratner

2003   Nomadic Justice? Restorative Justice on the Margins of Law. Social Justice 30(1):177–194.

World Bank

1989   Sub-Saharan Africa: From Crisis to Sustainable Growth. Washington, DC: World Bank.

REFERENCES

World Wildlife Fund (WWF)

2001   Center for Conservation Finance Business Plan: Building Conservation
            Capital for the Future. Washington, DC: WWF.

2002a   Building Conservation Capital for the Future. Electronic document,
            www.worldwildlife.org/conservationfinance, accessed September 24, 2002.

2002b   What the Center for Conservation Finance Does. Electronic document,
            www.worldwildlife.org/conservationfinance/does.cfm, accessed September
            24, 2002.

Worobcc, Christine D.

1991   Peasant Russia: Family and Community in the Post-Emancipation Period.
            Princeton, NJ: Princeton University Press.

Yanagisako, Sylvia

1979   Family and Household: A Review of the Anthropological Literature on
            Domestic Groups. Annual Review of Anthropology 8:161–205.

Young, Iris Marion

1986   The Ideal of Community and the Politics of Difference. Social Theory and
            Practice 12(1):1–26.

Young, M., and P. Willmott

1962   Family and Kinship in East London. London: Pelican.

Zehr, Howard

1990   Changing Lenses. Scottdale, PA: Herald Press.

Zeman, Thomas Edward

1981   Order, Crime and Punishment: The American Criminological Tradition.
            Ph.D. dissertation, History of Consciousness Program, University of
            California, Santa Cruz.

Zerner, Charles

1994   Through a Green Lens: The Construction of Customary Environmental
            Law and Community in Indonesia's Maluku Islands. Law Society Review
            28(5):1079–1122.

Zevallos Aguilar, Ulises Juan

2002   Indigenismo y nación: Los retos a la representación de la subalternidad
            aymara y quechua en al Boletín Titikaka (1926–1930). Lima: Instituto
            Francés de Estudios Andinos/Banco Central de Reserva del Perú–Fondo
            Editorial.

Zuidema, R. Tom

1977   The Inca Kinship System: A New Theoretical View. *In* Andean Kinship and
            Marriage. Ralph Bolton and Enrique Mayer, eds. Pp. 248–292.
            Washington, DC: American Anthropological Association.

Index

Abacha, S., 109
accounting, and discourse of
    criminal justice reform,
    207, 209–10, 216, 218
Achebe, C., 134
African National Congress
    (ANC), 51
Afro-Caribbean community,
    history and culture of,
    143–57
*Against the Romance of
    Community* (Joseph
    2002), 200
Agrawal, A., 35
Alcorn, J., 230
Alder, C., 226n15
Alderman, L., 246
Alhaji Asari (Niger Delta
    People's Volunteer
    Force), 111, 142n24
Allen, C. J., 84, 92, 97
Alonso, A. M., 144
Althusser, L., 223
Altink, H., 147
Amit, V., 43–45
anachronism, and diaspora
    narratives in Caribbean,
    170, 173
Andeanism (*lo andino*), and
    concept of *ayllu*, 78,
    86–88, 93
Anderson, B., 8, 22n1, 41,
    43, 44, 132–33, 195, 265
Andes region, and concepts
    of community and *ayllu*,
    77–97
Annales School, 32
anthropology: and critiques
    of community study
    method, 4, 28–29; and
    culture in studies of
    community, 143; and

debates on Andean *ayllu*,
    78, 80, 81–97; and revi-
    sionist critiques of com-
    munity in context of
    Caribbean, 164–74. *See
    also* ethnography
anti-Semitism, and concepts
    of community in sub-
    urbs, 178, 186–87
Apffel-Marglin, F., 91
apocryphal time, and Indo-
    Caribbean diaspora nar-
    ratives, 170–72, 174. *See
    also* temporal scale
Appadurai, A., 43, 44, 163,
    166–67
Arguedas, J. M., 86
Arnold, D., 84
arts organization, and com-
    munity in East London,
    49–76
Ash, R., 187–88
Ateke Tom (Niger Delta
    Vigilante), 111, 142n24
authenticity: and ghetto in
    community discourse on
    Orthodox Jewish *eruv*,
    192–95, 198n17; "peas-
    ant" and elite forms of in
    Caribbean context, 170
Awolowo, O., 133
ayllu, and concept of com-
    munity in Andes, 77–97
al-Azmeh, A., 136

Back from the Brink
    (ClearWater 2003), 110
Bailey, R., 254n3
Banfield, E., 30, 39–40
Barbados. *See* Caribbean
Barigha-Amage, N. B. P.,
    117, 119

Barrow, C., 147, 149
Bates, C., 154
Bauman, Z., 5, 46
Baumann, G., 156
Beauvoir, S. de, 273
Beccaria, C., 209–10, 211,
    212, 218
Bechofer, Rabbi Yosef, 182
Berger, P., 37
Berlant, L., 133
Bernstein, H., 29
Bhabha, H., 166, 168
Bharati, U., 272
Bilby, K., 155, 165
biodiversity, and community-
    based conservation, 232,
    238–39, 243
Blair, T., 50, 75
Bloom, S., 188
Bolivia. *See* Andes region
Borrini-Feyerabend, G., 230
bottom-up models, of con-
    servation, 227, 228
Boyarin, J., 176
Brah, A., 166
Braithwaite, J., 216, 220,
    222–23, 226n11, 226n13
Brenner, N., 108
Brereton, B., 160–61
British Journal of Sociology, 161
Brosius, P., 18
Burgess, E., 27
Byres, T., 29

Cadena, M. de la, 99n15
Calhoun, C. J., 22n3, 40, 43
California, and conflicts
    over Orthodox Jewish
    eruvin in suburbs, 185,
    197n10, 197n13
Cancian, F., 30
capitalism: and economic

School of American Research Advanced Seminar Series

PUBLISHED BY SAR PRESS

Participants in the School of American Research advanced seminar "Reconsidering Community: The Unintended Consequences of an Intellectual Romance," Santa Fe, New Mexico, April 12–18, 2003. Seated from left: Kate Crehan, Susan Lees, Mary Weismantel, Michael Watts. Standing from left: Elizabeth Chin, Miranda Joseph, Gerald Creed, Aisha Khan, Gyanendra Pandey, Peter Brosius.